THE

PSYCHIC

WORLD

Of

JOHN G. SUTTON

THE PSYCHIC WORLD
Of
JOHN G. SUTTON

John G. Sutton

First published globally in 2017
Copyright © John G. Sutton 2017
Psychicworld.net Limited
The moral right of the author has been asserted.
ISBN: 978-0-244-31103-2
Cover Design: John G. Sutton

CONTENTS

INTRODUCTION

INTRODUCTION

My name is John G. Sutton I am currently the feature editor of the monthly journal of Spiritualism 'Psychic World'. I have been writing a column for P.W. since 1992 when it was launched and have been the features editor for over twenty two years. This book is a selected compilation of my columns published in that newspaper.

My previously published works include books commissioned by many of the most prestigious publishing houses in the Western world: HarperCollins 'The Psychic World of James Byrne' 1993, Bloomsbury 'Psychic Pets' 1997, Element/Penguin 'Animals Make You Feel Better' 1998, Piatkus/Little Brown 'The Psychic World of Derek Acorah' 1999 and many more.

As an author I have toured the United States of America where my books were published by numerous publishers including Scholastic. In 1998 my publishers flew me to New York USA to appear on a number of network USA TV shows including FOX News and The Children's Network. Later that same year the Walt Disney Corporation flew me to Orlando Florida where I was the Special Guest on the International Animal Planet channel Disney TV Show 'Petsburgh USA'.

The columns featured in this book have been selected to offer the reader a reasonably comprehensive collection of my work over a period of more than two decades. The views expressed are my own and I have an absolute belief in the truth of eternal life and the power of spirit. I know that we do not die, we will all at some point in time to come cease to exist as a physical entity but our soul our spirit will survive and with that our personality. The next world is, in my experience and to the very best of my knowledge and understanding, completely secular, there is no religious force there. I realize that many may take offence at my observations and if that includes you then so be it, go grab a copy of The Bible or whatever and entertain yourself with tall tales of genocide, human sacrifice and all manner of abuses committed in the name of 'God'.

What awaits you in these pages has taken me over twenty years to compile and I have seriously studied the subject of Spirituality with some of the most qualified philosophers and Psychic Mediums in the UK. I sincerely hope you enjoy this work and thank you for taking the time to read about my psychic world.

Best Wishes

JOHN G. SUTTON

CHAPTER ONE

MY EARLY PSYCHIC EXPERIENCES

I believe that each and every individual on earth has hidden abilities that can be loosely termed as *Psychic Powers.* As children many people do encounter the paranormal that is for them, at that time in their development, normal. It is only as we become socialised, programmed if you like, into this increasingly material world that we deny our supernatural self. There may be those among you reading this that remember their early paranormal encounters. Many children do demonstrate some degree of supernatural awareness. Here, as an example, are some of my own personal psychic experiences. These demonstrate that, deny it or not, there exists an obscured doorway between this world and the next. On occasions that door opens and we, in our innocence, walk through.

Born in the shadow of Lancashire's Pendle hill, infamous for its witches, I was brought up to believe that the supernatural was evil and to be avoided. Perhaps there remained in the little village of Foulridge, where I lived, a kind of collective folk memory concerning the practice of witchcraft. I can clearly recall hearing my grandmother 'Eva Walsh' warn me that if I misbehaved then 'Old mother Demdyke' would appear and take me away. Demdyke being one of the Lancashire witches. My father, Francis Sutton, was by faith Roman Catholic and rather strict. The very last thing welcome in our family was a psychic encounter. But the spirit world had plans that extended beyond the belief systems and paternal rules that structured my young life. My grandparents lived in a 17th century stone cottage in the village of Foulridge, where I was raised. The house had, in the distant past, been the home of weavers who wove cloth on the premises. The cottage had a cellar the full length of the house and it was there that the hand-operated loom would have been sited. The cottage industry of weaving vanished with the factory system at the start of the industrial revolution. When I was a child the cellar contained only an old wooden workbench and various unwanted household goods. To me it was a wonderful place, full of cobwebs and mystery. Whenever we visited my mother's parents, Eva and Billy Walsh, I would head straight for that dark cellar to play. As a child of five years it seemed to me that there was nothing strange about the atmosphere in the dark corners of my friendly cellar. I was happy down there and would sit for hours playing. Then one day I noticed that someone had moved my toys, I had a tin train and some building blocks that were my favourite playthings. I recall searching for these and seeing a shadow moving in a corner. 'I'm Sammy' a voice said that seemed to come from within the darkness. Then a blast of cold air rushed by me. I wasn't afraid, just curious. When I looked again into the corner of the cellar there was nobody there. But in the shadows I saw my little tin train and other toys. From that day onwards I often saw the strange shadow in that dark corner of the cellar. It wasn't scary, I had heard the shadows name it was Sammy and we were friends. Sammy said he lived in the house and was happy here. I never told anyone about him because I somehow knew they wouldn't let me play down the cellar again if I did. I saw Sammy the shadow regularly until we moved away from the area. Then one day when I returned, he wasn't there anymore. I whispered his name into the cold corner where I used to play, but now there was only dusty cobwebs and a long abandoned broken tin train.

Many years passed before I told my mother about the shadow man that I used to see in her parent's cellar. I was amazed when she admitted that my grandmother had always thought that a ghost called Sammy haunted the house. It seems she too had heard and seen him. Whilst researching this book I checked the local records and there was a man by the name of Sammy Tummy who once lived in my grandparents old house.

BUILDING PYRAMIDS

The year was 1955 and I was a six-year-old boy full of the joys of life. The family had moved to Prestwich on the smart side of north Manchester. My father had entered the Lancashire Constabulary and was serving as a Police Officer. There were by now five of us; mother and father, myself John the eldest, my brother Martin and baby sister Frances Lesley. I was the wild one, the dreamer. I was the one that saw things that were not there. And I quickly learnt not to repeat that which I saw and heard.

The rules within our house were rigid and enforced. At a certain time, around 6 p.m., the children were dispatched to bed and the doors of the bedroom locked behind us. From then until next morning we did not leave the room into which we had been secured. During the summer months this was quite distressing as the nights were light and outside looked like so much fun. It was pointless complaining, as this brought unexpected and entirely unwelcome results.

My bedroom was separate from my siblings and I would lay in bed alone, staring at the wallpaper, wishing I were free. Night after night I lay aimlessly counting the pink paper roses on my bedside wall. Suddenly I was no longer in a tiny back bedroom locked in against my will, I was in a strange land where a river ran before me. The sun beat down from a clear blue sky and I sensed the heat and saw about me men dressed in unfamiliar clothes, leather belts and sandals. I seemed to be standing on a raised wooden platform bound together by what seemed to be ropes. Below me were countless hundreds of dark skinned men heaving and pulling huge stones along across a pathway of tree trunks. Fantastic as it may seem I saw these stones being heaved and dragged towards what I now know to be an unfinished pyramid. At the time I had absolutely no knowledge of Egypt and not a clue about the pyramids. But in the vision I was there, in some kind of position of authority, directing the work taking place. The strength and the joy of it all flooded through me. Then slowly the vision faded and I was back in Prestwich, a little lonely boy locked in my bedroom.

The next morning, when mother unlocked the door, I ran straight downstairs to tell her and my father all about that which I had seen. The reception I received shocked me. It frightened me a great deal to know that my parents considered that I was either inventing the visions or was in some way wicked. There was, as far as I knew, nothing evil about what I had experienced. However, I was left in no doubt that I must not talk of this again. I clearly recall wondering why I was thought to be so bad. To me the sights I had seen were both mysterious and wonderful. Like any child I just wanted to tell everyone about them. But the matter was, as my father so sternly said, closed. I was never to speak of it again.

That night I voluntarily went to my bedroom early and closed the door. Staring at the pale pink paper flowers that I had counted so many times I waited for the visions I had seen to return. Outside the early evening summer light faded and day became night. Still I stared at the wall waiting to be transported out of my lonely room and away to that strange land beyond the capacity of my imagination. It must have been midnight before I saw once more the sights of that far away and long ago kingdom. There again I stood watching the creation of something outside my childish comprehension. But the joy of being there was enough, I was there as a man, not as a boy. The experience was intense, thrilling, overwhelming. I was not viewing this vision, I was a real live living part of it. The sun, the river, the many dark skinned men all heaving and shoving and dragging and pushing huge stone blocks towards some distant place were happening now. I was there, in the midst of all this excitement and action.

The next morning I awoke exhausted. I felt dizzy, weak and unable to control myself. Staggering out of my bedroom across the first floor landing I fell from the top of the wooden staircase to the bottom. I vaguely recall trying to stop myself but could not do so. My parents were standing over me when I awoke. I was physically uninjured. Of the mysterious land beyond my bedroom I said nothing.

For months after the first visions came to me I would infrequently be transported into that world far away from my locked little room where I lay counting paper roses. But the intensity of my experiences had an effect upon my health. I would often waken feeling dizzy and fall down, as the room seemed to spin around me. My parents took me to the medical practitioners who said I was a perfectly healthy boy who was just growing up. I wonder what they would have said if I had told them about my nights spent building pyramids?

MEETING THE ANGEL OF DEATH

The year was 1968 and I was a young man serving as a soldier with the Royal Artillery in barracks at the small town of Sennelager, near Padderborn in Germany. The month was December and I caught a cold. The infection got rapidly worse and I had to report sick to the military Doctor. He diagnosed influenza and suggested I be admitted into the hospital, as my temperature was very high. Being a foolhardy youth I thought I would be better off in my barrack room with some medication. Reluctantly the Dr agreed and, carrying my supply of medicine, I was driven back to my barracks and confined to bed. It was a near fatal mistake.

The influenza overtook my ability to move and no sooner had I got into bed than I became almost comatose. The other soldiers in the barrack room, being young men, thought I was just enjoying a few days in bed. In truth I was very near to death and too ill to even take my medication. How long I was in this condition I do not know, perhaps two days.

Suddenly I was free from that lump of heavy body that was lying there in the bed. Looking down I could see it wrapped in untidy sheets and I felt nothing for it at all. In fact I was delighted to be out of it. Indeed I was out of my body and able to fly anywhere I wanted to. The feeling was almost indescribable. The joy of having no restrictions was fantastic. Then I heard a voice say to me 'Where do you want to go?' For some unknown reason I thought of Paris and the Eiffel tower, instantly I was there. Amidst the other tourists I walked around admiring the structure, I mingled with the crowds and it was real, I was there.

Having seen the Eiffel tower I thought I might visit the Taj Mahal and no sooner had the thought crossed my mind than I was transported there. Once again I looked around the grounds and the exterior of this magnificent building. But that wasn't where I really wanted to be. I was a young soldier, far away from my native land, my thoughts were now of home. I wanted to see and be with my beloved grandparents, in that little stone cottage where I had always been welcome.

Instantly I felt myself uplifted and flying through the atmosphere, soaring above the clouds and below me the blue seas of the wide world sparkled and shimmered in the heavenly light from above. It was an absolutely incredible and unforgettable experience. Suddenly I began to feel heavy and I could no longer fly. I felt myself falling, floating slowly to the ground. When I next looked I saw that I was standing on the long familiar road that leads from the town of Colne, in Lancashire, into the little village of Foulridge where I was raised as a child. But I couldn't walk another step. My feet felt as though they weighed a hundred pounds each. I was stationary, stuck on the final few hundred yards home to my village. Then I saw the most gloriously glowing beautiful lady I have ever seen in my life. Her shining hair fell in long dark tresses about her shoulders and she wore a brilliant white dress that seemed lit from within.

"I must ask you to make a choice" she said to me in a voice that was as calm and cool as a summer breeze. "You may continue on your journey to your village or return now to your body, which will you do?" she asked. For a brief moment I thought and made a decision "I'll go back to my body" I replied. As soon as I had spoken she reached out her hand and took mine. In that very instant I opened my eyes to see the grubby barrack room wall, next the untidy bed where I lay in my young soldiers body. The fever had passed and I was alive.

Since that day I have often thought to myself just what would have happened had I made the other choice? Perhaps then the angel of death would have taken me on to another home, in another world. One day I will know.

MATERIALISATION

On the 15th May 1973, at the young age of 44 years, my father Francis Sutton passed away. He had contracted leukaemia and died in hospital. His death was expected but it still came as a terrible shock. The man who had been the unquestioned head of the family was no longer with us. It seemed hard to believe at first. My father had been a Detective Inspector in the police serving in the town of Leigh in Lancashire where I now lived with my wife Mary. To me my father was the indestructible strong arm of the law. His death changed many things, including the dynamics of our extended family. No more would we be able to turn to him for advice and guidance. The rock upon which we had so often relied for support was gone.

It was early evening late in the month of August of the same year. I had just completed a days work and returned home to the ground floor flat that I shared with my wife Mary. She was in the kitchen preparing dinner and my mother, Sheila Sutton, was helping her. I stood in the main lounge area quietly watching the two of them fussing about with the setting of the table. It was a perfectly ordinary domestic scene not dissimilar from countless thousands of others in households throughout the U.K. That is before my father returned in his spirit body.

As I stood watching my wife and my mother, only half interested in what they were doing, I saw something move from the corner of my right eye. Turning quickly towards the centre of the lounge I saw, sitting in a chair, my late father Francis Sutton. For a very brief instant I was unable to speak. He looked directly at me and smiled one of his sardonic smiles as if to say 'I'm watching you boy'. He was dressed in his usual formal suit with a waistcoat, white shirt and dark tie. He was absolutely as alive as I was and this astounded me. Grasping for something to say I blurted out "What are you doing here dad?" Then as suddenly as he had appeared, he disappeared.

I felt faint, my pulse raced and for a moment I thought I would collapse. In my mind I questioned what I had just seen. It was impossible, yet it had happened, I had seen my father whom I knew to be dead. Searching for an explanation I thought that I had imagined it. But I did not imagine it. He had never entered our flat in life so it was not a memory of a former visit. The light was natural and the room well lit. No matter how I struggled to find an answer there was, to me, only one, my father's spirit had materialised and I had seen it.

From the kitchen my wife called "John, the dinner's ready" I sat at the table, half dazed, looking disinterestedly at my food. I was still in shock. "What's the matter John?" my mother said, "you look a bit pale" Little did she know, I had just seen a ghost!

A NEAR DEATH EXPERIENCE

In the year 1986 I was in hospital recovering from the removal of an embolism from my right leg when the site turned gangrenous. Despite desperate efforts by the medical team the infection quickly became life threatening and amputation was the only safe option. It was whilst I was sedated, following the removal of my right leg, that I underwent what I now know to be a near death experience.

The amputation procedure had been successfully completed and I remained unconscious. However, unbeknownst to me, my body had reacted to the drugs I had received and a minute form of fungi had begun to grow in my blood. So on top of the trauma of amputation I was now faced with a further serious infection. According to my brother Martin, who dared to ask, the odds against my survival were put at 20/1.

I can clearly recall stepping out of my body and seeing it motionless on the bed. There were tubes and wires protruding from it and I felt nothing but a desire to move onwards. Before me the walls of the intensive care unit opened and I stepped through them into an airport departure lounge.

There were many people in this airport lounge and I knew none of them. The seats were set in long rows and were filled with others who were just sitting there. Looking out through a series of windows I saw an aircraft standing on a runway. Then a lady dressed like a stewardess came to me and said I must follow her. Together we went to the rear of the seating area in the lounge to a door set into a white painted wall. "You're next" she told me "when they call you, go through that door".

I wasn't afraid in this situation. It seemed perfectly natural and, whilst I was curious, I was not overly concerned. Then someone called my name "Mr Sutton please". I stood and walked through the door that had been indicated. Within I saw three middle aged men seated behind a long wooden table. They were dressed in business suits and the eldest of the three, sitting in the centre position, had grey hair. They looked rather like senior civil servants ready to interview me for an official position. "Please take a seat" one of the three said and I duly sat down wondering what was next.

"You do know you are not in your body?" the man in centre said. " I know" I replied, though in truth it had not occurred to me. There followed a kind of benevolent examination of my life. Each of these three gentlemen questioned me in detail about why I had done this and how I felt about that aspect of my life. There was no indication that I was being judged, but a sense that I could have done better. "I'm not ready to die yet!" I said in defence of my lack of positive achievement. "Really" said the man on the right of the three "so tell us, why we should let you return?"

It was then that I knew that I was within the antechamber of eternity. These three men had the absolute unquestionable authority to send me to my destination in the next world. "I have a daughter, a wife, they need me" I said thinking as quickly as I could. That statement made no impression at all. "Everyone who comes in here tells us that kind of story, what are you going to do that will make it worthwhile letting you return?" My mind was spinning, this was it, wrong answer and I was out of the game.

The man in the centre with grey hair spoke to me very kindly "You do realise that if you return you will be an amputee" he said. The thought had never crossed my mind, but it did now. "Yes, but I can do many things despite that" I said. "I can help

14

the mentally handicapped, I was a nurse once" I ventured. "Now you are telling us something" the man on the left said "but there is more that you can do isn't there?"

For a moment I thought, then it came to me like a flash of inspiration, though why I will probably never know. "Yes" I replied "I will resurrect the pop singer P.J. Proby" (Proby had been my favourite singer from the 1960's when I was a teenager). The three men looked at me for a while and spoke quietly to each other. "Right Mr Sutton, just wait outside whilst we consider sending you back on a mission" the man with grey hair said. I stood and walked out of the room taking a seat directly next to the door. Time passed and I was not called back in.

As I sat in that airport lounge I heard the intercom announce that it was now time to board the aircraft. I remained seated, watching as all the others, every single one, stood, formed a long queue and boarded the plane. I had no doubt that they were en-route to the next world. I didn't move. "Will Mr Sutton, will Mr JOHN SUTTON! please take his seat on the plane, we are waiting to depart" a voice from the intercom was calling me. But I would not go, I was being considered for a mission and not until I knew what it was would I go anywhere.

I awoke in a hospital bed on the very edge of death. I was dreadfully ill, my kidneys had failed and I was on dialysis, if they did not start working soon I would certainly die. But they did. Much to the amazement of the medical staff I recovered. The odds might have been 20/1 against, but I made it.

In the year 1990 I was working as a Day Centre Officer caring for and teaching adults with learning disabilities. One evening I received a telephone call from a friend who told me that P.J. Proby was living just a few miles from my home, in the town of Bolton. I went to see the man who had once been voted the world's best male vocalist in the New Musical Express poll of 1964. He was in desperate straits, a washed up alcoholic mess. Somehow I managed to persuade Jim Proby to sing and wrote a song for him called *'Stage of Fools'*. Within just a few months I had P.J. Proby on Radio and TV with a new album on international distribution.

I had resurrected him just as I said I would. Granada TV even made a documentary about this and I was featured alongside P.J. Proby. However, that was not the reason I had returned from the borderland between this world and the next. I still did not know what that was though I knew it must be important and linked to spirit. Then from out of the blue a man called at my house, he said he was a Spiritualist medium. The man explained that he had been sent to see me by his spirit guides who had told him that I was to be instrumental in bringing the truth of spirit communication to the publics attention. This was to become my mission and it has been so since that day many years ago.

CHAPTER TWO

THE STRANGE LIFE OF BILL BROOKS

In the year 1968 I was a nineteen year old soldier 24138960 Gunner Sutton serving with the British Army stationed at Dempsey Barracks, Sennelager, Germany. My barrack room was on the second floor of a huge old four storey building that dated back to before WWII. I shared this room with three other young soldiers, we each had a corner with a military issue metal bed and a large dark green locker. It was long gone midnight and all of the occupants of my room were in bed sound asleep as I was too until something disturbed me. I woke on hearing the sound of footsteps walking across the bare wooden floor and can recall thinking to myself that it was the drunken Welshman that had the bed in the far corner by the window. Sitting up slightly I looked forward to see who it was, it was not Taffy. Standing at the foot of my bed was a horrible looking apparition that seemed to be lit from within it looked like an injured soldier as its head was half missing. I remember trying to scream but could not make a sound nor could I move, I was literally transfixed with terror.

It was January of this year and I was working in my office when the telephone rang and on answering it I heard a voice I recognised, it was a man called Bill Brooks. Bill had been a soldier with me forty eight years ago and I had neither seen nor heard from him since I left Germany in 1972. I wondered what Bill wanted and having exchanged the usual pleasantries he came to the point, he wanted to know if I had any memory of an incident in the barrack room when a weird ghost like entity had appeared at the foot of our beds. Of course I had perfect recollection of it the sight had really scared me and it had obviously done the same to Bill who had been sleeping in the bed opposite me. He asked me a number of searching questions about what we had seen and for a while I felt that he thought it had been some kind of a joke that I had played on him. It most certainly was not a joke and I had been as terrified as he obviously was. It seemed odd to me that Bill would take the trouble to find me after almost fifty years to ask about that mysterious sighting and I asked him what prompted this. Bill explained that he was writing a book about his strange life and wanted to check the facts with me concerning that particular paranormal phenomena.

In late July of this year I was pleasantly surprised to receive in the mail a copy of Bill's book it is titled '44 An Ex Soldier's True Story'. In this book he gives an account of our shared experience back in 1968 when we both saw that fear invoking apparition. I read this book with great interest and it really is an incredible story that Bill has to tell about his seriously strange life. You see Bill Brooks is man who according to his written testimony has been abducted by aliens many, many times. I realize that most people who make such claims are disbelieved and considered by some to be fabricating their accounts. But I knew Bill all those years ago and I shared one of his weird encounters with the unexplained. To me Bill seems to be as he was back then, an ordinary guy with a rather pronounced Black Country accent. So despite the extraordinary nature of his story I felt it must be as he believed it to be yet it is almost beyond belief. Let me give you an example:

In the chapter headed 'First Major (Mass) Abduction Event in the Army' Bill gives an incredible account of witnessing a number of soldiers being abducted into an alien space craft. There are his words:

' It was a late autumnal evening, around eight or nine when we noticed an orange-coloured mist coming towards our position which definitely got our attention. The soldier I was with Joe said he believed it was a simulated gas attack. We went back to the base camp to warn our section to put on their gas

18

masks. When we arrived we were surprised to find everyone asleep in their vehicles. We woke an NCO and reported to him what we had seen and that we thought this was a simulated gas attack. He said it was not possible as the training exercise had been cancelled and the section was on stand down. Joe and I then found somewhere to rest and as we lay back on some camouflage nets I saw an incredible scene. I saw a light and what looked like smoke coming towards us. As I looked away from the light my field of vision rested on a further site that I could make no sense of. I watched with incredulity a scene that I knew should not be possible and strained my eyes to make sure that what I was seeing was not a figment of my imagination. The men, as if under orders began leaving the vehicles they been sleeping soundly in which were parked a little closer to the field than we were. They seemed to be in a trance and looked for all the world as if they were floating towards some object with very bright lights in the field. Obscured by the brightness of the light, I struggled to make out any details of what I was seeing though it looked like some kind of vehicle. The guys had been on exercise during the day and were exhausted, yet here they were all moving in unison, but in an apparent state of sleep. Joe and I had a panoramic view because we were on top of a vehicle on the camouflage nets and very much awake. I decided to investigate and see where the men had gone and started down from the vehicle, but Jo said no, stay put. Don't go. I didn't know then that he could see armed men coming out of the woods, walking in our direction. Our vehicle was parked about 100 yards in front of the woods and to the right was the field where I now believe a UFO had landed. As I looked up and saw Joe staring towards the wood I quickly stared in that direction and was suddenly confronted by a man dressed in black coveralls with some kind of small blue square shaped badge at the top of the right sleeve. It soon became apparent that there were several of these men similarly dressed all with guns and as far as I could tell they were all blonde. This guy in front of me had a gun that he was pointing in my direction. He spoke and said walk towards the light. I hesitated because I could still hear Joe telling me not to go.

The following morning we were all standing on parade in the field with high ranking officers in front of us. Once again, I now know this to be very unusual, but it was still all in my first week in the regiment, so I had nothing to judge it by. I could see there were two rows of us on parade I didn't know any of them except Joe. He stood next to me asking in a whisper, if I remembered anything of what happened. As it turns out I didn't. I have no memory of anything at all, not even how I got on parade and so of course I had no idea what he meant, or that we've all been a part of a mass abduction. I noticed some of the guys on parade were wearing the old battle dress uniform from years before, though I was in the usual army fatigues. Again, I had no idea if this was normal or not, though I later discovered that the uniform had been phased out 10 years previously so that was very odd. I remember we were told in no uncertain terms by the senior officers that what had happened the night before must never be spoken about or discussed between us ever.

CHAPTER THREE

THE SPIRITUALIST CHURCH BRIDLINGTON

The wild westerly wind was blowing strong driving in hard cold rain the day my wife Mary and I visited the sea port town of Bridlington in Yorkshire . I was there for two reasons, firstly I had been invited by Katie the President of the local Spiritualist Church to give a talk to her members and secondly to meet with my old Army buddy 'Crazy Horse' James Howell. Let me start with meeting Mr. Howell a man I had last seen in 1971 at the Barracks in Sennelager, Germany when we were both serving with 39 Missile Regiment RA.

Through the internet facility known as FaceBook I had reconnected with James on the pages dedicated to our old Artillery unit 36 Arcot 1751 Battery . Exchanging messages over many months I was intrigued by the memories we shared of a time when life was less complex and Britain actually had an Army of over two hundred thousand men. Mr. Howell told me he was living in the Newcastle on Tyne area so when Katie at the Bridlington Church invited me I thought it an ideal opportunity to meet with James and his delightful wife Maureen. By the side of the harbour with a storm howling around us we shook hands again some forty five years since we last did so. James was no longer a somewhat svelte nine stone stripling he was now a strapping thirteen stone mature man and I, well I am a grey haired gimpy old Grumps.

In a local bar, over soft drinks, we spoke of incidents that had coloured our collective military past. James had a remarkable, if somewhat jaundiced, recall of one particular moment in time when I had conducted a very unwise Ouija Board session in a barrack room. On that night I had, inadvertently, connected with a discarnate entity from the dark side of the next dimension. There was a soldier in the room making jokes about the veracity of our communicator and the Ouija board spelt out this warning 'He will not be laughing soon'. That night, some hours after we had ended the connection to the restless spirit something diabolical happened to the soldier that had laughed. His barrack room was virtually destroyed, large steel lockers were thrown around and metal beds were twisted like Uri Geller's dessert spoon whilst the man cowered under his mattress in abject terror. The first I knew about this was the next morning as other soldiers told me of the destruction. Now, some forty seven years later, James Howell was remembering that incident and appeared convinced that it was not the work of some demonic discarnate force but an act of madness by yours truly. As I said rather an uncomplimentary observation but one that had remained burnt into his memory for almost five decades. James even recalled the other soldier's name as Stanley Browning the 36 Battery Runner.

James and I enjoyed some happier recollections of 1969 when in pre-Gaddafi Libya we both swam the bay of Tobruk . Subsequently we endured many months of hardship following the overthrow of King Idris. We were trapped in the base of RAF El Adem as the revolutionary army of Colonel Gaddafi surrounded the unit and refused permission for planes to land or depart. Then James reminded me of the time I had bitten a chunk of flesh out of his friend the fearsome and ferocious, but very tasty Scotchman, Charlie Mac. I was only defending myself having been soundly whacked on the head with a wooden mallet in a brawl then subjected to extreme violence. As I said 'Crazy Horse' had some rather dark memories of our distant days together, when we were young. In fact he told my dear wife Mary that he had great sympathy for her having put up with me for so long, wondering how on earth did she do it?
Number 5 Victoria Road Bridlington is the location of the Spiritualist Church and it was there on the evening of 29th June 2016 that I met with Katie the president of said church. The Church itself is a single story unit set slightly back from a residential road in its own neatly cultivated grounds. Within it has seating for approximately fifty in a wonderfully warm and spiritually uplifting atmosphere. On entering I immediately became aware of the scent of Patchouli, my favourite incense was delicately perfuming the interior. Katie, a glowing spiritual lady, told me how she and her family had refurbished the church that had been gifted to them by a former member. Looking out through the brand new windows I saw an immaculate peaceful garden for mediation

and remembrance, Katie explained how she and her dedicated daughter Debs had transformed this from a virtual rubbish tip. The whole Church had a brilliant atmosphere of peace and love that seemed to shine out from the very fabric of the building. I knew the moment I walked in that I was going to really enjoy my evening there and this was quickly confirmed. Taking the admission for the Church that evening was a delightful young lady called Shirley who gave me a rather old fashioned look then quietly assured me that she was looking forward to my talk, well so was I.

I was gently and very politely introduced on the platform by a kindly gentleman named Trevor. He told the congregation that I was an internationally published author and psychic as well as being the feature editor of this newspaper Psychic World. My talk I titled 'Exploring The Etheric' and for this I had prepared absolutely no notes whatsoever. Now I was facing over forty people and allowed myself to be inspired, you see I really was exploring the etheric as what I was about to say was completely unscripted and given to me as I spoke. The theme of my talk was how spirit will always find the right person to work with in their quest to bring enlightenment and the truth of eternal life. To better explain this I gave many personal examples of how I myself had been contacted by spirit and received directions and guidance.

In telling the congregation about my first near death experience I remembered the days when I was suffering from influenza as a young solider back when I was in barracks. The Army doctor had wanted to hospitalize me but I had asked if I could just sleep through this illness in my own bed, it was a mistake that almost cost me my life. Unknown to me I was in fact very seriously ill and once I went to bed the influenza took over my body. Suddenly I found myself standing outside my own physical form staring down at myself and a voice spoke to me asking where I would like to go. Being inquisitive about the world I asked to see The Taj Mahal and instantly I was there outside that mighty magnificent building. Then the voice asked again where I would like to go and I wanted to see The Eifel Tower in Paris . Within a split second I was at the very top platform of that tower mingling with crowds of people. The voice then asked me where I really desired to be and I recall saying that I would like to visit my maternal grandparents at their home in a 17th century stone cottage in the village of Foulridge , Lancashire . It was like being Superman, I began to fly through the air over England and came to earth some half a mile or so from my grandparents home. I felt as if I weighed a ton, I could hardly move and as I struggled forward I saw a most beautiful lady dressed all in white with long flowing dark hair approaching me. She stopped and said in the most reassuring tone that seemed to fill me with love 'John you have to decide, do you want to go on to see your grandparents or will you return to your body?' I knew then that I must continue being a soldier and told that angelic being I would go back. As she took my hand I again felt an incredible all pervading sense of peace and then I awoke. I was on the floor having fallen out of bed and I was cold, but the fever had gone, I had survived. I told the good people in the Spiritualist Church in Bridlington that if I had opted to continue on my journey to see my grandparents then I would, without any doubt, have walked into the world of spirit and they would have never heard of me or that incredible encounter. You see I believe that even then, when I was a young rather roughhouse soldier boy, the spirits knew I had a job to do for them and gave me the opportunity to return.

I would like to thank Katie the President of Bridlington Spiritualist Church for inviting me to speak. Thanks also to Trevor her gentle partner and to all who came to see me on that happy evening. I sincerely hope that my words brought some hope and allowed you to see that the spirits do guide us as they seek to explain that there is no death just eternal everlasting life in the light and love of God.

CHAPTER FOUR

POLTERGEIST TERROR

The area of Tyne and Wear is situated in the North East of England, there in late November of 2007, Mrs. Sabrina Fallon and her family were subjected to a truly terrifying ordeal when their house was haunted by a poltergeist. It started one night at about 11pm Sabrina was disturbed to hear footsteps in the loft of her council house as there should have been no one up there. These were distinct, loud and clear steps as if someone were walking across the attic. The footsteps stopped and, thinking she had maybe imagined them, Sabrina went to back to sleep. At around 5.15am she woke again to the sound of bangs, bumps and more footsteps all coming from the loft. Now this really scared her, so Sabrina dialed 999 and contacted the police. She was certain someone was up there in her attic. This worried her a great deal as perhaps it was a burglar and she had two young children in the house. When the police arrived they listened to what Mrs. Fallon had to say and went to investigate. As they approached the loft the sound of footsteps could clearly be heard so, with some trepidation, the youngest PC pushed open the trap-door, climbed up and shone his torch inside. The loft space was empty, save for cobwebs, a few old toys and couple of cardboard boxes. When Sabrina asked the police officers what they thought was causing the sounds they said 'we think you have ghosts'.

Sabrina actually thought the police were joking and that the noises were some form of natural phenomena, maybe wind getting in or something. She certainly did not believe in ghosts. Over the next few weeks the sounds in the loft continued but Sabrina, her husband Martin and the children did their best to ignore them hoping they would just stop. They didn't. Then on the night of the 15th December Sabrina was away staying with friends and left her house keys with her sister Jane and her husband Jason. They called in to check that the house was OK, as they opened the door a voice from an unseen source whispered something unintelligible to them and as the lights came on noises could be heard upstairs. Believing that there was someone in the house Jason shouted 'Who's there!' as he did so some invisible something was thrown down the stairs and hit the wall beside him with a loud thump. Having heard the story of the police saying the house was haunted he was now terrified, turned round and with Sabrina's sister ran out of the house and locked the door behind them.

The next day Mr. And Mrs. Fallon arrived home with their two children, Aimie age 15 months and Shannon age 9 years. It was the same house but inside it had changed. The atmosphere was tense, almost electric and the temperature was freezing. Sabrina put all the heating on but still the house was cold and a deep sense of unease hung like an anxious mist throughout the upstairs rooms. That night Sabrina recalls she hardly slept, but it was the next day that things began to become really weird.

Sabrina recalls the start of the tangible terror 'our baby Amie was in her cot asleep, I heard my bedroom door slam shut so I went upstairs to see why. The whole area next to little Aimie's room was icy cold. Suddenly I heard the horrible footsteps again only this time they seemed angry, thump! thump! thumping across the loft space and then a series of incredibly loud bangs and knocking echoed around the house as if a dozen children were hitting the walls with sticks. I went into Aime's room picked her up and ran downstairs. I was terrified that whatever it was would injure my baby girl'.

By now Sabrina had accepted the idea that there may well be some kind of unearthly presence in her home and not knowing really what to do about it she decided to look in her local

Yellow-Pages directory for help. There she found the name of Suzanne Hadwin listed under Clairvoyants and Psychics, she decided to try calling her and asking for advice. When Suzanne answered the 'phone she told Sabrina that she could sense the presence of two spirit children and a very evil man who was, she said, now a poltergeist or noisy spirit with wicked intentions. Suzanne identified the poltergeist as a man called Peter and said that death had occurred in the house and that this evil spirit was now trying to create fear and terror for the whole family but most of all it wanted to harm little Aimie. Suzanne agreed to attend the Fallon's home on the 19th December to conduct what she termed a 'spiritual cleansing' that would remove the wicked poltergeist and send it into the light. In the meantime Suzanne explained that she would ask her own spirit guide Romanoff to go and protect the Fallon family from any further attacks by the unquiet spirit she called Peter.

The next day Sabrina, who still half suspected that this was all too weird to be true, decided to go and ask the local authority housing department if they knew of any reason why her council owned property should be haunted. What she was told caused Sabrina Fallon's blood to run cold. According to the housing officer there had, in the past, been a murder committed in the house she now lived in. A man named Peter had strangled his young wife and then stabbed her to death with an iron poker. By now near to panic Sabrina asked the housing officer if the council would be prepared to meet the fee to be charged by the Psychic-Medium Suzanne Hadwin. It was that or Sabrina and her entire family were moving out. The council housing officer agreed to meet half the cost of the spiritual cleansing and rid the house of the poltergeist.

That night Sabrina telephoned the psychic-medium Suzanne to tell her what she had been told by the local council and advise that her fee would be paid in full but half would come from the housing department. As she started to explain about the murder a rough raspy voice shouted through the telephone 'Go Away!' and the line went dead. In the lounge of her home Sabrina had left her two children watching a TV programme, when she went in she saw to her absolute horror that the picture on the screen was a series of wavy fuzzy lines and her baby daughter Aimie was staring at it as if in a trance. Then the room went freezing cold and from upstairs the sound of banging and clattering came loud and louder followed by the frighteningly familiar thump! thump! thumping of angry stamping footsteps. Switching off the TV and grabbing her child Sabrina shouted at the unseen entity in terror 'Leave my family alone!'. Her husband Martin stood still, shocked out of his disbelief by the obvious evidence he had just seen with his own eyes.

In desperation Sabrina then tried to contact Suzane again and dialed her number, all she could hear when she placed the handset to her ear was a fiendishly horrible cackling laughter that sent shivers running down her spine. That night, following Suzanne's earlier instructions, the whole family slept in the main lounge. Upstairs the poltergeist was pounding and banging on the walls. Before sleep Sabrina had to go to the bathroom, taking baby Aimie in her arms. With husband Martin standing guard close by she dared to climb the stairs and enter the bathroom. Then as she tried to leave, holding little Aimie tightly, an immense invisible force pushed her in the back then hot stinging hands grabbed at her neck causing red welts and scratches to appear. The poltergeist had now started a new more physical reign of terror. With a scream of fear Sabrina ran with Aimie into the lounge and stood petrified as Martin secured the door. What followed was the most difficult, sleepless night of her life. Thuds and bangs, hammering sounds and discordant yells reverberated around the house till dawn finally broke.

That day Suzanne Hadwin and her assistant arrived to start the spiritual cleansing of the Fallon's home. As soon as Suzanne entered the house she was drawn to the upstairs rooms. This is how she described the sensation. "The house atmosphere was intensely cold and a sense of despair and depression hit me hard, almost like a blow in the solar plexus so strong was the negative energy. Prior to entering the property I had conducted a self-protection ritual and was secure, safe in the protection of my own spirit guide Romanoff. As I walked forward into the hallway I knew at once that the entity, the poltergeist, was in the upper part of the house and lurked there with evil intentions. The coldness was spreading through the house from that area and so I simply followed the invisible trail leading directly to the bedroom usually occupied by 9 year old Shannon. In there the discarnate being was hiding ready to cause harm with its wickedness.

For a moment I felt nausea, a vile stench of rotting flesh filled the room and sickness swept through me, then I heard my spirit guide speak 'Continue for I am here and you are safe'. The entity now knew that it was confronted. Without fear I spoke clearly and with forcefulness ordering the discarnate being to remain trapped in that room and not leave until I could return. I had to be ready to do battle with the poltergeist as I now knew exactly what I was facing. This was a lost soul locked into the limbo-land that exists between our material world that we call Earth and the next. This had been and indeed still was a vile and Godless spirit with murderous intentions doomed to haunt the misty purgatorial realms where its actions had condemned it to stay. In anger it now sought to inflict injury upon the innocent, just as in life it had done. Now I would banish it into the light of infinity and beyond. But I had to be fully prepared as this was a demonic spirit that would, if it could, seriously injure me.' Before she left the Fallon's house Suzanne saw all members of the family one at a time and placed protection around them to ensure that the poltergeist could not gain control of their bodies. Then she advised that she must now enter into her lengthy preparations readying herself to confront the evil spirit and cleanse the property.

Over the next few days the Fallon household did experience various attacks from the poltergeist spirit but all the noise was confined to the bedroom that had belonged to Shannon. Christmas came and went and the door to that room remained locked. From within came the occasional sound of stamping feet and loud thumping sounds as though the bedroom walls were being struck with great force by baseball bats. But the poltergeist remained trapped within.

On the afternoon of the 27th Decmeber 2007 the psychic-medium Suzane Hadwin returned to the house of the Fallon family ready to confront the poltergeist. This is how she describes what happened: 'I decided that the first thing had to be a direct confrontation with the poltergeist in the room where I had ordered it to remain. So with Martin Fallon and Sabrina alongside me I unlocked and opened the door. The atmosphere was unpleasant and an almost tangible sense of depression hung in the cold still air. Then I sensed a sudden movement, a rush of wind passed by me and I new the battle was on. The poltergeist was loose and I was about to cleanse this house and expel it forever. But there was going to be a fight I knew that'.

As Suzanne started to cleanse the bedroom Sabrina's daughter Shannon suddenly appeared at the top of the stairs staring hard at her with a look of absolute hatred in her eyes. 'Get out of here you bitch'. She said. But Suzanne knew that this was not the 9 year old girl speaking this was the voice of the poltergeist that had entered her aura. "Get Shannon downstairs now!" Suzanne said "I need to get the spirit off her". Mrs. Fallon did as requested and in the lounge sat young Shannon down as Suzanne instructed on a chair in the center of the room. Around this chair Suzanne sprinkled a circle of salt and then she began to remove the spirit of the poltergeist from the aura of young Shannon. Here is how Sabrina, Shannon's mother, described what happened next:

'I watched as anxious as any mother would, afraid that Shannon might be hurt but Suzanne assured me this was perfectly safe. Then she lit some incense and a candle which she placed inside the circle with her and Shannon who was looking a little scared. When Suzanne started she placed her hands, fingers stretched wide, at the back of Shannon's body and seemed to be pushing at a physical being. I saw her face contort and she began to order the poltergeist to leave my daughter alone then, to my absolute horror, young Shannon turned her head and shouted 'Leave me alone you cow!'. But it wasn't her voice. Then Suzanne gave what looked like a mighty push and I heard a voice inside my head shouting at me, just a stream of obscenities. I shouted to Suzanne and she indicated I should sit still. Then suddenly a great rush of wind burst from nowhere, the walls resonated with loud bangs and the sound of running feet echoed from the staircase. Upstairs I could hear again the awful thud, thud thudding of the poltergeist banging and clattering. Suzanne seemed perfectly calm and laid little Shannon on the settee telling me that all was OK now the poltergeist had left her. Indeed the room itself now felt so much warmer.'

Two local authority housing officers had by this time arrived as they wanted to witness Suzanne Hadwin expelling the entity from the council house. They, along with Martin Fallon who was now filming the spiritual cleansing, followed Suzanne up the stairs where she started in Shannon's bedroom.

To conduct the ritual of spiritual cleansing Suzanne set out a circle of salt and asked all those present to step inside. She herself sat on a chair and called upon her spirit guides, specifically naming Romanoff, to come and help rid these premises of the evil spirit of the poltergeist. As she spoke Sabrina felt something touch her. Here is what she said about that experience:

'I was inside the circle watching Suzanne intently when I felt some force pressing me, pushing me as if I were being crushed and a voice in my head shouted 'I'm Peter! Get that bitch out of here'. I was stunned, my head was spinning and I felt myself falling, down I slipped, hit the floor almost becoming unconscious. Then I looked up and Suzanne was helping me, she lifted me up and said that the poltergeist had gone out of the room now and I would be safe.'

Suzanne Hadwin went from room to room in the house and at each room she called upon her guides to take the evil poltergeist out and away to the place appointed in the light of love and understanding. When she had completed the ritual the hose was clear. This is what Sabrina had to say:

"After Suzane and the council officers had left I just sat down and cried. The whole thing had been too much for me and I was I suppose in a sort of shocked state. But the house felt warm again, like a home and I actually slept peacefully that night for the first time in ages. I can honestly say that Suzanne Hadwin got rid of whatever it was that was haunting our house and for that I will be eternally grateful'.

I asked Suzanne Hadwin what she thought of this poltergeist haunting and she told me this: 'The entity was the evil spirit of Peter, the man who had murdered his wife there many years before. In death he had failed to make his transition out of fear of damnation for his murderous deeds and so had become trapped in the nether world, the twilight zone that exists betwixt Earth and the next dimension of life that we know as heaven or hell. I feel that the physical youth and vibrant energy of the young girl Shannon had been used by the spirit of Peter to empower his malevolence and that he targeted the family as he saw them as intruders into his space. What I did was to call upon my highly evolved spirit guide Romanoff and his helpers asking them to remove the wicked entity and direct the spirit of Peter to his designated destination. This they did and now I am quite certain that the Fallon family can live in peace, the poltergeist has left the building, gone to its appointed place in the world beyond.'

CHAPTER FIVE

EXPLORING THE ETHERIC

A question I am frequently asked by individuals that come to me for private consultation is this: How is it possible for you to see the future when it has not as yet happened? The answer I give is this: what we perceive of as being reality is restricted or limited by our faculties. That is, as a general rule, we rely on our five senses: Taste, Touch, Vision, Sound, and Smell. You will agree that we can not see a radio wave with our eyes but you would also accept that they exists as when you tune in your radio using an aerial or antenna you can hear whatever is being broadcast. It is the same with your television, again we can not see the signal but it exists in the same way that a radio signal exists. So it is with your mobile telephone or other device such as an Ipad. The key to unlocking the transmissions is the device needs to be tuned in. So it is with the dimensions that we perceive using our five senses, Width, Height, and Depth. In physics this is termed 'three dimensional Euclidean space'. We tune in to this space using our five senses. However, it is my belief that there exists a fourth dimension that occupies space parallel to Euclidean space and the name of that dimension or plane is The Etheric.

Within the Etheric plane there exists I believe, through personal experience and extensive study, astral sentient entities that can and do communicate with certain incarnate human beings. I say astral entities as some, though not all, have never been incarnated in human form. Some astral beings are of other higher dimensions and enter the Etheric plane to guide and direct those whom they communicate with. The Etheric dimension is not a place of permanent residence, it is more a kind of intermediate plane between the material and the spiritual. It was the Theosophist Madame Blavatsky who first wrote of The Etheric. According to Theosophical teaching The Etheric occupies a plane which corresponds to the physical plane. It is by gaining access to The Etheric that human beings can communicate with evolved astral beings from other dimensions thereby acquiring knowledge and information that may, in some instances, contain details of events on this material plane that are yet to take place. That is the answer, that is how I and all other genuinely gifted clairvoyant psychics are able to foresee the future.

My personal experiences of exploring the etheric began when I was a child aged six years. My parents were rather strict and each evening I was required to go to bed before 7pm and remain in my room, in fact they locked the door. I recall it was a summers day, outside the sun was shining and I lay on my bed wishing I could play in the garden, but I was not allowed to. My bedroom had flowered wallpaper and out of boredom, as I lay on my bed, I began counting the flowers. I know now that what I was in fact doing was a form of meditation, distracting my mind by giving it a mundane task. The result was that suddenly I was no longer a little boy locked in his bedroom, I was flying through time and space into another dimension.

I can clearly recall the land I arrived at having left my six year old boys body behind me, it was a sandy desert and I saw a large powerfully built man standing on a raised wooden platform. This man was directing hundreds of near naked dark skinned men to heave and haul huge stones from a boat on the river dragging them on tree trunks over the sand. I looked at this man and saw he had scrolls in his hands then, I found myself entering his body I went in through the middle of his back and I became that man. The felling was incredible, I was strong, my mind was clear and when I spoke the people around followed my directions. This experience continued for some time until I awoke back in my room and it was the dawn of the next day. When I told my father what I had seen he became quite angry and said that on no account was I to speak of this again as it was the work of the devil. This really scared me, I knew nothing of satanic forces nor had I any dealings with demons. What had happened to me I could not understand and now I was cautioned never to mention it.

The experience of traveling into the Etheric continued over a period of weeks. Each night I would stare at the wallpaper, count the flowers and find myself transported to that mysterious land where I became a big strong powerful man. Each morning I would wake with the memory in my mind and unable to tell anyone. The strain of keeping that amazing adventure to myself made me ill and I began to start falling down in a kind of faint. I remember collapsing at the top of the stairs in our house and falling from the top to the bottom. My parents took me to the medical centre and the Dr. there advised it was nothing extraordinary and I would grow out of it. Meanwhile I continued to travel nightly into another dimension, until suddenly it stopped. I recall trying to find the hidden pathway by counting the flowers but it did not work.

In the year 1990 a Psychic Medium came to see me and said that the spirits had directed him as I was to be his manager. That man was James Byrne and I did indeed manage his career as a professional stage and television/radio psychic. I also wrote his biography 'The Psychic World of James Byrne'. Interviewing James in the process of writing the book he told me how as a child his father would beat and punish him then shut him up in a closed room. Within his room James, as a terrified young boy, began to experience communication with discarnate spirit entities.

Exploring the Etheric requires one to first find the door or pathway. Many psychics I have spoken with have told me stories not too dissimilar to my initial experience and that of James Byrne. Obviously as adults we will not likely find ourselves locked into a bedroom, unless that be a prison cell (heaven forbid). Though the late Nelson Mandela is reported to have told the guards at his jail that it was they who were in prison, he could, he said, transport himself through time and space to anywhere on Earth. No doubt what Nelson Mandela was referring to was his practised technique of Astral Travelling. That is he had discovered the key to freedom by accessing the Etheric dimension in his Astral Body. That is no doubt what happened to me when I was a child of six years. With James Byrne it would be the trauma of being abused that opened the invisible door allowing him to experience communication with evolved entities.

Today I practice meditation to enable my spirit to access the Etheric and I find that when the angelic beings require my attention they direct me. I pay close attention to their directions as there is a reason for them and it is my duty to comply to the best of my ability. One recent direction I received was to speak and write about the Etheric to encourage all to explore that parallel dimension and thereby acquire the truth they are seeking in life.

CHAPTER SIX

THE STRANGE CASE OF ANN/RUBY

The arguments for and against the belief in reincarnation are not confined to the Spiritualist religion. However for the purpose of this essay I shall confine myself to discussing this subject from a Spiritualist perspective. My personal belief is that reincarnation is the only thing that makes sense in the light of eternal life. You see I feel certain that this brief flickering, this fragile shadow that we call life is but a short step on our pathway to paradise. What we do here whilst incarnated on the planet called Earth builds our infinite and eternal spirit, shaping us into that which we truly are. I have previously stated that I utterly reject the idea that my sins can be forgiven if I would only believe and accept in certain religious teachings. What would be the point in my life if at the end all my deeds, everything I have done, all that I failed to do, each good thing and every bad thing were eradicated, just wiped away like a little child's tears for a lost toy. What could possibly be the use in cleansing me of my sins, did I not commit them wilfully? I do not consider myself to be a total fool, so must accept that all I have knowingly undertaken, both good and bad was of my personal volition. But what, you may ask, of those whose lives are short or blighted by illness? It is my understanding that we all live many, many lives, some term this reincarnation that is our spirit, our soul will incarnate in another body following our transition. "A little while, a moment of rest upon the wind, and another woman shall bear me" Kahil Gibran wrote that in his poem The Prophet. Let me now tell you of the strange case of Ann who became Ruby and please, ask yourself if you believe, for dear reader this really is a true story.

At an early age Lynda Lee became aware that her mother disliked her with an intensity that bordered upon hatred. Lynda's father loved her though and asked his older sister

Mary to help raise Lynda. So it was that Mary, Lynda's aunt, took the role that Lynda's mother rejected. The effect was that Lynda and Mary became very close and a bond developed between them that would last throughout the years. Mary had a kind caring husband called Chris who would help Lynda with her school lessons. It was almost as if her aunt and uncle were her mother and father, but they always kept their private life to themselves. It was a family trait, secrets were secrets and certain matters were never discussed.

As time passed Lynda, who was exceptionally bright and articulate, went away to University in the city of Johannesburg, South Africa. There Lynda married and very quickly gave birth to two children. Then, almost as quickly, she was divorced. Alone in the big city and with responsibilities Lynda found herself in the arms of a lover and again became pregnant. Due to complications with morning sickness Lynda sought the help of her aunt Mary who welcomed her into the house and cared for Lynda with great compassion. On 24th May 1993 Lynda gave birth to a beautiful little girl she named Ruby Jane. Aunt Mary was by her side and nursed both Lynda and the baby to good health.

Soon Lynda Lee was able to live independently again and moved into a substantial property with a large garden and swimming pool. Aunty Mary kept in constant touch by telephone and would on occasion visit with her husband Chris. It was during one such visit, as they sat in the entertainment area close by the pool taking an early lunch that Ruby began to speak. Always an extremely articulate child she sat looking at her great aunt Mary then said 'Aunty M, do you remember when you put me in that white box with my fluffy yellow duck?" For a moment there was absolute silence then Ruby spoke again "Why did I have a bandage on my back at Port Elizabeth?" aunt Mary who was aged 76 became extremely pale and in a trembling voice said "What bandage was that Ruby dear?" to which the child replied "The one that the doctor put on my back". As the words left the little girls mouth

Aunt Mary collapsed and fell from her chair to the floor in a faint.

Uncle Chris was on hand to help his wife Mary, he lifted her from the ground and carried her to a bedroom where she quietly recovered. It was later that afternoon that Lynda discovered what had happened to her aunt. It seemed that some years ago, over thirty in fact, in the year 1960, Aunt Mary and her husband Chris had a child born, they named her Ann. No one knew of this as the family were secretive and it had never been mentioned as some two days following the birth the baby Ann died, she had been born with Spina-Bifida. Ann had been treated at the hospital at Port Elizabeth where her badly deformed back had been bandaged by the doctor. Despite all efforts being made the baby died and Mary with Chris had buried her in a white coffin placing beside the tiny body of their daughter a yellow cuddly toy duck to keep her happy on the final journey into the next world. "We told no one in the family, no one about this, it is impossible for young Ruby to know these things" said Sylvia holding back her tears.

Some eighteen months passed and Lynda Lee had to visit the town of Port Elizabeth to attend the wedding of a cousin. As she was driving through the outskirts of the town with young Ruby by her side she noticed the child becoming agitated. "What is the matter dear?" she asked Ruby who quietly said "Look mum, that is the graveyard where I am buried, stop and I will show you where Aunt M. put me in the grave". As they walked through the hundreds of headstones, down many winding paths Lynda was sure they were lost but Ruby seemed to know where she was going. In a distant corner by a wonderful old tree Ruby stopped and pointed to the ground "This is my grave" she said. In the still silence of the cool morning air Lynda stood and gazing down to where Crystal had indicated she saw a pale white marble headstone with the inscription 'Ann Dubois, 24 May 1960 – 26 May 1960'.

Ruby Jane Lee was just over six years old when she took her mother Lynda Lee to see the grave where the baby of her Aunt Mary was buried. When Lynda asked her how she had been born again little Ruby explained, as only an innocent child could explain, "I came back in a beautiful, better body". Today, some fifteen or so years later, Ruby Jane Lee is an Internationally known model and yes, she is in a truly beautiful body.

CHAPTER SEVEN

HAUNTED HOUSES-v-EXORCISM

In the year 1973 I persuaded my dear wife Mary to accompany me to the cinema to watch a film titled 'The Exorcist'. I had, somewhat disingenuously, told her it was a romantic story concerning a priest and his forbidden lover. Those of you familiar with this film will know that it is in fact about a young girl being possessed by the demon Pazuzu. The plot centres upon the priest Father Damien Karras assisted by the experienced exorcist Father Lankester Merrin who collectively set about an exorcism to expel the demonic entity. The night we went to see this movie the theatre had in attendance a number of uniformed members of the St. John's Ambulance Brigade, Mary wondered why they were there. That was the very last time my dear wife and I ever went to the cinema together. More than forty two years have passed since that night and still she refuses to set foot inside a movie theatre with me.

The laugh a minute TV show 'Most Haunted' has popularised the idea that ghosts are everywhere, especially lurking in dark shadows within spooky looking old buildings. To attract their attention, according to this show at least, one needs night vision cameras, a few weird looking 'psychics' and a loud mouthed brassy blonde bimbo shouting 'If you are there show yourself'. Throw in the occasional screaming fit, have one of the team become 'possessed' by a discarnate entity, such as an ape or a dog, a fictitious character even and start uttering total gobbledegook then its Carry On Haunting. The problem is that the general public accept such nonsense as being the truth. As Spiritualists we know that there really are spirits that have become trapped between this material world and the next. Some spirits have deliberately declined to move on from this material world into the light and their appointed place, they remain between two worlds and at times those who are sensitive can see them. However, these discarnate spirits can and will eventually find their way to the eternal light of God's infinite love. In the meantime they are most certainly not going to act as unpaid TV show extras pushing wannabe famous ham acting fake psychics in the back. Nor would they start jumping into the physical body of an intellectually challenged moon howling half wit. However, there are spirit entities, there are actual real haunted houses and at times these do require an exorcism to be performed.

I was recently invited to conduct a psychic investigation of a huge Victorian mansion house with extensions and large gardens. This massive building was located in the county of Yorkshire just outside the town of Bradford and had, in its past, been the home of a rich mill owner. I was accompanied on this investigation by the new owner who had conducted some research into the history of the property, though he told me nothing of this. On entering the large oak front door I was instantly aware that in this house there had been many deaths and it was most definitely haunted. 'Many people died here' I said to my host 'this was at one time a form of hospital or nursing home' I sensed and he confirmed that was correct. I was drawn to a long corridor in an annexe off the main house and 'saw' there in a dimly lit room a vision of a lady on fire. As I described what I had seen I heard a voice tell me that she had taken her own life there by pouring petrol over herself and setting it alight. The gentleman by my side advised that he knew of this incident as he had spoken at length with the former matron of the house when it was used both as a nursing home and, in the annexe, as a treatment unit for recovering drug addicts. Deep within the main house in the darkness of the inner rooms I felt the presence of a spirit and an overwhelming sadness caused me to stop by an old exposed wooden beam. The atmosphere in that room was oppressive and cold I could feel the despair of the discarnate being that had taken his own life there, hanging himself by a rope attached to that grim oak beam. Again my host advised that he knew there had been a suicide within the property but more than that he did not know.

Once I had established that old dark house had unseen residents I agreed to conduct a form of exorcism, but first I had a duty to guide the discarnate lost souls out of their purgatory into the light of God's infinite love. It was too late in the day for me to do this and so a time was agreed when I would return and attempt to free the lost souls then cleanse the place of any residual negative energy. Some weeks later I returned with my wife Mary who always accompanies me as a kind of personal assistant. Together we visited the sites previously identified and I began to communicate with the spirit presence within. My aim was to guide them from this their earthly prison out of the mists of purgatory into the wonderful welcoming light of the divine power that we term God. My method is completely secular, in a gentle conversation with the spirits I make no mention of any specific religion or religious belief systems. My advice to the discarnate souls is straightforward as I explain that their life in this particular dimension is over and it is time to move on to the next phase. At times I have found that the spirit disagrees with my advice and on such occasions I call on my previous experiences in HM Prisons, I give them direct orders to move on or else!

It took me some time to persuade the two spirits within that large property to take the path into the light but eventually they did do so. The hanged man was a tragic soul who had been wandering the rooms where he died since he killed himself. I sensed his fear of walking into the unknown where he was convinced punishment for his suicide awaited. Once I explained that his ultimate destination was in the light of forgiveness and understanding the spirit of this man accepted. I did not see the discarnate spirit, but I heard a silent voice saying a form of farewell and the temperature of the room changed from oppressively cold to a fresh lighter feel. Also, strangely, the darkness that had filled the area switched to a new brightness as the sun shone in from a formally unseen window.

The next task for the completion of my duty as the exorcist was to remove from within those walls all residual negative energy. Mary had brought with her a number of sage bundles that she now lit and they produced powerfully pungent smoke. I had brought a small bell with me that I rang loudly as together Mary led us from room to room and I gave stern instructions in deep stentorian tones that this house was now a place of happiness and joy. I also sang a little song in the very heart of the house, this was a former ballroom with a massive white marble fireplace. The owner gave me a very old fashioned look as I began 'Knees up Mother Brown...Knees Up Mother Brown..Knees up Knees up....Don't get the breeze up...Knees up Mother Brown'.

At the end of the day as we all stood in the hallway I looked back towards the mighty dark oak staircase and saw shining there a brilliant sunbeam glimmering through a large ornate window. The whole house felt vibrant and in a way at peace with itself. You see I believe that everything in the universe is alive and has an awareness of what it is i.e. I know I am a human being, a pen knows it is a pen and that gigantic old Victorian house knew that it would once again be a mighty mansion.

Over the following months the new owner spent hundreds of thousands of pounds renovating the property and making it into a spectacular residence. It was converted to six large executive style apartments and is now a happy home to a number of contented people. I am told that no one has experienced any kind of distressing paranormal activity within those walls and it is a wonderful place to live. Though as for the owner, he tells me that every time he stands in what was the old ballroom a haunting melody pops into his head...'Knees up Mother Brown'...

CHAPTER EIGHT

A SPIRITUAL HEIRACHY OF NEEDS

Abraham Harold Maslow (1908-1970) was an American psychologist best known for his work on the hierarchy of needs, that is the basic needs to sustain life must be met before the higher needs of intellect can be achieved. Maslow depicted this as a pyramid showing them in ascending order starting at the base: 1. Physiological 2. Safety. 3. Love/Belonging 4. Esteem 5. Self Actualization. Put in simplistic terms what Maslow was saying is that before you can do anything beyond the mundane you have to provide for your basic requirements of life i.e. food and shelter in a safe environment. We in the developed Western world are today in a position whereby, in relative terms, our physiological needs are to all intents and purposes guaranteed. That is we will not starve on the streets, nor will we roam the land homeless and hungry. We all have, as a general rule, the basics to sustain our lives. As for safety, again in relative terms, we are reasonably secure and do not have to do battle on a daily basis to survive. That brings us up Maslow's pyramid to love and belonging.

As Spiritualists we understand that the essence of what we are is the spirit incarnate in a physical body. We are not the material body that has form as a human being we are eternal souls. Our current incarnation is but an ephemeral entity, a brief existence that we inhabit to extend our understanding into the infinite power that we know as God. What we do whilst we are 'alive' incarnated in our present form accrues to our spiritual essence that is who we really are. Thus our spirits, that is you and I, progress over time through the many mansions of eternity to ultimate perfection. It is my belief that this world that we call Planet Earth is an extremely elaborate mirage, an illusion if you will, created to enable us to spiritually evolve. As stated above in this Western world, in which most of us reading this live, there are today social support systems that virtually guarantee our two basic needs, as listed by Maslow. This situation has evolved over time, from the early stone age through the tribal hunter-gatherers to agricultural communities and eventually the massive cities created by the Industrial Revolution. No more do we have the likes of Oliver Twist asking for more, today we have the relative deprivation of no 50" flat screen TV with an 'X' Box. Even inmates of HM Prisons have computer games in their cells, compared to the bread, water and rats that were the lot of Victorian prisoners.

Love and belonging, level three on Maslow's pyramid of needs, is perhaps something so intangible that it can not be measured. Let me elaborate on this a little. For example what I may conceive of as 'love' may not be the same as how another perceives this. For me 'love' is the feeling I get when I hold my young grandson, when I stroke my dear wife Mary's hair first thing in the morning, when I shake hands with friends I have known for many years, or when I hear the sound of a lark ascending into a pale blue English sky. As for belonging I know where I was born, where I live, who my family are, my country, my land my home and I belong. I feel secure within that knowledge. But this may not be so for all, some will feel love in different ways, perhaps through desire and the realisation of physical contact. Some may identify belonging as being the possession of material goods. To each his own and so Love and Belonging are essentially needs peculiar to the individual. It must be so with esteem which is fourth on Maslow's pyramid of needs.

Esteem is the concept of being thought of with respect and admiration. However in today's crazy celebrity status conscious world being held in public esteem is perhaps no indication of worth. For example you dear reader may or may not be familiar with the term 'Diamond Geezer' which is most usually used to describe a villain such as 'Mad' Frankie Frazer.

Many people, mistakenly in my opinion, hold murdering convicted killers such as mad Frank in high esteem. Or pseudo singing groups such as 'The Monkees' who never actually played on any of their records, they were held in high esteem by their 'fans'. The truth is, I feel, that we each of us know what we are, being a fake and fooling the general public to attain fame and fortune is a lie. So any esteem we gain from that is utterly worthless. What Maslow's fourth need of esteem really means must be self esteem. As a man said, to your own self be true and it follows as night follows day you can then be false to no one.

Self Actualization is the highest of Maslow's hierarchy of needs and means that we achieve our full potential. The great man himself said this: 'If you plan on being anything less than you are capable of being, you will probably be unhappy all the days of your life'. I have outlined above the stairway that has to be climbed in life and to be honest we are truly fortunate today as we have a step up from the start. Yet so many of us are unhappy in our lives, now why is that? In my personal experience the sticking point is at Maslow's level two SAFETY. What many perceive of as safety is anything but, it is fear of failure. Taking a chance in life, in your life, means setting out to do something that will take you from where you are now to where you visualize yourself as being. The problem is that in so doing you risk losing the position you are currently in. So it is the fear of failure that is holding one back. However, look at it this way, if you were content being where you now are you would not be dreaming about being somewhere else, would you? Maslow said: 'One's only failure is failing to live up to one's own possibilities'.

Let me give you an example from my own turbulent life. Thirty years ago I suffered an accident that damaged my leg and resulted in gangrene. I had been a runner with many marathon races completed and a best time close to three hours. I once ran through the twenty mile marker in one hour fifty nine minutes. Waking up in a hospital bed as an amputee was something of a shock, believe me. But the worst part was being told I would never walk or work again as there were many complications including blood poisoning etc. I have to say that the medical team did a great job but I was discharged in a wheelchair and the social worker appointed to help assured me that my working life was over. They would ensure I was on all benefits available. I was, they advised me, perfectly safe. Now being safe and being alive are not, in my opinion, one and the same thing. I refused to claim disability payments and as I owned a large Victorian mansion style house I let out the spare rooms to students. My wife was worried, she did not complain though she trusted me. I next found myself a University course to get a teaching certificate in Special Needs Education and went there in my wheelchair. The thing was I did not see myself as a cripple I saw myself as a man that had things to do in life and nothing was going to stop me. Passing the course got me a good job with Lancashire County Council and within 18 months of being amputated I was in work earning a living.

The job with Lancs CC was very safe and I was looking after my family, again a viable human being nice and safe with a neat new bungalow. From there to staging shows at major theatres such as The London Palladium and The Liverpool Empire and having books published all over the world such as my best selling Psychic Pets was an experience. It was far from being a safe option to undertake such risky ventures and to be truthful none of them made me a great deal of money. On the way I met and worked with many interesting and incredible characters that have enriched my life. Let me tell you it hasn't been safe, at times I was sailing very close to the wind. But as one of my showbiz associates Hollywood star Steve Rowland says 'if you are not living on the edge then you are taking up too much room'. As for esteem, well I have no doubt that I have done my best and made a real effort against the odds. Regarding my self actualization, it ain't over till it's over, there's time yet. Now what about you?

CHAPTER NINE

THE RAINY DAY

Henry Wadsworth Longfellow (1807-82) in his poem 'The Rainy Day' wrote the immortal words: 'Into each life some rain must fall'. I am sure we can all relate to that, as one door closes and another one just slams us right in the snotter. Sometimes, it seems, our days are dark and dreary, but behind the clouds the sun is always shining. The idea is to keep on keeping on till you make a breakthrough from stormy weather to walking on the sunny side of the street. The trick is, so it seems to me, never ever give up trying, as one fine day you will find yourself dancing along sunnyside lane. That is my theory and as I travel down Route 66, following my recent birthday, I am as hopeful as ever of achieving what I personally perceive of as success. You see, in my opinion, gaining the love, affection and respect of the people that matter in ones life is success. Let me give you some examples from this wide, wild and sometimes wonderful world that we call Planet Earth.

As a professional psychic consultant I have met and spoken with many people that would perhaps, at first glance, appear to be affluent and successful. One young lady I helped was immensely wealthy, her credit card had no upper limit if she needed more she just contacted the bank. Outside her residence in the city of Oxford UK was a shining new chauffer driven Bentley, by her doorway stood a huge personal bodyguard. In material terms this lady was rich, in spiritual terms she was impoverished. It was not that she did not want to follow the pathway to enlightenment, her position prevented her from so doing. This young woman was the daughter of a Middle Eastern Royal family and as such was a virtual prisoner, locked away behind golden bars. Over the years that we spoke I did all that I could to bring hope to her life, all she really wanted was to be free, to be in the arms of man that loved her for herself. I wish I could tell you that she found her Romeo, but she did not, she eventually accepted the husband her father arranged and moved into a remote palace in a distant land where she would forever be a beautiful princess in a gilded cage. You may see her, or others like her, seated in the back of a glittering Rolls Royce, being driven through the streets of London. Next time you do, think not that there goes a fabulously wealthy woman, understand that there goes a prisoner in emerald handcuffs.

In the year 1990 I sent a song I had written to the trouser ripping Texan pop-singer P J Proby with a view to recording him singing this. The song was titled 'Stage of Fools' and Jim Proby liked it, said he would sing it but needed to see me. I was pleased to connect with PJP as he had been my favourite singer back in the sixties when he had top ten hits with songs such as 'Hold Me' and 'Somewhere'. What I found when I arrived at his broken down terraced house in the back streets of Bolton, Lancashire was an alcoholic old man on the edge of despair. Jim Proby had been a big star once upon a time, he featured alongside The Beatles on their very first TV Special 'Around The Beatles' in 1964. John Lennon and Paul McCartney wrote a song for him 'That Means A Lot' and Proby was voted the best male vocalist that year in the New Musical Express poll. By 1990 all that fame and what had been his fortune was gone, the fairy tale was behind him, what remained was exceedingly grim. However Jim Proby could still sing, his voice was as brilliant as ever and so I agreed to help him rebuild his career, though how I could do it I did not know at the time. What I then did was get him into the recording studio and put his amazing voice onto tape. Within three months I had sufficient songs to release an album we called 'THANKS' featuring the incredible voice of P J Proby. I even managed to get Jim on TV, BMG in Europe agreed to distribute the album, in the UK The John Menzies group got the CD Album into all the record shops. Suddenly Jim Proby was back, with a summer season at Blackpool I had signed him to and Granada ITV were filming a documentary about him. Success! You dear reader may well think so but the truth was that P J Proby had another issue far bigger than mere alcoholism, he was hell bent on self destruction. What had taken me a year and a lot of money to create he wrecked completely by refusing to promote or sing any of the songs. Then he almost killed himself by drinking a full bottle of Jack Daniels, collapsing with a heart attack, that ended his Blackpool season. And that dear reader was the end of that, Jim Proby well and truly rained on the parade.

To say that the episode with Proby earned me nothing but distress is perhaps something of an understatement. My wife Mary went ballistic. But she loves her crazy husband so on with the motley. Never a man to give in and be what one might term a 'normal' person I decided next to promote theatrical presentations of psychic powers featuring the very gifted medium James Byrne. Again I managed to succeed quickly getting James onto Lancashire's biggest commercial radio station at Red Rose Radio in Preston. I arranged with the amazing John Myers who was then the station controller for James to do a series of Psychic Phone in late night shows. This was the first time a commercial station had done this and we were featured in the national press. James Whale picked up on this and we were invited on to his Network UK TV show. I sent an outline for a book about James to HarperCollins the publishing house and got us a contract for me to write 'The Psychic World Of James Byrne'. The book was published in 1993 shortly after James Byrne was in my co-production 'A Psychic Experience' at The London Palladium. We were on a roll, BBC Radio One had James on a one hour special, he was selling out theatres across the UK. We even flew to Ireland and he appeared live on The Gaye Byrne Show the top light entertainment show in the Republic of Ireland. This was what one might call success and, though I say so myself, I believed I had been instrumental in creating it. What happened next was something else. I began to get psychic mediums from all over the UK pleading with me to manage their careers, one such was the Liverpool performer Billy Roberts, another was a man called Derek Johnson also known as Derek Acorah. As for James Byrne, well Jim was at heart a Bolton lad who wanted to live a quiet family life and father children with a woman that loved him. James Byrne got married, moved to another town and settled down. He sometimes writes for Psychic World and is now mainly working as a healing force helping people with health problems. But let me tell you this, when James told me he was throwing his hand in and leaving my management it was a rainy day indeed, I was seriously upset. Over two years of hard work building his name and he was gone. I had to start all over again from scratch with a new idea, a new client and I had not the first clue how I could repeat the success I had created for James Byrne.

Meanwhile it never rains but what it pours. I am sure you have all experienced that feeling, I know I have. But, as a man said, into each life some rain must fall.

CHAPTER TEN

FREE WILL-V-CIRCUMSTANCES

Some years ago, whilst visiting the author Colin Wilson we were discussing the philosophy of positivism as opposed to the nihilism of Sartre's existentialist doctrine of despair. Wilson argued that Jean Paul Sartre's statement in his book 'Being and Nothingness' that 'Life is a useless passion' totally misses the point of our existence. As human beings we have free will to be what it is possible for us to be within the confines of our given circumstances.

However, what we may construe as difficult circumstances should not deter us from attempting to attain what we perceive to be success in life. As a good example of progression through determined effort consider the achievements of Colin Wilson himself. He was born into a working class family in the industrial midlands where he originally worked at various mundane jobs. It was whilst he was employed as a laboratory assistant that he became so disillusioned with his lot in life that he contemplated suicide. Wilson went so far as to prepare a phial of acid that he was intending to drink, with the glass at his lips he suddenly realised that he must live, he had real work to do. Wilson then escaped the factories and nine to five taking himself to London where he slept rough on Hampstead Heath as he read for and wrote his masterpiece 'The Outsider'. During our discussion Wilson explained that it was at the moment of his intended suicide that he had a momentary vision of what he could be if he dared to dream.

The philosophical belief that we are spiritual beings incarnated in a physical body existing within the confines of this material world is incorporated in what we term metaphysics. 'Cogito ergo sum: I think therefore I am' Rene Descartes (1596-1650) explains that we are more than the mortal body that we inhabit. Yet this physical being that is, to all intents and purposes, what we are comes with circumstances that are utterly beyond our control. For example if I were the first born child of say the Queen of Great Britain then, assuming health and mental capacity, my life would be one of service to my country. To do otherwise would require an immense effort of will and determination, as evidenced by the abdication of King Edward VIII in 1936. That, in philosophical terms, perhaps explains why it is the norm for individuals to accept their birth circumstances and proceed in life accordingly. The saying that 'the fruit does not fall far from the tree' offers a widely accepted insight into the way that many, if not all, allow the circumstances of their birth to dictate the way they live their lives.

In my August 2015 feature column I wrote of my paternal ancestor Richard Sutton whose extraordinary life story was used by Emily Bronte as the basis for her character Heathcliff in her novel 'Wuthering Heights'. Richard Sutton achieved a great deal in his life rising from virtual poverty employed as a boot-black amongst the slaves in his masters mansion house to being the owner of vast estates. Sutton eventually bought his masters mansion 'West House' at Dent in Yorkshire along with numerous farms including Rigg End. It was at Rigg End that his sons William and Robert were born to his wife Eleanor. I am the direct descendant of Robert Sutton who became the head of many important estates, including Hornby Castle. Robert was also a gamekeeper and in those Victorian times would have been a man of considerable standing in the local community. His brother William Sutton emigrated to Canada in the year 1851 and resided initially in a small town called Kincardine where he built a saw mill, created a dam to supply water and was generally an energetic organiser. There exist to this day streets and areas named after my Great Great Great Uncle namely: Williamsburg, William Street and Sutton Street.

In the year 1867 William Sutton (1828-1896) was appointed as Sheriff of Bruce County and he moved into a house in Walkerton that had a cell block incorporated into the building. Subsequently a purpose built jail was built and William Sutton was in overall command as the Sheriff. Sutton held that position until the year 1892 when he was charged with abusing his office. It seems, from records held in the Bruce County Museum that Sutton had been absenting himself from his place of duty to spend time setting up a lumber business. I am indebted to my erudite distant cousin Jan Bridget for this: 'It does leave a huge cloud hanging over William Sutton. Further investigation into affairs in British Columbia (the other side of Canada) reveals that William Sutton had been visiting British Columbia for twenty years and spending some considerable time there setting up a lumber business at Cowichan, Vancouver Island. He had visited enough times for the local newspaper to state, in his obituary, that he had lived in British Columbia for 20 years, yet he did not actually move there until 1893, three years before he died.' The point I am attempting to make is that William Sutton the son of Richard Sutton (1782-1851) was very like his father, a determined adventurer and a man to be reckoned with. The fact that circumstances surrounding him on arrival in Canada would have been difficult did not halt or hinder him as he quickly became a man of substance.

My father Francis 'Frank' Sutton was by trade a blacksmith in the 1940s when they used anvils and heavy hand held hammers to beat the metal into shape. After military service with The Parachute Regiment' Frank Sutton married his wife and my mother Sheila then soon after I arrived. To improve his circumstances my father joined The Lancashire Constabulary becoming Police Constable 1772. Frank quickly achieved promotion transferring to the Criminal Investigation Department or CID where he became a Detective Inspector. Frank Sutton overcame the tough circumstances of his early life as a blacksmith and gained a position of good standing in the police force. His son, my brother Martin Sutton also joined the police service in 1970 and he served in many departments including as a team leader in The Tactical Aid Group in Greater Manchester and as a CID Detective Inspector. As you can see there is a pattern here, the apple did not fall far from the paternal tree.

In my own case I served for some years as an NCO in the British Army and was the Middlewight Boxing Champion of my Regiment. My father's brother Alfred Sutton was also a Middleweight boxing champion in the Army. On leaving the Army I went into the Home Office Prison Service where I was employed initially at HM Prison Wormwood Scrubs and subsequently Strangeways Prison Manchester where I became a Hospital Officer. For a time I ran the assessment ward at Strangeways Jail where inmates were sent by the courts for psychicatric assessment. This was a difficult position for me as I was always sensitive and as the psychic insights came to me the visions were at times incredibly intense. One inmate on the ward was charged with arson, he had tried to persuade the local council to change his local authority house as he claimed the neighbours were threatening him. To persuade the social workers that he was telling the truth this man had an idea, he set fire to his own council house by pouring petrol through the front door. Unfortunately the house had only just been painted and the woodwork was emitting fumes that instantly ignited burning the place down along with his three children that were upstairs asleep. I took this man to Booth Hall Children's Hospital to visit his daughters. They were in an isolation burns unit wrapped up like Egyptian mummies, as I stood by these children with the man at my side handcuffed to me I saw as in a vision the tragic flames surrounding them. For those children there would be no more circumstances.

I think, therefore I am, as a man said and I arrived at the considered conclusion that though I was fully physically capable of being a jailer I had other objectives in life. So whilst I did initially allow my trajectory to be within the close proximity of my historical family tree there was within me something more. Perhaps that something is what drove my ancestor Richard Sutton to be the man he was, as his son Sheriff William Sutton was and Robert Sutton was and my father was. Circumstances, I make the circumstances as Winston Churchill said and each of us can do something special if we try. Life is not a useless passion it is, as Colin

Wilson told me, an experience that we can make positive if we would only dare to dream.

CHAPTER ELEVEN

HEATHCLIFF
The Origins Of Emily Bronte's Character

Numerous polls have shown that of all the romantic heroes in literature the character that is most frequently voted as number one is that of Heathcliff from the novel 'Wuthering Heights' by Emily Bronte. He was even the subject of a chart topping pop song by the brilliant Kate Bush which contains in the lyrics lines from the novel 'Heathcliff, let me in at your window'...'bad dreams in the night' etc. For the character of Heathcliff is, if you read the book, one mean, moody, brutal, aggressive and at times almost demonic individual with dark swarthy looks. He is a tortured loner, an outsider, obsessed by his love for Catherine. For some reason many women find Heathcliff one extremely sexy man. Emily Bronte was a very proper young lady from a clerical family, she would have no personal experience of anyone like Heathcliff. So how did such a well educated, rather protected lady dream up such an unorthodox character? What follows is, I believe, the answer.

As a Spiritualist it is part of my belief that I am totally responsible for my own actions and I do not accept that my sins belong to anyone else, they are mine. As a general rule I also believe that as you sow, so shall you reap. In other words if my deeds are destructive then what follows will be negative, I sincerely hold that to be true. Of course I try to do good things, to help others and be a kind, compassionate soul, but now and then someone comes along that needs special attention. We all have that within us, at least I believe we do and in my case most certainly. It is a strange paradox, is it not, that a spiritual individual can switch from being gentle and forgiving to being an agent of retribution. How can this be? Is it nature or is it nurture? That question has puzzled psychologists and psychoanalysts for as long as there has been scientific inquiry into the human mind. One well known idiom or wise saw that suggests an answer is this 'the fruit does not fall far from the tree'. In my personal experience that has often been proven to be an unfortunate truth. As an example, whilst working in HM Prison Wormwood Scrubs I was dealing with a young man who had just been sentenced to life imprisonment for murder, he had poured a can of petrol over his victim and burnt him to death. The strangest thing was that his prison record showed that his own father had also been sentenced to life imprisonment many years previously for committing a murder in exactly the same way. Now as I said I am by nature and by my belief in Spiritualism a forgiving and kindly soul, but there is something within me that, when the time comes, alters my personality quite dramatically. Could it be, I have often wondered, that my physiological and psychological genetic composition predisposes me to be a man for all seasons? If so where then did this interesting and at times highly volatile nature bear its genesis? What strange family tree bore this mysteriously motivated individual fruit-cake?

Inspired by the television series 'Who Do You Think You Are?' I set out to research into the history of my own family, The Sutton's, starting at my paternal line. I was already aware, having spoken briefly to my cousin Keith F. Sutton, that our line could be traced back many centuries. Keith had already discovered that we shared a direct ancestor, one Charles Sutton, who was the father of my grandfather. This man had been in charge of a country estate at Old Langho in Lancashire acting as the gamekeeper, a trade and job he had learned from his father Robert Sutton who previously held that position. This seemed to me about what one might reasonably expect as the Sutton family were residents of the countryside in Yorkshire and Lancashire. So going back to my Great Great Grandfather there was nothing particularly remarkable. The occupation of gamekeeper and estate manager was though one requiring a certain firmness of character, especially in late Victorian England. But there was something more that Keith wanted to tell me about The Sutton family, he said that we shared a direct line ancestor named Richard Sutton of West House in the town of Dent in Yorkshire. There was, Keith advised me, something really quite unique about this Richard Sutton, he was, according to certain serious academics, considered to be the source material for the dark, rather brooding character of Heathcliff from the novel WutheringHeights by Emily Bronte.

The Bronte sisters actually lived some fifty or so miles to the south east of Dent in the town of Haworth where their father was a minister. However the Bronte family had wide social connections throughout Yorkshire and Lunesdale and the brother of Emily and Charlotte Bronte named Branwell Bronte was an artist who paid a visit to Hartley Coleridge the brother of Samual Taylor Coleridge the famous Lakeland poet. In his article for The Sedbergh Historian Mr. Christopher Heywood in 'Hartley Coleridge and the Bronte Novels' concludes that the remarkable story of Richard Sutton and his rise to prominence was passed to Branwell at Nabb Cottage on Rydal Water during the occasion of his visit there. It is assumed that Branwell subsequently recounted this story to his sister Emily. This was the true story of Richard Sutton a man both infamous and important in his time who climbed from being little more than a boot-black to being a land owning gentleman of substance. A great deal of painstaking detailed research has been conducted into the life of this man by another of my distant cousins a rather erudite lady named Jan Bridget of Todmorden in Yorkshire. Jan has discovered that our ancestor Richard Sutton (1782-1851) was orphaned at a young age and taken in to work amongst the slaves owned by the powerful Sill family of Dentdale. Edmund Sill, the master of West House and owner of many farms in the Yorkshire dales, was a slave trader with two ships trading with Jamaica where he was associated with a sugar plantation. From Jamaica Edmund Sill brought slaves through the port of Liverpool to work on his lands in Yorkshire. When Richard Sutton, then little more than a boy, was taken to work for the Sill family he worked alongside the slaves enduring extreme harsh treatment.

Richard Sutton in his position as general hand for the Sill family is recorded as being subjected to a flogging for some misdemeanour, so he was not treated with great favour by the family. There is a DVD film made about the Sills and the use of slave labour in Yorkshire titled 'A Regular Black: The Hidden Wuthering Heights' in which it was claimed that Richard Sutton went on from being a slave to becoming the richest man in Dentdale and was of an unpleasant nature. The generally accepted story being that Richard Sutton was in love with Ann Sill the daughter of his benefactor Edmund Sill. Richard and Ann would have been virtually raised under the same roof albeit in vastly different quarters. This is no doubt the source of the gossip about Richard Sutton that was current during his lifetime and would have been discussed by people in the area. The film suggests that Richard Sutton may have been a black slave but this is wrong as Jan Bridget discovered he was baptised in St. Oswald's church at Thornton-in-Lonsdale. The mythology surrounding Richard Sutton was clearly evident during his lifetime as he gradually achieved great prominence in the Dentdale locality owning properties such as Rigg End Farm and buying the mansion West House the former home of Edmund Sill. In her will Ann Sill left Richard Sutton a considerable amount of money and he did indeed die a rich man in the year 1851. His story has, it seems, been embellished and elaborated by Emily Bronte as there are many similarities between the character of Heathcliff and Richard Sutton. As undoubted proof that he attained social prominence his rather grand raised gravestone can be seen under a cherry tree in the graveyard of the 14th century church of St. Andrew's at Dent, Yorkshire. It says 'Richard Sutton of West House'. Inside the church are a number of plaques dedicated to the Sill family mentioning the plantation in Jamaica. One such plaque is in memory of Ann Sill who may have been the inspiration for Cathy in

WutheringHeights with Richard Sutton as her Heathcliff. I am a direct line descendent of Richard Sutton, he is my Great, Great Great, Great Grandfather.

CHAPTER 12

THIS SCEPTRED ISLE

Recently we will all have seen in the news features, articles and discussions concerning the continuing membership of Great Britain in The European Union. You will no doubt have your own thoughts on this one way or another, here are mine. As a Spiritualist I believe this to be the absolute truth it is the 7th Principal of Spiritualism: 'We affirm the moral responsibility of individuals, and that we make our own happiness or unhappiness as we obey or disobey Nature's physical and spiritual laws'.

There is a problem I perceive, that is we are simply not at liberty to obey or disobey Nature's physical and spiritual laws as we are all, in effect, prisoners of society. Nor are we at liberty to follow our personal ideas of moral responsibility, we must do what we are told to do in accordance with the laws under which we live. In 1762 the philosopher Jean-Jaques Rousseau published his work 'The Social Contract' which starts with these words 'Man is born free and everywhere he is in chains'. You see in our current society we are dominated by economic and social inequality, dependency on the state, regulations, rules, highly sophisticated legal restrictions, laws, statutes and an enforcement system designed to ensure that the status quo is maintained. You may or may not be aware of this but The European Court of Justice can require foreign police forces to be deployed in Great Britain to enforce European Law. You and I have no choice in this matter, we are bound in this extended society, to adhere to the man made rules that are made not to promote our spiritual development but to lock us in to a system designed to control us. George Orwell wrote in his seminal novel of a dystopian world '1984' If you want a picture of the future, imagine a boot stamping on a human face, forever'. What Orwell was saying, in effect, was that the people, that is you and I, will either comply with the rules of society (Big Brother) or suffer the consequences. Please ask yourself this, how can any individual hope to make their own happiness within Nature's physical and spiritual laws when one is subjected to man made rules and regulations that prohibit and profoundly restrict virtually all of ones actions.

It can of course be argued that there is an accepted general will of the people to live within an ordered society and that this will, in the UK , is best expressed through the ballot box at a democratic General Election, such as we have just seen. However, as you will no doubt have noticed, nothing ever seems to change very much for the better and those that have the positions of power maintain them. All this, to me, seems very disturbing as I would sincerely like to believe that my elected representative in Parliament was there to ensure that our country was a good and happy land in which to live. Yet I see much evidence to the contrary. For example the last Labour Government allowed employers to introduce 'Zero Hour' contracts that effectively reduce the workers rights to nothing as they have no guarantee of a wage at all. Any questioning of the Zero Hour contract and that is what you get, zero, nothing at all. Now that disgraceful nonsense came about under a Labour Government. I can imagine that Kier Hardie would be rotating rapidly in his grave if he was aware of such shenanigans.

There also exists another tier to our Government and that is the European Union which has the authority to pass binding legislation restricting and controlling the people of Great Britain . For example the EU, as a basic principal, allows free movement of workers between all member states. I am not a racist, my wife's distant ancestors were Irish, but I am lately becoming concerned at the influx of central European people into the towns and cities of the UK . It is now a statistical fact that in the city of London the indigenous British English speaking population is in the minority. Go there and observe for yourself that the streets of our capital city are full of immigrants begging and propositioning people for cash. I was there recently and a fully fit man of Romanian appearance with a large dog, smoking a hand rolled cigarette stopped me and asked for money. Now I am a disabled man and was being helped along by my wife so I calmly advised the uncouth ruffian that it was a damn disgrace when the fit and healthy were begging off cripples. Who benefits from the UK allowing in such wasters? The employers benefit because such immigrants are more than willing to work for low wages on Zero Hour contracts as even at such poverty line rates they are being paid five times or more than they would be receiving in say Bucharest .

At the risk of being thought xenophobic it is my personal belief that the country I was born in is my home and as such I would like to see it protected by the Government representing me. The Treaty of Rome that came into effect on the first of January 1958 created the European Economic Community, this was subsequently amended in 1993 by The Maastricht Treaty which the UK duly signed. Whilst the following explanation is perhaps an over simplification in effect the resulting membership of The European Union requires the UK to allow the people of other member countries free access to enter this kingdom to work and enjoy all other benefits. Now if I suggested to you that it was perhaps a good idea to leave all the doors to your house open so that any of your neighbours could walk in and help themselves to your hospitality you would perhaps think I had lost the plot. It is my personal opinion that the Government of this country did exactly that when they signed away our rights to stop immigrants from countries party to the EU from entering the UK to work or otherwise indulge themselves in our benefits. As a Spiritualist I believe that there is a law of Nature, that we all, no matter what colour, creed or nationality we are have an absolute right to live life and make our own happiness. My ancestors fought and died to protect this country so that future generations would be free to do just that, safe from the undue influence of those who would invade this land. Please ask yourself this question, what was the point of going to war when the ultimate result has been almost total capitulation. As a member of the EU we can not resist the demand of entry into this sceptered isle by any individual from any of the member countries of the EU. This fortress built by nature has been sacked by barbarians and our culture is being rapidly eroded as a direct result.

It is my belief that to make progress, to spiritually and materially improve, we require a degree of freedom so to do. If our British society, our culture, our heritage is eroded and the rule of law that enables this to happen is enforced from a foreign land then we British people are reduced to a form of slavery. To progress one must be free from the chains. There will in the next two years or so come a time when you can vote on the question of the UKs continuing membership of the EU. It is my personal intention to say no to the European Union as I feel it has become a direct threat to my country, to all the British people and our way of life. This is the country of my ancestors whose feet walked in ancient times on England 's green and pleasant land. I feel it is my moral responsibility to speak my truth and hopefully help protect this sceptred isle from those that would reduce it to penury.

'King Richard II' Act 2 Scene 1. By William Shakespeare

This royal throne of kings, this sceptred isle, / This earth of majesty, this seat of Mars, / This other Eden, demi-paradise, / This fortress built by Nature for herself / Against infection and the hand of war, / This happy breed of men, this little world, / This precious stone set in the silver sea, / Which serves it in the office of a wall / Or as a moat defensive to a house, / Against the envy of less happier lands,- /This blessed plot, this earth, this realm, this England.

CHAPTER 13

THE GHOSTS OF BODMIN JAIL

In February of the year 2015 my wife Mary and I were visiting Cornwall investigating the spiritual power of the area. We had been well and truly lost on Bodmin moor where I had inadvertently managed to drive us up a steep dirt track to Hawk's Tor. That Tor, with its standing stones and remote crag had an intense eerie supernatural atmosphere which electrified my psychic senses. Once we found our way out of that desolate location Mary suggested we proceed to the actual town of Bodmin and visit the old jail. She had previously read a brief history of this decommissioned prison and I had seen the ridiculous episode of 'Most Haunted' featuring the jail in which Derek Acorah pretended to be possessed by the spirit of an imaginary former jailer. The parapsychologist Dr. O'Keefe working with the 'Most Haunted' investigators had laid a trap for Derek by getting his assistants to discuss a supposedly infamous, but completely fictitious, South African jailer called Kreed Kafer. Derek had obviously heard this fabricated story, swallowed the bait and when the TV cameras were filming him he faked a trance and fraudulently acted out possession by the non existing spirit of Kreed Kafer. The name is an anagram of Derek Faker which he proved himself to be whilst filming in Bodmin Jail. I recall watching that episode and laughing out loud at the utter stupidity of it. You have to hand it to Acorah, he is a natural comedian.

Bodmin Jail was initially commissioned in 1778 as a CountyJail, a Debtors Prison and House of Correction. The population of the jail increased dramatically following the end of the Napolionic Wars in 1815 so that by the 1820s all the cells were occupied. There were sixty executions at the jail and many of these were open to the public. The usual method was to fasten a noose around the neck of the condemned and drop them a distance so that the large knot in the rope snapped their neck killing them instantly. At one point the jail had a new execution shed built that was ruled unlawful by the inspectors of prisons and it was not sufficiently open to the public view. In those days 'justice' had to be seen to be done, if you can possibly call hanging someone for stealing a sheep justice that is. On one occasion over 20,000 people attended to watch two condemned men hang. The year was 1840 and two brothers William and James Lightfoot, were strung up and hanged before the mob.

Inside this old jail they have created a form of chamber of horrors with numerous mannequins dressed in period clothing depicting disgusting scenes from the prisons grim past. There are silent enactments of floggings, of strangulations and beatings, force feeding etc. All manner of man's inhumanity to man is to be seen there. Mary and I managed to see inside the main cell block and I did experience there a sense of being observed as a certain area had a distinct and noticeable lower temperature. It has often been my experience that when entities from the spirit world are present there is around the specific area an actual chill and also an unearthly stillness. As we passed through the jail and came close to the long dark corridor of cells I felt that unmistakeable sensation.

This part of the main cell block had been the central location for inmates and something wicked walked within those walls. I felt that there had been a malevolent force, possibly the nature of the harsh regime itself, that had seeped into the stones themselves. Mary had the camera and agreed to help me so with some slight trepidation I entered a particular cell that had an unusual atmosphere. Using psychometry I tuned in to the memories there placing my hands against the cold brick walls and allowing the images to enter my mind. As I did so a name came to me I heard this quite clearly 'Everest'. At first I thought this was connected to the Himalayan mountain but then I heard again 'John Everest'. This was clear in my mind and I asked Mary to make a note of that. The cell I tuned in to appeared to be full of dark images of despair, misery and desolation, I felt the sadness of long dead prisoners impregnated into the very fabric of the jail. Within that cell countless hundreds of inmates would have wailed their lives away in the interminable gloom of this dirty dungeon.

During renovations to restore the jail a horrible discovery was made they found an 'Execution Pit' that is a specially constructed unit for hanging prisoners. You can visit this disgraceful testimony to a time thankfully passed and see where many met their awful ends in Bodmin Jail. Mary and I stood there and looked at the noose and noted that it is fully working as the hanging pit has been fully restored. Just standing by the side of that dark place I felt again the unearthly chill and saw for a moment a dark shadow shift across the far corner of the room. There is no doubt in my mind that this area and the main cell block unit at Bodmin Jail are impregnated with human despair. The invisible power of the highly charged emotions experienced by prisoners about to die has imposed an unearthly atmosphere on the area. That is it actually feels closely connected to the next dimension of life and is, I feel, a portal through which troubled discarnate souls may communicate. Hence there are numerous reports of ghostly encounters at this old jail.

In conclusion I would say that yes Bodmin Jail is in the generally accepted use of the term 'haunted'. There is certainly a presence within those ancient walls that tingles ones psychic senses. There are also entities present as when Mary checked on the name I had heard in that dark lonely cell she found that John Bentham Everest was the Governor of Bodmin jail for many years during the early 19th century. You really should go and see this old prison if you are in Cornwall as it is a brilliantly presented museum depicting the horrors of life behind bars two hundred years ago. The jail is open 364 days a year from 10am to dusk, just call this number for further details 01208 76292

There is available at Bodmin Jail a regular 'Ghost Walk' that is professionally organised and can be booked in advance. I believe the cost is £75 but for that you get an overnight adventure inside the jail and your tour is led by an experienced Psychic-Medium. If you are interested in such an encounter then the number to call is 01208 76292 or you can book online at the website WWW. Bodminjail.org

CHAPTER FOURTEEN

VISITING SPIRITUAL CORNWALL

I last visited Cornwall in 2001 along with the authors Ron Ellis (Ears of The City) and Professor Joe Cooper (The Case of The Cottingley Fairies). We were meeting with the philosopher and writer Colin Wilson (The Outsider) at his home in Goran Haven to discuss, among other matters, metaphysical poetry. I was struck then by the almost otherworldliness of the land. There is a subtle but discernable eerie essence in the air. As one enters the rugged Cornish landscape with its craggy coastline and strangely silent sleepy villages, a sense of the supernatural begins to creep into ones subconscious. February of this year my wife Mary I set out to explore the spiritual heart of Cornwall. We could feel the paranormal power as we drove deep into this kingdom by the sea. It is not quite tangible, yet we both felt just a little uneasy as we stopped to study the map by the side of a wild misty moor land some distance north of Bodmin. We were close to our destination, a hotel inland from the town of Newquay. Our quest to discover the preternatural power of Cornwall was about to commence.

The spray from the Atlantic Ocean was quickly caught by the westerly wind and blown across the rocks of Land's End, giving me a wet welcome to the edge of the country we call Britain. This was Cornwall; the original Celtic name is Kernow, considered to be a mystical kingdom of which the author Thomas Hardy wrote: 'It is pre-eminently the region of dreams and mystery'. I had arrived with my dear wife Mary to tune in to this ancient landscape, where some say the legendary King Arthur was born and died. As I stood for some time looking out over the turbulent waves, out to the far horizon beyond which lay the continent of America, I let my mind drift open to the deeply atmospheric environment. There, where the salt sea heaves and the wild gulls call, where the wind is like a whetted knife, I fleetingly experienced a vision of life as it would have been countless centuries ago. Legend has it that there once was another land stretching out from this lonely place over twenty eight miles adjoining the distant Isles of Scilly to the far west. They say this land had many towns and churches, thousands of people lived there, before the deep Atlantic staked its watery claim. As I stared across the waves in my mind I saw a far away spire and heard a distant bell tolling. Then a blustery ozone heavy blast of wind captured my hair and blew me instantly awake.

Some few miles east of Land's End by the town of Praa Sands there are the remains of a castle. That castle is what many consider to be the most haunted in Britain. Pengersick castle stands somewhat forlornly with what remains of its old grey stone tower surrounded by an overgrown garden. Its history is indeed bleak, the original owner, Henry Pengersick, is reputed to have murdered numerous individuals there most notably a monk visiting from Hailes Abbey who called to collect tithes. There have been numerous sightings of a ghostly hooded monk in and around this castle and grounds. Henry Pengersick was considered to be of a psychopathic nature and when he took a bride, the very beautiful Engrina Godolphin, he proved to be a villain and destroyed her will to live. There have been many reports of her spirit haunting the interior of Castle Pengersick. On the day that I visited the castle was quiet, almost malevolently silent, stark against the billowing white cumulus clouds scattered in the otherwise cornflower blue Cornish sky. I took a moment to contemplate the remains of this darkly ominous castle and gazing at the upper windows saw what I took to be the light of a candle. This side of the stone walled tower was in shadow yet I saw something glimmering, a brief yellow light in the cold darkness there. As I looked there came a slight subtle tingling sensation at the back of my neck and a quiet voice spoke to me: 'Something wicked this way comes'. I wasn't waiting to find out what that something was in a matter of seconds I was back in our car with Mary and we drove off at a reasonably rapid rate, away from the grim malevolence of Castle Pengersick and the ghosts that haunt within.

Some two miles south of the village of St. Buryan in Cornwall off the B3315 there stands a Neolithic stone circle known as 'The Merry Maidens'. According to legend these stones are the petrified remains of a group of young women who broke the holy Sabbath day by dancing on a Sunday and as punishment were turned to stone. There are in total nineteen stones, granite megaliths and they form an almost perfect circle. On the day Mary and I visited the sun was high in an almost cloudless sky and a sense of peace pervaded the area. Placing my hands on the surface of the stones I used psychometry in an attempt to gain insight into the history of this ancient stone circle. Standing there hand to stone I closed my eyes and allowed what visions may come to enter my mind. Within moments I had a brief image of a man dressed in rough stitched animal skins, a thick black belt around his waist and long unkempt hair. There seemed to be many people around him, carts loaded with sacks, the circle was full and noisy like a market. Shouting rough voices in a language I did not know, cattle, horses and a feeling of vitality, of happiness. 'John, your hat' Mary said handing me the black fedora that had blown off my head and I was back in 21st century Cornwall. I could not say with any degree of certainty that what I saw at The Merry Maidens stone circle was an accurate vision of a scene from ancient times. However I do know that there exists a theory that these ancient stone circles were in fact meeting places where the hunter-gatherer tribesmen and women would meet to exchange foodstuffs and animal skins, axe heads and hand made tools etc. So it is quite possible that my vision was of a long ago market day from a time when the ancient Cornish people lived by hunting wild deer and other animals.

It was early in the month of February 2015 when my wife Mary and I set out from our hotel near Newquay in Cornwall to visit the village of Trebetherick. I knew of this place only through the poetry of Sir John Betjeman who wrote an evocative poem about his youth there where he would spend his summer holidays. As with many of Betjeman's poems 'Trebetherick' is rich with place names identifying the area, which made it absolutely ideal for me as I conducted a psychic search for the spiritual essence of Betjeman's Cornwall.

'TREBETHERICK' by John Betjeman: 'We used to picnic where the thrift/Grew deep and tufted to the edge/We saw the yellow foam flakes drift/In trembling sponges on the ledge/Below us, till the wind would lift/Them up the hill and o'er the hedge./Sand in the sandwiches, wasps in the tea/Sun on our bathing dresses heavy with the wet/Squelch of the bladderwrack waiting for the sea/Fleas around the tamarisk, an early cigarette.' That is the first verse of the poem and the place is there just as Betjeman described it, the salt sea air, the sand, the foam flakes in the breeze. As I stood by Mary's side watching the waves washing over the stones where once John Betjeman ran his heedless way I sensed a little of what it must have been like for him and his trusty young friends. For the area is unspoilt, almost untouched by the eighty or more years that have passed since: 'Ropes around our mackintoshes, waders warm and dry/we waited for the wreckage to come swirling into reach/Ralph, Vasey, Alistair, Biddy, John and I'/Then roller into roller curled/And thundered down the rocky bay/And we were in a water world/Of rain and blizzard, sea and spray/and one against the other hurled/We struggled round to Greenaway/Blessed be St. Enodoc, blessed be the wave/Blessed be the springy turf, we pray, pray to thee/Ask for our children all the happy days you gave/To Ralph, Vasey, Alistair, Biddy, John and me.' For a brief moment, as the sunlight danced on the incoming tide I was there with John and his young friends and they always will be thanks to Betjeman's poem.

From the beach Mary guided me over the springy turf across what is now a golf course to the 12th century church of St. Enodoc mentioned in his poem. Pausing at the gateway I looked into the graveyard where, to the immediate right I saw a black marble headstone with one name carved elaborately JOHN BETJEMAN 1906 1984. I had with me a copy of his

'Collected Poems' and with some help from Mary managed to take a seat on the ground by the side of the grave where I read aloud his poem 'TREBETHERICK' as I did so a group of people visiting the church came over to listen. There was a certain magic in the air by Betjeman's grave that mystical afternoon as I read his words. At the end of the reading many came to me saying they had been pleasantly surprised and delighted to hear the poem and some said they found it a spiritual experience. I know I felt something special was happening and though I would not claim that the spirit of John Betjeman was with me as I spoke, I did experience a sense of inner tranquillity.

The following day as the sun continued to shine we decided to journey inland to the town of Bodmin. I had studied the maps and saw that to the east there was remote moorland that I instinctively knew was charged with a form of paranormal power. Strangely, despite being certain of the direction to Bodmin Moor I managed to get us well and truly lost. Our SatNav had decided that it was having a day off and would not function so in the middle of nowhere there we were. My dear wife Mary is quite accustomed to me losing my way so, having advised me what a plonka I was, she closed her eyes and took a nap. Meanwhile I managed to drive down a long and increasingly narrow winding road that took us to a steep hill. All around I saw gloomy grey stone walls in disrepair with dark shaped cottages overhung by bushes and broken old trees. This was a seriously silent land, no birds were singing, no sounds at all, it was unearthly. The atmosphere became almost electrically charged mesmerising me. As I drove up a very steep incline I heard a terrible scream 'Stop the car you maniac!' Mary shouted shocking me back to reality. Somehow I had managed to go off the road slightly and our car was on the edge of a rubble stone scattered track leading towards a huge rock outcrop. Just looking at this pile of ancient stones, obviously placed there countless ages ago, I began to feel uneasy.

Having stopped the car where it was I took the map and attempted to orientate myself. To the south east I could see a lake and beyond a road, the map told me I was near the top of a hill and it showed me the name as Hawk's Tor. Standing by the car I slightly shuddered though the day was warm and the sun shone right there near to top of Hawk's Tor there was a chill that I recognised as belonging to another dimension. Staring at the stone formations I saw for a fragment of a second images of a time long past, there were many people all in rough clothing of animal skins, yet they were not there. I looked again to confirm this and saw Mary staring at me camera in hand. She said I had been stationary for some minutes and had looked to be in a trance. Yet to me it had seemed only seconds. Hawk's Tor is one powerful paranormally charged site that deeply disturbed my emotional equilibrium.

On our way out of that mysterious moorland Mary told me that she too had experienced something unusual. As she had stood looking at me in my semi-trance state a discarnate voice had spoken to her and said one word that she said sounded like 'rockash'. I later researched this and found that there was an old Cornish language phrase that included a similar word: Ud roacashaas. The meaning roughly translates to 'gloomy place'.

CHAPTER FIFTEEN

WHEN ELEPHANTS WEEP

Animals have emotions, of that I am absolutely convinced. Those of us that have lived alongside pets will know that they share our happiness and also our sadness. My own bulldog Grumbles used to recognize whenever I was feeling low and often would come and place her head on my knee and look up as if to say 'don't be sad, I am your friend'. It was a kind of telepathic link that we shared and I still miss that old dog.

Scientists term the attributing of human emotions to animals anthropomorphism which is a form of criticism, as if to believe that our pets have feelings like we do is mistaken or wrong. One book that challenges this is 'When Elephants Weep' by Jeffrey Moussaieff Masson and Susan McCarthy. I was given this book by Barry Cunningham the managing editor of Bloomsbury Children's Book and he suggested I read it as part of my research into the paranormal powers of animals when he commissioned me to write 'Psychic Pets'. I was deeply moved by many of the examples given by the authors and found the book truly inspirational. Here is a sample:

'A game warden in Tanzania was doing 'elephant control work' when he saw three female elephants and a half-grown male in tall grass. Since his job was to keep the elephant population down, he shot the three females-and slightly wounded the the half grown animal. To his dismay, he suddenly saw two elephant calves, who had been with the females but hidden in the long grass. He moved towards them, shouting and waving his hat, hoping to drive them back to the larger herd, where other elephants would adopt them. The wounded elephant was dazed and helpless and did not know which way to turn. Instead of fleeing, the orphaned calves pressed themselves against him and supported the wounded elephant away from further danger.'

The elephant calves, as described above, were acting in a manner that clearly indicated they were consciously helping their injured friend. Such action is contrary to what many scientists would have us believe about animals i.e. that they act instinctively. Surely the natural instincts of those two elephant calves would be to run away from the clear and present danger. But they did not do so, they acted to aid and protect their fellow creature, rather like a soldier may do on a battlefield. Such actions indicate that the elephants had feelings for without them they would surely have turned and run.

Freedom is one of the great joys of life that we will all have experienced at some time. Thinking back in my own life I recall the sheer exhilaration I used to feel waking on the first morning of the summer holidays knowing that there was no school and I could go playing in the fields with my friends. Animals also feel joy experiencing freedom as illustrated by this anecdote:

'In spring, when the chimpanzees at Arnhem Zoo are allowed out of their winter quarters for the first time, there is a scene of exultation as they scream and hoot, clasp and kiss one another, jump up and down pounding on each others backs. They are not free, but the additional space, the relatively greater freedom, thrills them. It looks as if it gives them joy'.

Anyone who has owned a dog and taken it for a run in a park will doubtless have witnessed something quite similar as the dog charges here, there and everywhere. That sense of freedom, clearly demonstrated by the dog's delight, is an emotion and is as real as our own feelings of joy at being free.

The great naturalist Charles Darwin in his book 'The Expression of the Emotions in Man and Animals' stated that emotional weeping was a 'special expression of man'. He did however note one exception reported to him by Sir E. Tennant that some Indian elephants, newly captured in Ceylon (now Sri Lanka) when tied up showed 'no other indication of suffering than the tears which suffused their eyes and flowed incessantly. One captured elephant sank to the ground uttering chocking cries, with tears trickling down his cheeks'. The emotion being expressed by the captured elephants was perhaps of frustration and sadness at the loss of liberty and segregation from their family. As human beings we too would likely shed tears in such a situation.

If we accept that animals have emotions and express them with their own particular physical attributes we should also accept that they are sentient creatures capable of making value judgements. That is animals posses the ability to act altruistically i.e. in a way that helps others but may endanger themselves, as in the example above with the elephant calves.

During the years that I have been working as a psychic author I have met many people who tell me that they have seen the spirits of their pets who are passed into the next world. We buried our pet bulldog Grumbles in a quiet corner of the garden where, in life, she used to rest in the shade and snore loudly. Last summer I was myself snoozing on the hammock that stands by that corner and as I began to wake from my nap I heard quite distinctly the familiar sound of Grumbles snoring away. Half asleep I looked up and saw, for one brief moment, that happy old friend flopped out paws before her head fast asleep. Then I remembered that she had gone and as I looked she disappeared into the shadows of the late summer afternoon.

Animals have souls, our pets, like us, do not die. The next world is as real to animals as it is to us and to think otherwise is just pure arrogance. We ourselves are animals, human animals and as such will take our natural place in the kingdom beyond this material plane that we call Earth. Elephants may indeed weep, as may we all, but in the next dimension our God will dry those tears as we become one with the eternal love that awaits all living creatures.

CHAPTER SIXTEEN

POSSESSION AND DEMONIC PACTS

Over the last few years, on many supposed Psychic-TV programmes, there have been featured what we are asked to believe are 'possessions'. That is the so-called medium becomes possessed by the spirit of some infamous character, such as say Dick Turpin the highwayman. This obvious nonsense is plainly ridiculous to those that know the teachings of Spiritualism, but to the general public it may appear plausible. As Barnum said, there's one born every minute. As for the fakes that play on the susceptibility of the public, they are bringing the beliefs of Spiritualism into disrepute. It is a sad truth that some people will do anything for a chance at fame and fortune.

As unbelievable as it may seem there are those that seriously consider it is possible to become successful, rich and famous by selling ones soul to the devil. This belief dates back into time immemorial but perhaps the best known account, albeit totally fictional, is the German mythological character of Faust. In Latin the word 'faust' translates as 'lucky' and it was a change of luck and good fortune that the character Faust sought. In the story Faust seeks all knowledge and worldly pleasures. To obtain these Faust enters into a contract with the devil offering his soul in return for earthly success. The representative of the devil is Mephistopheles and through this agent Faust gains his desires, seduces innocents and attains what he perceives as a position of eminence. In the end though Faust pays the ultimate price and is dragged screaming to hell. There is an opera that tells this story it is 'The Damnation of Faust' (1846) by Hector Berlioz.

Urbain Grandier (1590 -18 August 1634) was a Roman Catholic priest at Loudun in France who supposedly made a pact with the Devil. He was said to have desired to enjoy carnal knowledge of the nuns at the nearby Ursuline convent and according to reports of the time he did just that with many of them. It was claimed by the nuns that Grandier sent the demon Asmodai to them during darkness. Grandier was tortured and subsequently burnt at the stake convicted of witchcraft by a court convened by Cardinal Richelieu. This is the wording of actual pact that was submitted as evidence in the trial of Grandier: We, the influential Lucifer, the young Satan, Beelzebub, Leviathan, Elimi and Astaroth, together with others, have today accepted the covenant pact of Urbain Grandier, who is ours. And him do we promise the love of women, the flower of virgins, the respect of monarchs, honors, lusts and powers. He will go whoring three days long; the carousal will be dear to him. He offers us once in the year a seal of blood, under the feet he will trample the holy things of the church and he will ask us many questions; with this pact he will live twenty years happy on the earth of men, and will later join us to sin against God. Bound in hell, in the council of demons. Lucifer Beelzebub Satan Astaroth Leviathan Elimi The seals placed the Devil, the master, and the demons, princes of the lord. Baalberith, writer.

Niccolò Paganini (27 October 1782 – 27 May 1840) was a world famous violinist who many believed had entered into a deal with the devil. He certainly achieved international success as both a violinist and composer, so popular was Paganini that wherever he performed the standard ticket price was doubled. He amassed a huge fortune which he subsequently lost by investing in an ill fated casino. He also owned a number of highly prized violins that he acquired by dubious means i.e. he won one in a music reading challenge contest and another was gifted to him by a rich admirer. These were, in today's values, million pound instruments and Paganini had a number of them. As a point of interest Paganini was a friend and associate of the composer Hector Berlioz (see above). When he died it was on the grounds of Paganini's association with the devil that his body was denied a Catholic burial in Genoa. It took four years, and an appeal to the Pope, before the body was allowed to be transported to Genoa, but was still not buried. His remains were finally put to rest in 1876 in a cemetery in Parma.

Many well known artistes, actors, singers etc. have stated that they believe that they are, in some way, possessed by spirits whilst performing. James Dean, the double Oscar winning actor was reported as stating that whilst playing his part in front of camera he actually became the character he was representing. Dean stated 'I have a fairly adequate knowledge of satanic forces' his co-star and himself a brilliant character actor Denis Hopper said of Dean 'he used to say that he would leave himself open to the spirits...to be possessed in effect'. James Dean was killed in a car crash on 30th September 1955 when his Porsche 550 Spyder hit an oncoming vehicle head on. The 1960s Amercian folk-singing sensation Bob Dylan in a recent interview made comments that may indicate he believes he himself has a contract with some discarnate entity. Here is a verbatim record of his interview: Q: So why do you continue to tour: BD: It goes back to the destiny thing...I made a bargain with it a long time ago and I am holding up my end. Q: What was your bargain: BD: To get where I am now. Q: Who did you make the bargain with. BD: With the Chief Commander. Q: On this Earth. BD No Sir! In a world we can't see.

The extremely successful popular rock music group The Rolling Stones have themselves been linked to satanic practices and beliefs. During 1967, shortly after their release from prison on drug related charges, the Rolling Stones recorded an album entitled 'Their Satanic Majesties Request'. This was followed by probably their most controversial recording, 'Sympathy For The Devil', written by Mick Jagger and Keith Richards it tells the story of Satan's walk through the world, it recounts his exploits over the course of human history and warns the listener: "If you meet me, have some courtesy, have some sympathy, and some taste; use all your well-learned politesse, or I'll lay your soul to waste." Jagger stated in an interview with *Rolling Stone* magazine that he wrote it 'sort of like a Bob Dylan song'.

CHAPTER SEVENTEEN

THE PHILOSOPHY OF OPTIMISM

As we enter a new year I thought how many of us will be thinking 'here we go again'. Perhaps looking ahead to the next twelve months with a gloomy sense of pessimism as if we expect nothing good to happen. We each have our burden to bear in this life, some more than others, but surely we owe it to ourselves to positively affirm our existence by personal effort. It is easy not to try, to look on our misfortunes as a kind of inevitable curse from which we are doomed never to escape. So adopting a negative attitude we accept failure and as Christina Rossetti observed, wonder 'Does the road wind uphill all the way? Right to the very end?' Thus turning our lives into a daily grind as we endure the struggle instead of enjoying the challenge.

Life should not be just drudgery and toil. We are, each one of us, an individual miracle. Why then do so many of us allow ourselves to be disheartened when faced with what are really minor difficulties compared to the odds against our being born in the first place? The answer to that question has been sought by numerous philosophers over the centuries with many seeming to see the human condition as one of pointless desolation. Consider what Aristotle (384-322 BC) the Greek philosopher said 'It is better not to have been born, and death is better than life'. Then we have John Paul Sartre (1905-80) stating almost that life is meaningless and 'man is a useless passion'...'hell is other people'. Sartre's hopeless existentialism offers this thought to mankind: 'Human life begins on the far side of despair'.

Arguing against the pessimistic philosophy of Sartre and his school of existentialist doom and gloom is Colin Wilson and his philosophy of optimism. Wilson, who first found literary fame in 1956 with his international best-selling book 'The Outsider', offers a far more hopeful antidote to Sarte's despair. Wilson proposes that there should be a philosophy of optimism that is based on the teachings of the psychologist Abraham Maslow. Whilst practicing as a psychologist in the USA Maslow arrived at a unique conclusion. He realized that all the patients he was seeing were suffering from some form of malaise be that depression, anxiety, paranoia or whatever. He, as the psychologist, was attempting to bring them back to normality. Then he asked himself the question why was it that many people were not depressed, paranoid etc. What was it about these people that stopped them suffering from anxiety etc. So Maslow began to study 'normal' people in an attempt to find why this was so.

One thing that Maslow noted about individuals who were coping with life was that they reported enjoying moments of delight. That is they had periods of enhanced perception, peak experiences that made them feel good about themselves and the world in general. Such experiences encouraged them to be optimistic. Those that were not coping, the clinically depressed, did not report such moments and were morbidly pessimistic.

We may imagine that it is difficult to achieve a peak experience, when we perceive that we have just received absurd good news and the world is wonderful place. Wilson argues that it is not as problematical as we may think. Citing the writer Mark Twain, Wilson gives an example of the character Tom Sawyer who is required to paint a fence. Now painting a wooden fence is, one would think, a rather mundane task and hardly likely to bring any form of inspirational insight. But Mark Twain has Sawyer undertake this task with great enthusiasm, whistling whilst he vigorously paints making the job seem so much fun that people passing ask for a go with the brush. Some pay Tom Sawyer to let them enjoy the experience of painting that fence and give him strange things that any boy would love, such as a dead cat, a ball of string, a penknife etc. The point that Mark Twain is making and Wilson is explaining, is that most situations in life can be turned into wonderfully rewarding experiences if we apply ourselves to them in a meaningful manner. Tom Sawyer made it appear that painting a fence made him happy, he did this by adopting a carefree attitude and displaying this to the world by whistling a jolly tune. By so doing he became happy, turning a mundane task into a peak experience.

The argument that Wilson is putting forward to support his philosophy of optimism is relatively simple. If we adopt a positive frame of mind and pay attention to the detail of the daily duties, tasks and personal interactions that constitute our days, then we will alter our perception. Most of us do not do that, pay attention that is. We allow our lives to run on automatic pilot, missing 90% of the detail seeing only the outline of the life we are supposed to be living. By concentrating on each task, each conversation, each moment in fact we become aware and by so doing enjoy even the most boring of duties.

As an example from my own life, I recently decided to valet my car. This is hardly an intellectual exercise and I imagined it would be extremely dull, but I set about the job enthusiastically. I bought chrome cleaner for the wire wheels, special wax for the body, Canadian bees-wax for the leather seats and all manner of dusters to polish the paintwork. Then, one fine morning, I went out and started work. I washed the car down with light shampoo, hosed it off and buffed it dry. Then applied the Simoniz Wax and polished the bonnet etc. It was as I was applying the chrome cleaner to the wire wheels that I noticed someone was standing behind me watching. 'What an amazing car' the elderly gentleman said 'I used to have one of these in the sixties, can I sit inside?' Having done so the man told me how much fun he and his wife had all those years ago driving round in their own car. We passed a happy half hour exchanging anecdotes and then he had to go. As I stood watching him walk away I thought for a moment what a happy morning I had just enjoyed and all because I had undertaken a mundane task with optimistic enthusiasm.

Might I be so bold as to suggest that we each make a resolution to adopt Wilson's optimistic and positive approach to our lives in the New Year. We do owe it to ourselves to pay attention to what we do with our limited time. If we put in 100% effort to even the most seemingly boring of tasks we will enjoy life so much more. So the next time you paint a fence, clean your car or undertake any duty do so enthusiastically and you may be amazed at how much joy you get from the experience. One thing is for certain, adopt the philosophy of optimism and you will never be depressed again, you won't have time!

CHAPTER EIGHTEEN

BILLY'S WILLY

As Spiritualists we accept that we own our deeds. We believe that our sins belong to us and actually help us to develop spiritually. We also own the experiences that form our characters and make us what we are. What we do with our lives, the product that is the result, belongs to us. By their fruits shall you know them, so the Bible says; St. Mathew Ch.12 V.33 'The tree is known by his fruit'. The enigmatic comic genius that is Billy Connolly presents his fruit, nuts and all, via an idiosyncratic, highly original interpretation of life to audiences around the world. His internationally broadcast television programmes, such as 'Billy Connolly's World Tour of Australia' etc. have been viewed by tens if not hundreds of millions of people. So the man is doing something right and that something, in my opinion, is a lot more important than just making people laugh. Billy Connolly makes people think and he does so by expressing, in highly exaggerated, outlandish language many of humanities innermost foibles and fears. The innocent honesty with which Billy exposes his own self, both physically and emotionally, enables his audiences to relate to a sometimes terrible truth and it is that truth which sets them free to laugh out loud at its obvious absurdity. When we laugh at fear, any fear, it loses its power over us. I believe that Billy enables us to do just that.

A cursory glance at Billy Connolly working on stage in front of an audience would likely give one an initial impression of a long haired, wild-eyed, belligerent, intimidating, aggressive, verbally abusive, Glasgow/Scottish 'See-You-Jimmy' buffoon. If that were truly it then he would never have succeeded and won over the entire English speaking world and half the rest too. The foul-mouthed expletives used by Billy Connolly in his work as a comedian would, in other circumstances, offend many people. Yet the man has a way of making even offensive language laughable. I had often wondered what made the man capable of doing this. I found the answer in 'Billy: The Complete Life Story Of A Comic Genius' by Pamela Stephenson, his wife.

Pamela Stephenson holds a Ph.D in Psychology, though she is probably best known as the beautiful blonde comedienne in the long running television series 'Not The Nine O' Clock News' in which she starred alongside the likes of Griff Rhys Jones, Rowan Atkinson and Mel Smith. Her book about Billy Connolly reveals a dark and insecure side to his life that has undoubtedly molded the man in a truly mysterious and, in my opinion, magnificent way. Read the book and you will see why I believe that one has to admire his indefatigable determination to overcome the kind of start to life that would have broken most people's will to live never mind to seek international success.

Born in a Glasgow slum tenement, where the entire family had to wash in the kitchen sink, Billy experienced real deprivation, hardship, physical and sexual abuse as a child. His mother was an alcoholic given to bouts of violence and his father, who shared a bed with Billy, would frequently interfere with him. Eventually things became so bad Billy was sent to live with two of his aunts who beat him without mercy for any minor or even imagined misdemeanor. Amazingly Billy coped with all this and did so by disassociating himself from what was happening. That is his mind switched its perception from subjective to objective viewing the abuse as though it were happening to someone else. He survived, but the mental scars remain and can occasionally be seen as Billy Connolly bares his soul, consciously and unconsciously, before audiences around the world.

The horrendous childhood Billy suffered has, I believe, given him the ability to observe and articulate humour in even the most difficult subjects. He brings a kind of sub-conscious release valve to the unspoken terrors of today. I think of his hilarious account of having a rectal examination of his prostate gland, in which Billy described in minute and excruciatingly embarrassing detail how he had to bend over whilst someone he had never met before inserted a rubber gloved hand into his rear end. 'What a way to make a first acquaintance'. Then he explains how he was caught masturbating and attempted to explain that a spider had jumped on his willy and he was swatting it off. Pamela Stephenson, who has likely seen more of Billy on stage than anyone else, comments in her book that she has wondered if some invisible demons are whispering in his ear as he prances about the stage spouting inspired, unrehearsed, yet meaningful meanderings.

It is Billy's gift to make us all smile at even the little odd things in life that is one of his main attributes. Which brings to mind his television series 'Billy Conolloy's World Tour Of Scotland'. In this he was again seen doing what he appears to enjoy doing a lot, that is either playing with or exhibiting his willy. In that series he confidently whipped off his kit and danced starkers round a group of standing stones on some remote Scottish island. Now, from what I have seen Billy's willy is not anything to write home about, one would not be struck dumb at its appearance, which seems fairly normal to me and I should know having been a nurse for many years. But when his willy makes an appearance people smile. Now that is, in my humble opinion, an amazing achievement.

Throughout his early adult life Billy Connolly was a drunk. Today he is sober, but for many years he suffered from a form of alcoholism. That is he could survive without drink but chose not to do so, he simply enjoyed being a crazy, out of control, drunken, brawling, outrageous, Oliver Reed type individual. Eventually Billy realized that if he continued to drink he would lose his new wife Pamela, also his children and ruin any chance he had of long lasting happiness. So he quit. Anyone who has ever been hooked on the booze knows that takes some doing but Billy did it and his career continued on from success on television to even bigger things in Hollywood and many movies including the voice of Billy Bones in 'The Muppets: Treasure Island' which is among my own very favourite films of all time.

CHAPTER NINETEEN

ORWELL PREDICTED BIG BROTHER BRITAIN

In his classic novel '1984' George Orwell described a future world where the population existed under the constant observation and control of an all powerful government headed by Big Brother. The world of '1984' is now, as amazing as it may seem, almost a reality. This reality is gradually turning our country into a form of open prison, where our every social interaction is observed, registered and ultimately controlled by the state. Our absolute right to live our lives in freedom has been removed and soon we will not even be allowed out of our own homes without proof of our identity. The police, and soon maybe even traffic wardens, private security guards, hospital receptionists, bank tellers, members of the military etc. will be empowered to demand to inspect our ID cards. If we cannot produce the card we may be subjected to a period of detainment in custody pending proof. Now you can believe this or not, certain major chain stores are being fitted with prison cells in their basements to hold anyone detained for failing to carry the compulsory ID cards. There will be fines for failing to comply and as all offences are now arrestable i.e. anyone can be arrested and locked in a cell for something as minor as dropping a cigarette butt if a police officer so decides, you could end up behind bars. If this sounds like fantasy consider this from The London Evening Standard:

'Under Section 44 of The Terrorism Act 2000 in London 7,566 people and vehicles were searched under the act between April 2001 and April 2002. That figure rose to 33,800 in 2003-04 approximately 100 people a day. The Terrorism Act 2000 allows police commanders to declare the whole of London an area where stop-and-search can be deployed at any time.' That is anyone can be stopped and forcibly searched i.e. have their clothing removed and their pockets and perhaps even their physical bodies inspected by the Police. If you have never experienced this practice you may find it difficult to comprehend how disturbing it can be to have ones person violated in public by a stranger in uniform. You may say that as you are an honest and innocent citizen you have absolutely nothing to fear from this and support the authorities and their actions. Try telling that to the family of Jean Charles de Menezes, the man killed at Stockwell station on the London Underground when police officers fired eleven shots into him having mistaken this man for a terrorist suspect. At the time the Metropolitan Police Commissioner Sir Ian Blair went onto national television and had the bare faced audacity to say that we should all expect 'more of this' in the future. I fear that he may be right!

It was on the Scottish island of Jura, between 1946 and 48 that Orwell wrote '1984' He was at the time a sick man suffering from TB, the disease that would eventually kill him. Educated at Eton Orwell, whose real name was Eric Arthur Blair, missed out university due to financial constraints and joined the Indian Imperial Police Force in Burma. In his novel 'Burmese Days' he sets out his utter distaste for imperialism. Perhaps his experiences with the Imperial Police helped him to understand that given too much power, too much authority, the British Police would potentially become as oppressive as the Indian Imperial Police. Whatever did colour Orwell's mind his vision of Britain in the near future that he depicted in his novel '1984' has become almost a nightmare reality. Here are some of the things that Orwell foresaw with my explanation of how they actually exist today:

TELESCREENS: Orwell describes these as being within the living quarters of homes and able to see and broadcast instructions to people. Today: INTERNET PC SCREENS: These sit in the homes of millions of people and with a webcam, microphone and speakers the individual can be observed and directed from anywhere in the world via a computer connected to the internet.

THOUGHT POLICE: Orwell wrote of 'thought crime' which was an offence against Big Brother. Anyone speaking treason or anything construed as anti Big Brother was said to have committed a 'thought crime' and was arrested and tortured. Today: **POLITICAL CORRECTNESS:** We have in the UK laws that are forcing us to accept many previously unacceptable things and we may not speak out against them for fear of offending. For example one may not openly criticize homosexuality. One may not speak out against immigrants occupying council property for fear one would be accused of racism etc. There have been cases where the police have actually cautioned people that they are thinking the wrong things and need to be 'educated'.

GENERAL PUBLIC SPYING: Orwell wrote that people and even young children would be encouraged to report on their neighbours and family if they in anyway transgressed against Big Brother. Today: **DSS BENEFIT FRAUD CAMPAIGN:** This is just one example of how the British Government has openly encouraged the public to spy on each other. On television the DSS ran an advertising campaign supposedly showing people working whilst claiming benefit and at the end gave a telephone number asking the public to 'phone in and report anyone they suspected.

ROOM 101: Orwell wrote about a room where anyone who had offended would be taken and subjected to torture to make them love Big Brother. Today: **GUANTANAMOBAY:** This is a lock-up concentration camp style jail where unconvicted, ostensibly innocent individuals are held and openly abused. Whilst this is not a British prison information that has been extracted from tortured inmates has been used by the British Government.

CAMERAS IN PUBLIC PLACES: Orwell described how the public would be constantly watched by Big Brother with hidden cameras and microphones placed in the streets and parks. Today: **CCTV:** Look in any city center and you will see CCTV cameras, they are linked to a central observation unit. There are cameras in shops, at petrol stations, even in the toilets at public houses. There are even hidden microphones placed in lampposts in some cities. The Speedcams on our roads can read number plates and linked to a central computer can check instantly for any vehicle that is not taxed and insured.

We are today all living in a massive prison and George Orwell predicted it. The ability of Big Brother government to observe our every activity is increasing week by week and soon each and every car journey we make, every financial transaction we undertake, everywhere we go will be fed into a computer and if there is a slight variance from what they decide is the norm then we will be taken in and questioned. Give the wrong answers and you could well end up in room 101, or Belmarsh Jail, Guantanamo Bay etc. Orwell predicted all this, I predict a riot.

CHAPTER TWENTY

RUTH PARRISH: SPIRITUALIST MEDIUM?

It was Christmas Eve morning in the year 1988 and on the Isle of Angelsey in North Wales Mrs. Attwood was suddenly taken ill and rushed to hospital. In the ambulance with her was a young boy who had similar symptoms, blinding headaches, vomiting, nausea, dizziness, acute pain, but the cause was unknown. The medics caring for her on the way to hospital said that across Angelsey there had been a number of such cases and they suspected viral meningitis. Mrs. Attwood was a very poorly lady when she was eventually admitted to a ward.

The doctors gave Mrs. Attwood three lumbar punctures attempting to gain a better diagnosis so they could treat her symptoms but they remained baffled. There was no rash evident, as is usual with meningitis. Yet still she suffered from the intense and almost unbearable headaches and a severe sensitivity to light. Gradually the strain of fighting this pain overcame Mrs. Attwood and she began to drift into and out of a state of semi-consciousness. Any slight movement brought on the nausea causing her to vomit violently. At this point the physical existence of Mrs. Attwood was in the balance, she was at the very verge of death.

As it was Christmas the hospital had discharged as many patients as it was possible to do and Mrs. Attwood was the only patient on her ward, effectively excluded as she awaited diagnosis. Over her face the nurses had placed a towel to shield her eyes from the light. A constant watch was kept over Mrs. Attwood as her condition remained unstable though she continued to cling on to life.

On the morning of the 26th December, Boxing Day, she woke to hear the sound of someone walking across the hospital ward, the heels click, clicking and gradually getting louder as they approached. Suddenly awake Mrs. Attwood peered beneath the towel covering her eyes to see who was coming in her direction. She saw, standing by the foot of her bed, a smartly dressed woman and behind her an equally well dressed man. She recalls noting that though the clothing was neat, kind of tweedy, it appeared slightly old fashioned in design, rather like the clothes worn in the 1940s movies she enjoyed so much. Both the man and the woman looked to be aged in their late middle years and had friendly faces that seemed to smile at her in a gentle but knowing way, as if they understood.

The lady at the foot of Mrs. Attwood's bed quickly ran round the side and grasped both of her hands in hers rubbing them together. 'Now don't you worry my dear' she said 'you will soon be well and I promise you will have a long and happy life'. Then she went on to tell Mrs. Attwood that there were certain important lessons that she must learn and that all people had to understand. These included tolerance and consideration for others, but in her state of fever Mrs. Attwood forgot the rest. She did remember the name that the lady gave her, she said that she was called Ruth Parrish and was a Spiritualist Medium living at Blaenau Ffestiniog. At the time Mrs. Attwood had never heard of Spiritualism and had no idea what a medium was.

Over the next few days Ruth Parrish was constantly at the side of Mrs. Attwood telling her many things about Spiritualism and the spirit people, explaining that she too could see them. Ruth advised that Mrs. Attwood herself could experience the spirit folk and she then saw her own guardian and described in detail this man as being a Chinese Mandarin with the name of Ching.

During the days leading up to New Year Ruth Parrish constantly stayed by the side of Mrs. Attwood encouraging her to get well and telling her that in this life there were many important things that she had to do. Though she was not specific Mrs. Attwood knew that these important things were in some way linked to the lessons that Ruth Parrish had been discussing with her regarding Spiritualism and Mediumship. Soon she began to feel stronger and by New Year's Day the doctors told her that she would discharged the following morning.

Feeling weak, but much better than she had been, Mrs. Attwood prepared herself to leave the hospital and go home. Her rapid recovery was, she thought, due to the kindness and compassion of Ruth Parrish the lady who had effectively nursed her back to life. As she slowly packed her toiletries away Mrs. Attwood looked round the ward to see Ruth and thank her for all she had done. But the lady was nowhere to be seen, in fact, apart from herself, two nurses and one other elderly patient, the place was empty.

Before leaving the ward Mrs. Attwood stopped at the Sister's office and asked the staff nurse there where Ruth Parrish was so that she could thank her for the kindness she had shown. The nurse just looked baffled, 'There is no such person on this ward and, as far as I know, there never has been'. Mrs. Attwood tried to explain that Ruth was a smartly dressed matronly type in a tweedy outfit that had been sitting by her bed every day since she came onto the ward. The staff nurse had no explanation to offer, she herself had been on duty throughout the time on that very ward and had seen no one that fitted the description given by Mrs. Attwood of the lady she called Ruth Parrish. As far as the hospital was concerned there simply was no such person, neither as a patient or staff member.

Mrs. Attwood eventually made a full recovery and found that not only had she become physically stronger she was now an emotionally whole and healthy individual. Something had happened to her during that period in hospital that had changed her from being a rather selfish and bitter person to being one that cares, is compassionate and kind. She has become rather like her mysterious mentor Ruth Parrish, who came to help when she needed it most all those years ago.

FOOTNOTE: Despite extensive enquires in the Blaenau Ffestiniog area Mrs. Attwood could find no record or trace of a Spiritualist Medium by the name of Ruth Parrish. If you have any information that may help in this continuing search please do contact me.

CHAPTER TWENTY ONE

THE GENIUS OF COLIN WILSON

In early December of the year 2001 myself, the author Ron Ellis along with the wonderfully talented and highly amusing Professor Joe Cooper went to visit Colin Wilson at his home Œtetherdown[1] in the little Cornish village of Goran Haven. I had long been a great admirer of Wilson's work and must have read ŒThe Strength To Dream[1] (one of his lesser known titles) at least six times as it is, to me, simply inspiring. The idea to go see Colin Wilson was in fact Joe Cooper's he had been a personal friend for many years and so after a few tentative telephone calls it was agreed that we three men in a car all go to visit. It was an incredible experience for me as it is not often one has the opportunity to meet with a living legend and believe me Colin Wilson is at the very least that. Let me tell you just a little about this incredible man and his genius as both a writer and a philosopher:

Colin Henry Wilson was born on the 26th June 1931 into a working class family in Leicester where his first job was shifting stock in a warehouse. Wilson went on to work in the chemical industry but was so ill at ease with his position that he at one point contemplated ending his life. The shock of holding a flask of poison to his lips rocked young Colin into realising that not only must he live he had to do something of serious significance with his life. By the mid 1950s Wilson had managed to get into and quickly out of the RAF, where he was called up as a conscript, by pretending to be actively homosexual (a practice that was at the time unlawful). No square bashing for Colin, he knew he had a mission and set off with a rather tatty old sleeping bag and slept rough on Hampstead Heath whilst spending all waking hours in The British Library researching his first book 'The Outsider[1]. When Victor Gollanz published this in 1956 it rapidly became an international best seller propelling the 24 year old Wilson to instant fame. It was though something of a poisoned chalice as Wilson soon found out. OxBridge, the home of British intellectualism, does not like outsiders and young Colin Wilson with his seminal anti-sarte philosophical examination of social alienation was very soon an outsider himself. He even managed to get himself horsewhipped by the father of his beautiful ladyfriend Joy who challenged Wilson, whom he believed to be a seriously disturbed beatnik, brandishing a riding crop. So Colin Wilson was literally one of The Beat Generation in both senses of the term. The popular press went to work on Wilson and soon he was making headlines for all the wrong reasons. Labels soon followed as he became one of the original Angry Young Men of English literature alongside John Brain (Room At The Top) and John Osborne (Look Back In Anger). He fled London in absolute disgust at the vilification he was receiving and found peace with his Joy in a rented house overlooking the sea in far distant Cornwall. He was to remain there forevermore along with his new bride Joy.

In the year 1971 Wilson published a book that many readers of Psychic World may be familiar with 'The Occult: A History' in which CW covered numerous topics ranging from potted profiles of Helena Blavatsky, Daniel Dunglas Home, William Blake and P.D. Ouspensky to sections on magic and spirituality. If you have not read this book then really you should it is an erudite attempt at a reasoned examination of psychic and supernatural phenomena. Which brings me back to the year 2001 and my meeting with the man himself.

Colin Wilson presents as a typical professorial type, tall, imposing, slightly imperious but remarkably warm and friendly. He welcomed the three of us into his home and quickly introduced his wife Joy who is a delightful lady with sparkling wit. The house itself Wilson has named ŒTetherdown' and it is just what you might expect a nutty professors home to be like, extremely eccentric and stuffed top to bottom and back to front with books, records and CDs. There were book shelves in the kitchen, in every room, they lined the walls, jam-packed must have been ten thousand books or more. The bathroom had book shelves! Outside stood three mighty wooden sheds full of, you guessed it, books. Lots of the books in the sheds were written by CW himself as they were first editions sent to CW by the publisher. Imagine my delight when Colin invited us to select a few and he would sign them. Colin is also an amazing chef, he personally cooked us a simply brilliant meal of rich dark meat and we washed it down with more red wine than I can ever recall drinking in one sitting. What a wonderful kind and interesting host. And everyone who is anyone has been to see Colin Wilson, he told me that my favourite poet Sir John Betjeman had been sitting in the same chair I was in and he had even started to write a poem for Colin and, believe this or not, CW gave me the first few lines and suggested I complete it. So I did and here it is:

TETHERDOWN: The Home of Colin Wilson. By John G. Sutton When the wind from Gorran Haven/Blows across to Tetherdown/Sweeping in sea salted ozone/From that cobbled Cornish town/And the sacred scent of fishes/Fills the early morning air/Then let me be in that safe lodging/For my joy is ever there. When the insults of this world/Can touch me nevermore/And the curfew sounding bell/Calls me to an unknown shore/Close in then The Outsider/Keep the wildest storms away/Be they errant human nature/Or the gales from Veryan bay. Wrapped in stone and ancient oak/Where the peace lies ages deep/Let me rest by Gorran Haven/In that long eternal sleep/And if some speak my name and whisper/Of a fleeting world renown/Let their comments catch the wind/That blows across to Tetherdown.

Colin Wilson kindly signed a copy of my poem for me and it is beside this computer as I write now of a happy day not so long ago when I met the genius that is Colin Wilson. CW wrote: For John with admiration Colin Wilson. I suspect that what he really meant was that he admired my absolute audacity in finishing the work of Sir John Betjeman and then having the nerve to present it to him.

Do read Colin's work, he has written over one hundred and twenty books and you can find them all in your local library. I personally recommend 'The Strength To Dream' and of course 'The Occult'. He writes like a dream and as his autobiography says he has been dreaming to some purpose. Now go discover The Genius that is Colin Wilson.

CHAPTER TWENTY TWO

PLASTIC GANGSTERS & PERSONAL RESPONSIBILITY

As Spiritualists we believe that as we sow so shall we reap, in other words we are personally responsible for all our actions both good and bad. This is not the way that some religions teach responsibility, in the Christian faith for example they state that by accepting that 'The Lord Jesus Christ' is the saviour all sins shall be forgiven. Now I don't know about you but I am absolutely certain about me and I have indeed committed many sins but they are my sins, a part of what makes John G. Sutton the person that he is. I am not hiding away behind a 'saviour' I did what I did with clear intent and accept full responsibility for my admittedly sinful actions. With me we are not talking murder or molestation of under age children, my sins mainly involve administering physical retribution on those making a good case for a beating and to be totally honest, I would do it again. So what would be the point in forgiving me, I am unrepentant, I half enjoyed dealing with those that had the gall to provoke me, so what is the point the Christians are trying to make offering absolution to someone like me?

I confess my, at times. aggressive nature has overtaken my spiritual side, let me give you an example: I was walking along an avenue in East Acton, London, the month was June, the weather fine and sunny I was in a really happy mood on such a glorious day. As I walked alongside a hedge by the side of an open grassy area I heard the loud screaming of a woman who sounded to be terrified and calling for help. The screams were coming from directly behind the hedge so I pushed the bushes aside and stepped through to see a large man holding a woman by the front of her dress in a threatening manner. Without hesitation I immediately confronted the man and as I did so the situation changed as he let go of the woman and turned on me. Not only did he begin to approach me in a menacing manner but so too did the woman. 'Wallet mate or you get it' the large lout demanded and his female accomplice moved forward alongside him. I almost laughed, what a treat I thought as I smacked him straight in the mouth and dropped him to the floor where his lady friend started to scream all over again. I realise I could have left it there but sometimes the temptation is too much, I mean he was intending to assault and rob me, so I slapped him, very gently of course, till he too started to scream. I confess it was perhaps a little more than was called for, I am a sinner, but those two would have stolen my money, possibly injured me if they had the chance. Who knows maybe I taught them a lesson, I hope I did, but I seek no forgiveness for enjoying thumping that thug.

Recently I saw a documentary film made by Donal Macintyre titled ; 'A Very British Gangster' which featured as its main subject a bloated low life villain from the broken back streets of Manchester. I will not name the disgraceful cheap bully but suffice it to say that this 'plastic gangster' has made a somewhat dubious reputation for himself by terrorising the immature, often intellectually challenged and docile residents of housing estates in the Greater Manchester area. His crimes that he openly boasts about are numerous, they include armed robbery, police assault, fraud, possession of firearms, handling stolen goods etc. etc. His general modus-operandi involves intimidation, brutality and bullying. In this documentary the petty hoodlum announces that he is so tough that Strangeways Jail can not deal with him, whilst at the same time showing images of this goon in a body-belt locked up in The Block of that notorious Victorian prison. What we are shown in this film is an obnoxious, egotistical, mindless thug who has no intention of redeeming himself in the eyes of society. Indeed a close member of his family was recently shot dead in cold blood in revenge, it seems, for some violent crimes committed elsewhere. The man in question is seeking retribution whilst at the same time accepting absolution for his previous acts of violence from his local Christian parish priest. The documentary actually shows this brute and his fellow thugs in a Christian Church where they state that they are confessing their sins for forgiveness before they go out and commit some more!

The doctrine of personal responsibility is, in my humble opinion, the only thing that makes sense and I have been there during a very near death experience. I have been interviewed by what we may term angelic beings about my incarnation on Earth and they did not mention religion, they asked me to briefly detail what I had done with my life. As Spiritualists we believe absolutely in the survival of the personality after the death of the physical body so we must therefore also believe that if we are good people here, then we will be good people there in the next dimension and vice versa. So the wicked will be faced with their personality intact as villains, thugs, murderers, rapists etc. There is simply no way to escape that fact, I know I have been there and I was myself, I stood before a panel of three quite reasonable ordinary looking individuals who questioned me about my life and I had clear recollection of all that had transpired. Not only did I know what I had done with my life I knew that it was with me, I was now answering for all my actions. As I said at the start of this column I am an unrepentant sinner who has committed sins and whilst I seriously do regret some there are others, such as thumping the would be mugger, that I actually enjoyed and would likely do again. What I am I am, cogito ergo sum, I think therefore I am and we all are, believe me there is no escaping what you are.

The point is that personal responsibility for our deeds is something that should be taught to all, each individual must accept that whatever they knowingly do will be with them into infinity and beyond, as Buzz Lightyear said. Any religion that teaches the forgiveness of sins is without a shadow of any doubt, misleading its adherents and potentially placing them on a difficult pathway to perdition. That cheap 'Plastic Gangster' from Manchester is in for a terrible but well earned shock as he offers to the angelic beings in explanation for his life of violent crime the excuse that he was forgiven by a Parish Priest in the name of The Lord. As you sow so shall ye reap and I would not want to be facing an accounting of my life if I had wasted it on sinful debauchery and wickedness. As I stated above, some say they are too much, too tough for the likes of Strangeways Jail to deal with. But be assured, there awaits something after death, in that undiscovered country, far worse than any mortal punishment that exists here and it is waiting for such fools.

CHAPTER THWENTY THREE

AUTOMATIC WRITING

It was in the year 1996 and I had just been commissioned to write a book titled 'Psychic Pets' for the publishing house of Bloomsbury . J K Rowling and I shared the same managing editor Mr. Barry Cunningham. I can recall meeting her in the office there and passing the time of day, she was just working on her first Harry Potter novel and no one had any idea that this was going to be the sensation it turned out to be. But I could see something about the lady, a quiet determination and she had an aura of success even then. For me 'Psychic Pets' was something of a turning point, the book became an international best seller and suddenly I was in demand. The strange thing about my writing skills was that although I always did my research carefully when it came to putting the words around the facts and building the book I found I was helped by my unseen guides. The words just seemed to materialise on the page before me as I sat with all my notes and often I would be so astounded at aspects of the story that I would laugh out loud. You see it was as if I were reading the book for the first time, not writing it. The book wrote itself almost as if I were an automaton pressing the keys to the instructions of another. It was in fact a form of automatic writing and it is a gift that is with me to this day.

Following my success with that book I was commissioned to write as series of titles by Mr. Barry Cunningham who had moved to Element Publishers. One book that took a lot more research than usual was an Astrology based children's title 'Star Signs For You and Your Pet' which was a fun look at astrology and how it may apply to pets and their young owners. That book took a little time to get right and to ensure I had not made any very obvious errors I asked a reasonably well known Astrologer to proof read my first draft. This they did and said all I had done appeared correct so after some minor adjustments and added humour supplied by my automatic writing I packaged the book and sent it off to my literary agent. Some time later, much to my surprise, I received a telephone call from Rosemary Bromley my very genteel literary agent and she told me that an extremely strange thing had happened. She said that she had just received a book submitted to her by another author and that when she began reading was horrified to discover that it was exactly the same as my book. She wondered how could this be? She knew I would not steal or copy someone else's work. It was when she told me the name on the book that I realised what had happened, the professional astrologer that I had asked to proof read my book had removed all reference to John G. Sutton from it, substituted his name and sent it to a literary agent as his own work. Unfortunately for the crook he had been guided to send the book to my literary agent and she immediately alerted me. I will decline to name the cheap thief that did that to me but you will all know his name.

There are various ways that I use my ability to practice automatic writing and one is the more usually accepted method of placing a pen on a blank sheet of paper and allowing it to write. When I first tried this all I got was a lot of wild uncontrolled scribbles that made no sense. I could though feel that there was a slight power, a kind of cold tingle on my hand as I held the pen so I knew that I was receiving communication but I was not getting it under control. Time solved that and after many months of applying myself to the task I found that not only words but full sentences were being written. I also found that if I allowed the pen free reign I could ask questions and get answers that were correct. I told a certain lady, who shall for reasons of my own safety, remain nameless, about my ability and she asked me to prove it. I was open to this challenge and therefore suggested she ask the pen a question as I held it to the blank sheet of paper. The lady said 'What it is my weight?'. The pen instantly came to life and began to write a statement of some serious poundage and at the end wrote 'too fat'. I showed the lady questioner the answer given and was somewhat surprised to receive a very angry response. She later told me that she had that very day weighed herself wearing only her birthday suit and was not amused to think that my spirit guide had been watching her.
There is a way that you too can test your ability to practice automatic writing. First take an ordinary black or blue biro pen and lay it alongside a plain white A4 sheet of paper. Now allow

yourself to meditate and concentrate on the pen and the paper, stare unblinkingly at he pen, consider every aspect of it and open your eyes wide, get the image of that pen in your mind. After say ten minutes of meditation take the pen in your writing hand, hold it very loosely yet at the same time maintaining control of the balance if not the exact movement. Now place the point of the biro at the top left of the blank paper and in your mind ask your guide to give you a message. You may find that the pen moves very quickly with erratic stops and starts making scribbling loops and swirls. In your mind say 'Calm Down' do this, perhaps even speak out loud. You will find that after some rather hesitant starts and stops the pen begins to write clear words that will, in time make sense. This is not something that you can hope to achieve overnight it takes time and you must be very patient. Eventually you will find that the pen will not only produce clear handwriting but it will also answer your questions.

In have found that I can now communicate with specific spirits using my automatic writing and each has a distinctive handwriting style. You will, with years of practice be able to do this yourself. I have found that with my main guide doing the automatic writing I can achieve messages for others from their departed loved ones. It is an absolutely brilliant aspect of my personal psychic gift and one that I feel many others can use with dedication, constant practice and time. Note that please, TIME, it takes time and the results are by no means instantaneous. But if you are determined to succeed and willing to spend an hour each week training then you too will be able to access your psychic gift through automatic writing.
I now find that when conducting a one to one personal consultation that using automatic writing is a wonderful way to initiate a connection. Often for me the pen has written astonishingly accurate information that is pertinent to the subject. For example one lady came to see me and the pen wrote 'Deep water and I am here, accident'. The lady was instantly in tears when I showed her what the pen had written as her well loved elder brother had recently drowned in a river having fallen in during a walk home on a stormy night.

CHAPTER TWENTY FOUR

THE GHOST CLUB

Over the last twenty or more years myself and my dear wife Mary have been photographing what we believe to be discarnate spirits and also elemental beings. A number of our photographs have been published in this newspaper 'Psychic World' but other than one single example of a Goblin photo featured in a magazine there has been little mainstream media interest. I believe that with the new multiple mega-pixel digital cameras it is now more possible than ever before that anomalous phenomena can be captured on film albeit in a digital format. I include in this article an example for you to see for yourself this image shows what I believe to be an elf or fairy materialised in my hair. The image is untouched other than having been cropped to enable you to better see the elemental entity.

The problem I have found with presenting out photographs of fairies and spirits etc. to scientific sceptical experts is that they claim not to be able to see the anomalous phenomena that I can quite clearly see. Now this may well be because I am a psychic clairvoyant with an advanced facility trained over many years or it may be that there are none so blind as those that will not see. I seriously suspect the latter to be the case. In one instance I took a number of selected images that, to me at least, clearly show either materialised spirits or elemental beings. The result was that the photographic expert took a look, declared he could not see anything unusual in the images and pointed out to me that to believe otherwise was to be taking a step on the path to insanity.

I am quite certain that my wife Mary is a sane and sensible person, despite being married to me and she would be the first to point out my mistakes if she believed I was jumping to incorrect or fanciful conclusions. So I decided to test my belief in the existence of spirits and elementals captured on camera and sent samples of the files to various high profile sceptics and parapsychologist etc. To date not a single one has had the decency to respond. Then I came across an internet site dedicated to The Ghost Club. The following is taken directly from that internet website:

THE GHOST CLUB:

The club has its roots in Cambridge when in 1855 fellows at TrinityCollege began to discuss ghosts and psychic phenomena. Formally launched in London in 1862 (attracting some light hearted ridicule in "The Times"), it counted amongst its early members Charles Dickens and Cambridge academics and clergymen.

This group undertook practical investigations of spiritualist phenomena, which was then much in vogue and would meet and discuss ghostly subjects. The Ghost Club seems to have dissolved in the 1870s following the death of Dickens but it was relaunched in 1882 simultaneously with the Society for Psychical Research (SPR) with whom there was an initial overlap of members.

The Ghost Club was revived on All Saints Day 1882 by A.A.Watts and a famous contemporary medium, the Reverend Stainton Moses. Whilst the SPR was a body devoted to scientific study the Club remained a selective and secretive organisation of convinced believers for whom psychic phenomena were an established fact. Stainton Moses resigned from the vice presidency of the SPR in 1886 and thereafter devoted himself to the Club which met monthly, with attendance being considered obligatory except for the most pressing reasons. Membership was small – 82 members over 54 years – but during this period the Club attracted some of the most original – and controversial minds in psychical research, serving almost as a place of refuge for those who were unable to pursue activities elsewhere. These included Sir William Crookes who attracted scandal after investigation into Florence Cook, a medium.

Since its founding in 1862, the Ghost Club has welcomed many luminaries to its membership. The list includes Charles Dickens, Sir William Crookes, Air Chief Marshall Lord Dowding, Arthur Koestler, Dr.C.E.M.Joad, Donald Campbell, Sir Julian

Huxley, Sir Osbert Sitwell, W.B.Yeats, Sigfreid Sassoon, Dennis Wheatley, Dennis Bardens and Peter Cushing. Present members include the explorer and founder of Operations "Drake" and "Raleigh" Colonel John Blashford-Snell, OBE, and noted paranormal investigators Maurice Grosse, John and Anne Spencer and Reverend Lionel Fanthorpe, as well as author Lynn Picknett . A previous chairman of the Ghost Club was W.T.G. (Tom) Perrott, a life member of the club and an eminent figure in the field of psychical research. The club has investigated many famous locations during its lifetime, such as BorleyChurch, Chingle Hall, The Queen's House, RAFCosfordAerospaceMuseum, GlamisCastle, Winchester Theatre, WoodchesterMansion, Michelham Priory and the Clerkenwell House of Detention.

The chief investigating officer of The Ghost Club is today an erudite gentleman called Mr. Derek Green and on the website is listed his contact email address. So having been ignored and or ridiculed by many supposed experts I decided to send Mr. Green an email including a small selection of photographic images in JPG files. Some short time passed and I received a reply from Mr. Green advising me that my submissions to The Ghost Club had been forwarded to the committee. I am awaiting a considered response and hope that our photographs will be properly examined and evaluated. There has been no tampering with the files and if you met my wife Mary you would instantly understand that fraudulent tinkering for effect would be out of the question. So I will keep you all posted on developments and if you get the chance I highly recommend you visit the website of The Ghost Club: WWW. Ghostclub.org.uk It must be a brilliant organisation as my friend the author Colin Wilson was a member.

CHAPTER TWENTY FIVE

WAYNE ISAACS: My Early Psychic Experiences

The well known television psychic Wayne Isaacs and I collaborated on writing a book about his life and the title we used is I'M NOT MAD, I'M PSYCHIC. Since publication in December of 2012 this book, published on Amazon Kindle has been in and out of the top ten best selling books on the subject of Spirituality. There are 28 Five Star reviews on Amazon with many readers saying that they found the book to be a gripping read that was addictive reading. I wrote the words, but it is, in my opinion, the astonishing story of Wayne's early life that has made our book a success. Here is a sample from the book in which Wayne tells how he first began to receive messages from the world beyond:

It was at this time during my 13th year that I began to receive information about others that was not conveyed to me through any of my five senses, I just seemed to know. I recall clearly being in the school playground and running up to a boy in my class and saying 'Grandfather John sends his love' those words just came to me and I had to say them to the boy who instantly started to weep. I did not know that his beloved grandfather, whose name was John, had died the week before. The message just appeared in my mind. On another occasion I was sitting in the English class looking at the teacher when I saw a car crash and shouted out 'Look out Sir the road works are there'. After the lesson ended the teacher called me over and asked me to tell him who had been talking about his accident. I did not know, no one had said anything to me I just knew. I tried to explain that to him but he said I was a naughty little liar and he would find out who told me as yes he had crashed his car the day before hitting a big hole in some unmarked road works near his home. This kind of thing was happening to me all the time around my thirteenth birthday and onwards. It was absolutely beyond my control, I had the information bounce from nowhere into my mind and had to speak it despite not understanding where it came from or what it might really mean.

There were to be many problems for young Wayne as his ability to comprehend exactly what was happening to him was limited to the verbal and often physical abuse he received from both his peer group and the school teachers who thought he was spying on them. His parents thought he was delusional and took him to see a psychiatrist. This is an example of the kind of phenomena that Wayne was experiencing taken from his book I'M NOT MAD, I'M PSYCHIC.

The night terrors began and so did the waterworks. I was just too scared to get out of bed as all around me the dark shadows shifted and twisted into monstrous shapes that seemed to be grabbing at me pulling me down into the darkness and no one believed when I told of the weird things I could see. No one would listen and who could I tell. My parents were loving, kind and caring but to them I must have seemed like a right basket case. Things just got progressively worse and on one night of absolute horror I was woken by a long black hand crawling up my body and reaching for my throat. There was no body attached to this frightful appendage just the arm with a great grabby hand trying to throttle me. As I tried to scream I looked and saw my toy monkey that I called Mr. Boo jumping around on the bed, his eyes were lit by a strange dark red light and they moved up and down from left to right. I was absolutely terrified by this and next morning my soaking wet bed sheets were clear evidence of the horrors I had experienced. Of course I tried to explain to my parents what I had seen but they could not understand. How could my dear mother understand that her young son was haunted when I did not myself comprehend the complexity of what I was being subjected to. I realise now that I was a wide open psychic channel, but then I was just a very frightened little boy. So desperate and despairing was I that in a fit of frustrated anguish I ran into the main lounge where my parents were sat watching TV threw myself at the wall then began to bang my head and body against it I just needed to die I could not live with this it was torture and no one knew, no one to tell. It must have terrified my parents and they just did not know what to do with me.

Wayne had to cope with the problem of being an open psychic channel as best he could but his highly emotional nature could take only so much. In his 20s Wayne was taken by his parents to a secure psychiatric hospital where he was located in a locked ward. The initial diagnosis was bi-polar disorder and the senior psychiatrist there advised that for the rest of his life Wayne Isaacs would be on medication. But Wayne knew differently he knew that he would one day be well and it was this self belief that protected him inside that institution for the clinically mentally disturbed. You can read how Wayne gradually improved and was helped back into society where he joined a Spiritual Awareness class and managed to get his extraordinary powers under control.

Today Wayne Isaacs is a well established and respected professional psychic-medium and he has appeared on numerous television shows worldwide. His story is inspirational and one that all interested in paranormal powers should read. I'M NOT MAD, I'M PSYCHIC is available on Amazon Kindle and as a paperback.

CHAPTER TWENTY SIX

THAUMATURLOGICAL HEALING

During the early hours of one morning In the summer of the year 2013 I woke from a deep sleep shouting loudly these words 'I Will Not Do It!' My bedroom was in almost complete darkness but I saw standing at the foot and side of my bed a number of semi-translucent spirits that emitted a slight golden luminescence. As I looked, now in silent wonderment, I heard a loud somewhat sombre voice say in deep commanding tones 'Yes You Will'. At that instant from directly above my body a brilliant beam of glimmering, shimmering white light shone down upon my chest. I was momentarily mesmerised as this almost tangible beam of brilliance appeared to be entering my being. The next instant I was wide awake, the sunlight filtering through the half closed curtains sparkled and it was dawn. I clearly recall wondering what had happened, who were those spirits and what was it that I had been told I must do. Later that day I was to find out.

As part of my work as a professional psychic-medium I present a series of on-line discussions in a internet chat room on a website called WWW. Oranum.com In this chat room, which is totally free to enter, there came this day a lady, her na me is Michelle, who told me she was with her son whose name was Ashley. I heard a voice telling me that Ashley had a serious problem with his nose and was forever having to wipe away fluid, the medical term is Rhinitis. When I told Michelle what I had heard she explained that Ashley had been troubled with his nose for many years and despite seeing many specialists at the NHS Hospitals no cure had been found. I then heard the same voice telling me that I would heal this young man, Ashley or Ash as he prefers to be called, who is in his mid twenties, so I asked his mother if she would like to conduct healing for her son. Michelle agreed, so there and then I asked her to direct Ashley to look at my image visible on her screen via my webcam. What happened next was as though I was being used by an unseen force, I raised both my hands pointing my fingers directly into the webcam moving them gently and as I did so I felt a tremendous tingling vibration through my hands into the tips of my fingers. It was as if some mysterious invisible energy was being transmitted. Michelle told me that she had experienced a strange tingling sensation as I sent the healing power and her son Ash said he felt something vibrating his body.

I am, in many respects, a man that has a developed sense of humour and I do really enjoy a good practical joke. Please believe me that this is not in any way shape or form a joke, I am absolutely serious when I tell you that two days later, into my chat room on WWW. Oranum.com there came Michelle to tell me that since I gave her son Ash the healing his nose had stopped running and he was totally healed. She was astounded as over the years she had taken her son to every kind of medical doctor and specialist she could and still his nose would not stop running. But it had stopped now. The question in my mind when I heard that amazing report from Michelle was this, am I really supposed to heal people? It would appear that indeed I am being directed to do and as a psychic-medium I trust and follow the messages and guidance I receive from my discarnate spirit guides.

Michelle soon began to tell people about the incredible healing powers that I had used to heal her son and soon my chat room on WWW. Oranum.com began to fill with people seeking healing from me for themselves and their loved ones. One dear lady called Tiffany was in absolute despair she had been suffering breathing difficulties and when she went to the medical doctor had been diagnosed with bronchial pneumonia, she was in fear of losing her life. Again my guide spoke to me and advised I should heal this poor lady, raising my hands I advised her to touch her computer screen look at me and receive the healing I was to send. As I did so once again the intense sensation of a powerful vibration passed through my hands into my fingertips out into cyberspace where it connected with this sick lady. Days passed and each time the lady came into my chat room I gave her more of the healing power. It took a little while but she recovered and was certain, she said, that it was the healing she received from me that had healed her. Till then she had been fading fast despite all manner of anti-biotics.

There are, for reasons best known to themselves, professional psychics that seem to get some strange twisted delight in giving people bad news. Some weeks after I had healed the lady with pneumonia she came to see me in my chat room on WWW. Oranum.com and told me that someone had advised her to prepare herself for sadness as her father was about to pass to spirit. This horrible advice deeply disturbed the dear lady as that week her 72 year old father had been taken seriously ill and the intial diagnosis was pleurisy. As I had healed her she asked would I be so kind as to heal her father. Now it is one thing to preach to the choir as all who have stood on a Spiritualist Church platform will know, but it is quite another to deal with long established very sceptical people. Tiffany's father was exactly that, an elderly gentleman who had worked all his life and was a no nonsense down to earth individual who called a spade a spade. I agreed to speak with her dad, his name is Ted, and so that very evening she brought him to my chat room and we had a friendly discussion. I sensed he was desperately ill but my guide told me I could do this I really could heal him. But first I had to allow Ted to understand that I was serious and a normal man intent on helping as best I could. So I got my George Formby style Banjo, plunked it and sang him a song 'I'm leaning on a lamppost at the corner of our street...etc' Ted was soon laughing with me as we talked about the good old days when beer was a shilling a glass and Wodbines were passed round smoky pubs as men in flat caps shuffled the dominoes. Then I gave him the healing, my hands went to the webcam and I experienced the amazing surge of intense energy as the force within me passed through my fingertips over cyberspace to poor old Ted. I completed that and then I heard my guide tell me to advise him that the Dr. would send him for a scan and that this would be completely clear as I had healed him. So I did that, I told Ted he was cured and go home have a good nights sleep. I am sure he thought I was nutty as a fruitcake.

The next day I was delighted to be advised by Ted's daughter that he was actually feeling a great deal better all his chest pains had eased and he could get his breath. I asked to see Ted again in my chat room on WWW. Oranum.com and he came along again on two more occasions. Some weeks passed and I heard no more about old Ted until one day his daughter Tiffany came to my chat room and told me that her father's Hospital Report had arrived, he had been sent for a scan and the results showed that there was absolutely nothing wrong with his chest. The lady said that Ted and the doctors dealing with him were all astounded as they had fully expected to see serious lung damage due to the pleurisy. It seemed that the healing I gave Ted had worked, though how this works is a mystery it is a kind of magical miracle, the correct term is Thaumaturlogical Healing. The spirits have empowered me to heal and though I may have shouted 'I Will Not Do It' the commanding voice of my angelic guide proved to be right, 'Yes You Will' and yes I am so doing. It is an astonishing thing to have happened to me and I will from this moment on be making available the incredible healing force that passes through me to those in need. It is not of me, I am not a magician, I make no claims to be anything special but I have, so my guides tell me, been sent to heal those that are in need.

CHAPTER TWENTY SEVEN

THE SPIRITUAL POWER OF POETRY

I have recently been broadcasting a network USA radio show called Psychic World in conjunction with WWW. Transformationtalkradio.com out of WBLQ from New York city. The feedback has been very encouraging and one thing that my American audience tell me they like a lot is the poetry I read on air. In my programme broadcast on he 15th January the main subject matter was poetry of the soul, a subject that is very close to my heart as I truly believe that some poets are effectively mediums inspired by angelic discarnate entities to write poems that have a spiritual message for mankind. As a poet and professional psychic medium myself I have on many occasions woken from a dream with the words of a poem in my mind almost fully formed. This happened to me quite recently and I had to immediately transcribe the words onto a Word Document writing the poem that is called 'FLOWERS'. It tells the story of a love that is eternal through the stages in life when we would typically give flowers to our loved ones. This is the poem it bears my name but was, I know, created in the dimension of spirit by beings far more gifted than I.

FLOWERS
By John G. Sutton

Flowers in the fields, wild roses grow/God's way of letting us know

The most beautiful things sent from above/Flowers show us the power of love

I was just a child, aged only three/Out in the garden by the old oak tree

Picked some daisies growing there free/Made a little posy for my dear mummy

As I gave them to mum, said I love you true/These are the flowers I picked them for you

I was eighteen years, she was sweet sixteen/The loveliest girl I had ever seen

She held my hand my heart beat fast/I had found the one for me at last

That Valentines day, the roses were red/Gave them to my girl, with love the card said

On our wedding day my bride wore white/The flowers were glorious colours so bright

She held my hand Yes I will, Yes I Do/Together forever with a love so true

Her pink rose bouquet she threw to a friend/That night we knew our love would never end

Through the years gave her flowers to say/Our love is true just like our wedding day

Each Valentines the roses were red/Sent them to her, with love the card said

Anniversary's came, the silver and gold/Time passed but dreams don't grow old

Our children all grown, sent us flowers to say

To our Mum and Dad on your special day

But time is a thief, and to all it will come

The final journey for us had begun

Now we lie side by side our spirits are free/And the roses above are placed there with love

Flowers in the fields, wild roses grow/God's way of letting us know

The most beautiful things sent from above

Flowers show us the power of love.

The craft of poetry is, in my personal opinion, an art form that is at its best divinely inspired. I think of the poetry of William Shakespeare whose Sonnet 18 'Shall I Compare Thee To A Summers Day' is among my favourites. In the poem Shakespeare tells us that though 'ever fair from fair sometime declines/By chance or nature's changing course untrimmed' the eternal summer of our beautiful youth will never fade when captured 'In eternal lines....so long lives this and this gives life to thee'. Shakespeare's work is as potent today as it was in the days of Elizabeth the first because it is inspired and inspirational. Think of his works and how many Shakespearian quotations fill the English language and our culture. Sonnet 18 gives us 'The Darling Buds Of May' that became the title of a popular TV series featuring Catherine Zeta Jones and David Jason.

The recently deceased author and philosopher Colin Wilson (The Outsider/Beyond The Occult etc.) once told me that when he sat down to write there very often came over him a sense that he was being guided. There can be no doubt whatsoever that Wilson's research was conducted to a fine degree prior to his application to paper but a mountain of facts do not make a readable and informative article of book. What Wilson was saying is that despite all his intense erudition the final spark of inspiration to formulate the work came from a discarnate source. Colin Wilson was always a philosopher first and an author second, he told me he was guided in a way to tell the world that the nihilistic philosophy of the Existentialists was totally misguided and that life was far from meaningless. In his book 'Below The Iceberg' Wilson explains that John Paul Sarte, the founding philosopher of Existentialism, was in fact arguing against an eternal truth that is we must live in hope. Tomorrow is always another day and if we can believe that then we can overcome all odds. Colin Wilson passed to spirit on the 5th December 2013 I met with him for just a few days when I was researching my own published work back in 2001.

The work of Colin Wilson, especially his philosophical works, will live on and, in the years ahead, I am quite certain his genius as an anti-Sartre philosopher with a dynamic positivistic philosophy will be internationally recognised. Do read 'The Strength To Dream' by Colin Wilson it is beyond doubt an inspired and inspirational book.

CHAPTER TWENTY EIGHT

INTERESTING TIMES

May you live in interesting times, is an ancient Chinese curse and it seems that for we who are alive today it is materialising. Japan is currently facing the biggest national crisis since WWII when America dropped two Atomic Bombs on Hiroshima and Nagasaki killing tens of thousands of innocent people. Now, as I write, the massive earthquake and subsequent tsunami that hit Japan has caused the Atomic reactors at Fukushima massive damage and they are nearing meltdown, set to explode radioactive waste into the atmosphere potentially endangering not only the thirteen million residents of Tokyo but populations as far away as Europe and the USA. The Japanese Emperor Akihito has made an unprecedented television broadcast to his people pleading for calm and assuring them that all will eventually be well. This is a very serious matter indeed for His Imperial Majesty The Emperor of Japan is still considered by many of his people to be a divine being. This belief dates back to pre WWII times when the nation of Japan had what was known as State Shintoism as the only recognised religion. America, during its occupation of post war Japan dismantled the Shinto shrines and removed State Shintoism as the standard religion of Japan. Imagine that! Yet it still survives today as Shinto is the most widely practised religion of Japan along with Buddhism and, to a lesser extent, Christianity. Religious beliefs and prayers are not providing an answer to this terrible crisis and despite his supposed divinity Akihito appears to be powerless to halt the increasingly dangerous situation at Fukushima.

Some few weeks ago in Tunisia there started a series of public demonstrations against the dictatorial regime of President Ben Ali. The riots started when an unemployed graduate was stopped by the police from selling vegetables and fruit from his market stall giving him no means of supporting himself. In a desperate act of defiance this young man set himself on fire in the centre of Tunis. The result was an instant recognition by the people that they too were in a hopeless situation because of the fifty year dictatorship and they set about rioting. The predominant religion of Tunisia is Islam and the majority are of the Sunni belief group. The mosques are/were all controlled by the Tunisian government and the President himself appointed The Grand Mufti or religious head of Tunisia. So when the people began to riot they did so in direct opposition to the instructions of their religious leaders. Within days that dictatorship had fallen and the President, Ben Ali had been ousted.

Just days after the people of Tunisia had overthrown their leader the population of Egypt, no doubt having seen that all was possible, set about rioting, demanding freedoms that had been denied them under the strict dictatorial rule of Hosni Mubarak. The primary complaints of the Egyptian people were of low wages and police brutality, the usual repressive regulations and lack of hope. They set out to overthrow the rule of President Mubarak. Around 400 or so Egyptian rioters were shot dead but despite this they continued until at last Mubarak was forced from power after thirty years as a dictator. I personally watched Hosni Mubarak making his final televised plea to the people to just calm down and go back to work then all would be well again. The audacity of this speech near took my breath away as it was quite clear that Mubarak was completely out of touch with reality. Within just hours of making that broadcast he was gone. The predominant religion in Egypt is Islam and the vast majority of the population are of the Sunni belief group. Since the year 1980, when the Egyptian constitution was amended, the State Religion has been Islam. According to the constitution all legislation must agree with Islamic Law. So when the population of Egypt set out to overthrow the Government they did so almost in direct defiance of Islamic law.

Following the exit of Hosni Mubarak from the presidency of Egypt there came an even greater shock as the people of Libya began to demonstrate and attack the regime of Colonel Gaddafi. I was in Libya during September 1969 when Gaddafi staged a bloodless coup and ousted King Idris. Forty two years later he is still in control of Libya but as I write is facing what is effectively civil war as opposing factions seek to remove him from power. Things are now starting to look bleak for Gaddafi as the U.N. has authorised the imposition of a No Fly zone on Libya and the use of all necessary force to stop Gaddafi from killing all who oppose him. He meanwhile is broadcasting to the people of Libya   telling them it will soon be time for them to rejoice and dance in the streets. I fear he may be wrong. As I write the U.S.A. and the U.K. are bombing the airports of Libya. The religion of Libya is 97% Muslim of the Sunni belief group and subject to the law of Islam.

These are indeed interesting times and very worrying too as the UK U.S.A and France are now bombing the Libyan military bases in what will be seen by many as an act of war. But what really is all this about? We are told by the UK Government that Gaddafi is brutalising his people, that the Egyptian President Mubarak was a wicked dictator. We were also told (wrongly) that Iraq's former leader Sadam Hussain had weapons of mass destruction and was killing his own people, led by General 'Stormin' Norman Schwarzkopf we went to war and killed tens of thousands of Iraqi people. We were told that in Afghanistan the Taliban were training international terrorists, we went to war (the opium production increased) and still we are losing our brave soldiers lives over there. The concern I have is that following on from the overthrow of Gaddafi in Libya, which is a foregone conclusion, there will be yet another Islamic country that we in the Western world will get involved in. The last time Iran was controlled by Western powers was as a result of Operation Ajax that, in 1953, overthrew the democratically elected Government of Mosaddegh. This C.I.A. action was, in part, led by Major-General Schwarzkopf the father of 'Stormin' Norman. The reason Mosaddegh had to be replaced was, in simple terms, oil. His government had taken over the British Petroleum (BP) owned oil-fields and nationalised them. The religion of Iran is Muslim with 95% of the population belonging to the Shia Islamic belief group.

As a Spiritualist and practising professional psychic I do see future events through my clairvoyant gifts. What I am now seeing in my visions deeply concerns me and I only hope that I am wrong but I see an endless religious/oil war without frontiers. I am a clairvoyant not a political or revolutionary leader but I know, as you too should know, that we are heading towards hell in a basket unless we stop attacking and invading other countries. Turn on your television and have a look, you too will soon see what I am seeing as the Eton/Public School educated, hereditary Multi-Millionaires that control us cry havoc and let slip the dogs of war.

CHAPTER TWENTY NINE

LADY ZARA: The Horse Healing Equestrian

Last month I asked if any reader had an interesting psychic/supernatural pets story that I may be able to use in my book: PARANORMAL PETS published by Amazon/Kindle. I was delighted with the response and one reader suggested I speak with Lady Zara Barton a horse healing equestrian who has an amazing gift for helping horses. When I spoke to Lady Zara she was pleased to agree an interview so I immediately booked a flight to the Isle of Man where she lives and this is her wonderful story:

Age just one year Lady Zara Barton could ride before she was walking. Her first horse was a little Shetland Pony called Lucky, jet black, gentle and a brilliant easy ride for young Zara. The ability she displayed even at that tender age really impressed her trainers who were amazed at her incredible control as the horses just seemed to understand what young Zara wanted them to do. By the age of three years Zara was considered to be an equestrian prodigy as she mastered the art of jumping her ponies winning numerous 'Lead Reins' competitions in and around her home in the leafy suburbs of Cheshire in the UK.

Early success
By the age of tweleve years Zara was frequently featured in the journal of equestrianism Horse and Hound as she won many events at county shows throughout the North of Engalnd and Wales. Following numerous successes with her name being mentioned in the top training circles Zara was asked to start teaching other riders. Despite just being in her teenage years many of her clients were adults who were frequently astounded at the way this gifted girl could improve their horses attitude.

Zara won her first Grand Prix Dressage competition age 18 years of age riding her horse a black mare called Pretty Woman, this is the highest level you can compete at and is the recognised international standard. This determined young lady was now driving her own 4 X 4 SUV with a horse trailer from show to show and winning time after time. Her home now was a huge mansion house on the outskirts of Southport in the county of Lancashire where Zara stabled five horses her favourite being Frank a mighty seventeen two hands bay coulred gelding. At this time people started to ask Zara what was the secret of her success as it seemed she had an almost magical touch. Zara was able to take even the most unresponsive horse and produce a balanced managable ride with many going on to win at county show level. The answer she always gave was this 'sensitive empathy, discovering the problem and working with the horse to resolve it'. Zara insists that horses are in many respects similar to human beings, if they are sick or have been mistreated they will invariably react accordingly.

Living on The Isle of Man

Lady Zara Barton is now resident on the Isle of Man located some thirty or so miles from the coast of the UK where she breeds and trains horses. Her riding successes are continuing and she is also running her own school of equestrianism there where her talent to train others is nationally recognised. The world reknowned equestion trainer of numerous Olympic champions Conrad Schumaker guides Zara's work. Conrad has been watching over Zara from a distance for the last ten years. Many believe that Lady Zara Barton is destined one day to become an Olympic Games rider herself. However it is Zara's ability to take a seriously disturbed or difficult horse and working with it produce a manageable mount, that is her speciality. Zara says 'the problem with many troublesome horses is that they have often been abused in training'. Zara explained to me that in the not too distant past some trainers used physical corrective measures to train horses to respond in certain ways. This negative programming, beating with sticks, hitting and even punching a horse creates an animal that may very well react in a required way, but out of fear. This is rather like training a human being to move to the left by smacking them round the head every time they move to right.

Such cruelty has, in the past, been relatively comon practice in the conditioning of horses, much in the way that the psychologist Pavlov programmed dogs to respond to the ringing of bells. However, when it goes wrong and the horse fails to accept the abuse the result can be a terribly troubled animal potentially posing a serious threat to anyone attempting to ride it. Lady Zara Barton owns such a horse, his name is Wizard and he was, until she re-trained him, considered to be too dangerous to be ridden.

Zara heals a horse

Zara bought her the horse Wizard, a seventeen one hand chestnut gelding as a three year old and when she brought him to her stables he was one brute of a beast, kicking, rearing, bucking and more like a bronco mule in a wild-western rodeo show than a potential equestion dressage champion. But there was something very unique about this big chestnut horse that Zara could sense and she was determined to give him her very best efforts. Wizard though had more problems than even Zara had envisualised, some months on and he was not making the expected progress so Zara new something was wrong. Her close observation of the horse indicated that Wizard was not relaxed in the company of its stablemates. He appeared restless, unsettled, grumpy, lacked anything like an acceptable attention span and was still rearing up. Holding Wizard in her arms one morning to calm him Zara suddenly realised that not only was this big horse nervous he was also in pain. There was no brightness in his eyes, Wizard's ears were flat and lacked any sign of alertness, the horse was sick, she sensed that very strongly. When the veterinary surgeon gave Wizard a close inspection it was found that within his sinus cavity at the right side of his head there had developed a large cyst. It was this cyst that was now causing the continuing distress to Wizard and it had to be removed by surgery.

It is now over two years since Wizard survived his operation on the sinus cavity when his horrible and painful cyst was removed. Zara nursed him back to health and when he was once again fully fit recommenced the training. Zara was simply determined that this brilliantly beautiful horse would succeed and she is not a lady that gives in. It took time, it took patience and it was worth all the ffort for Wizard is today a star of Dressage at Grand Prix level, he has qualified to compete at the Hickstead Derby, a seriously prestigious event and has been valued at £500,000.00 by Zara's mentor the highly respected international equestrian Hans Schmelder.

A future cahmpion

I asked Lady Zara Barton what her plans were for the future, did she intend to continue training horses or would she concentrate on riding. This is what Zara told me: 'I will always be training and nurturing horses, breeding them and producing Grand Prix level champions, it is one of the reasons I am here. Another is to ride and I sincerely believe that one day I will be good enough to be a member of the Great British Equestrain team representing the UK at the Olympic Games'. Having seen what Lady Zara Barton can do when she puts her mind to it I must say we should all be ready to applaud as she brings home an Equestrian Gold medal from some forthcoming Olympic Games.

CHAPTER THIRTY

INSOMNIA: ABSENT HEALING

Over the years of working with clients seeking clairvoyant insights into their lives I have frequently found that many are enduring the unpleasant experience of sleep deprivation also known as Insomnia. For various reasons such as anxiety, depression, stress, physical pain, emotional upheaval etc. they simply can not enjoy a complete nights rest. For a few nights this lack of sleep is difficult but it can be dealt with, however for some the problem is one that is constant and often, despite medical intervention, it continues, sometimes for years. The term for long term sleeplessness is Chronic-Insomnia and it is a well known medical condition that should always be reported to ones medical practitioner.

There may, in certain instances, be physical conditions, such as hyperthyroidism and obstructive sleep apnea that cause the insomnia, these can be treated. It is therefore essential that if you suffer from insomnia your first approach for help should be to your general medical practitioner. However, once you have taken the responsible and correct action in notifying your G.P. and have followed their advice you may decide to consider the power of Spiritual Healing.

In the North West of England, close to that little seaside town known as Blackpool, noted for fresh air and fun, there lived a very gifted Spiritual Healer by the name of Bill Parker. For many years Bill had been healing and helping others by using his gifts in conjunction with his guides from the world beyond and his ability to alleviate both physical and emotional problems has been proven many times. I first met Bill when he was awakening as a force for healing, almost two decades ago, when he was receiving his initial visitations by the spirits that would soon become his mentors. Two of these guides have since identified themselves as former Native American Indians known in previous life as Sitting Bull and White Eagle.

Sitting Bull was a member of the Native American Sioux Indian tribe and was their Holy Man who led the tribe in their resistance to the American Government. He is perhaps most noted as the War Chief that defeated Colonel George Armstrong Custer at The Battle of The Little Bighorn on 25th June 1876.

White Eagle is a Native American Pawnee Indian chief name given to the leader of the tribe at a particular time. The Pawnee tribe were known as The Great Plains Indians and lived mainly along the banks of the Missouri river. The Pawnee practised human sacrifice believing that the richness of the soul and success of crops would be improved by sacrifice which involved an arrow being shot into the heart of a young girl at dawn on a certain Spring day. It was known as The Morning Star Ritual and was last carried out, according to records, in the year 1838.

Bill Parker has had his guides names confirmed to him many times by various mediums who have received messages for him. On one occasion a lady medium from the town of Lea near Preston was out shopping when she saw a statuette of an Indian and felt a need to purchase this as a gift for her friend Bill Parker. When she handed it to him she explained that it was an irresistible urge that made her buy it and she had been guided to give it to him. The statuette was of Sitting Bull.

I first began referring my clients to Bill many years ago and have received a very positive response from those that have called him. Whilst Bill is willing to see people on a one to one basis he finds that this is time consuming as his home is not on a main motorway route so the way he works is most usually by absent healing. This is perfectly simple and involves nothing more than an individual suffering from, say insomnia or pain, maybe back ache etc. telephoning Bill direct at his home on his BT landline number 01995 670124. Bill then writes down their name and some brief details and places this on what he terms his Absent Healing List. Then at night Bill contacts his spirit guides and says prayers to heal all those that are on his list.

Bill was a deeply spiritual man who sincerely believed in his ability to heal. I know, having referred many clients to him that he was successful. Some few months ago I was speaking to Ms. L. a long term client of mine who lives in London and works with the security services as a senior consultant. The pressure of her work and the stress of personal issues had been taking a toll on her emotional equilibrium, I knew she wasn't sleeping properly and suggested that she call my friend the spiritual healer Bill Parker. Ms. L. did that, though I sensed her reluctance. It was less than a week later that Ms. L. called me again to say that as amazing as it might seem since she had spoken to Bill her sleep pattern had changed and she now was able to enjoy a full nights rest.

Bill helped countless hundreds of people over the years that I have knew him and he assisted in the cures of individuals with damaged backs, psychological problems and all manner of illness. He sometimes travels to Scotland, near to the granite city of Aberdeen and will, if you ask him, perhaps see people there. He makes no charges. Bill gave his powers of Spiritual Healing without taking a fee, nor would he directly accept any payments. Bill would send money to one of the Fresh Water Aid charities that he raised funds for but he would not accept anything for himself.

Bill Parker recent;y passed to spirit this is his obituary published in the monthly journal Psychic World.

IN MEMORY OF BILL PARKER (1929-2017)

I write to celebrate the life and kindness of a wonderfully gifted compassionate spiritual healer that I had the absolute pleasure of knowing. In the North West of England, close to that little seaside town known as Blackpool, noted for fresh air and fun, there lived a very gifted healer by the name of Bill Parker. For many years Bill was healing, helping others by using his gifts in conjunction with his guides from the world beyond. This gentle unassuming man had an amazing ability to alleviate both physical and emotional problems. I first met Bill when he was awakening as a force for healing over two decades ago, as he began receiving his initial visitations by the spirits that would soon become his guides and mentors. Two of Bills spirit helpers were Native American Indians known in their previous incarnations as Sitting Bull and White Eagle.

Bill Parker would help anyone and at no time did he accept payment. If anyone were to give him money he would donate that to the Water Aid charity helping to bring fresh drinking water to the developing world. For that charity Bill raised many thousands of pounds. Over the past twenty or more years Bill featured many times in my 'Off The Cuff' column here at 'Psychic World' as I wrote about his numerous success stories. Bill had an amazing gift that enabled him to project absent healing to those seeking help from all corners of the world. Each night Bill would take his long list of people that had sought help and pray for them. The results would often be amazing but Bill was not a man to take personal credit for these marvellous miracles, he knew that the spirits deserved the real praise.

There may be those among the readers of this newspaper that benefitted from the healing help of Bill and his spirit guides. At times he helped me as I struggled with my own infirmities and I will always remember him as a good man, a friend and an inspirational healing force. His son David called me with the news that Bill had passed to spirit and was obviously upset to have lost his loving father. Can I please ask all who read this brief tribute to a fine spiritual man to say a prayer for Bill Parker's family, they, like me wish him well in his new happy hunting ground, somewhere over the rainbow.

If you have insomnia or other needs you can also contact your local Spiritualist Church and attend on their healing evening where I am certain you will receive the help that you need on a direct one to one healing basis.

CHAPTER THIRTY ONE

IS THERE ANYBODY THERE?

In his poem 'The Listeners' the poet Walter de la Mare wrote these lines: 'Is there anybody there? Said the traveller, knocking on the moonlit door'. Those words have become synonymous with the practice of communication between travellers incarnate in human form and those discarnate spirits waiting behind the moonlit door between this world and the next. We, the incarnate, are all travelling in one direction towards the discovery of what awaits when the door is opened. Is there anybody there? The answer will not be a surprise for Spiritualists as we know that there is another dimension of life that exists. The communication between the material world and the spirit world is a reality that we accept as fact. The visions, messages and insights that many prominent Spiritualist mediums were given as guidance have been written and recorded for centuries offering all who truly seek a reasonably comprehensive library to research. Yet there are those that not only question the evidence of life after life, many make a profession of attempting to disprove the eternal truth. How sad is it that?

There is, strange as this may seem, a group of educated erudite individuals who have formed themselves into a society to disprove the veracity of psychic phenomena. They call their group The Skeptic Society. This is what they have to say about themselves:

The Skeptics Society is a nonprofit scientific and educational organization whose mission is to engage leading experts in investigating the paranormal, fringe science, pseudoscience, and extraordinary claims of all kinds, promote critical thinking, and serve as an educational tool for those seeking a sound scientific viewpoint. Our contributors—leading scientists, scholars, investigative journalists, historians, professors and teachers—are top experts in their fields. It is our hope that our efforts go a long way in promoting critical thinking and lifelong inquisitiveness in all individuals.

One very telling statement endorsed by the intellectually gifted founder of the Skeptic Society Dr. Michael Shermer is this: 'When we say we are "skeptical," we mean that we must see compelling evidence before we believe'. By compelling evidence what Dr. Shermer appears to be seeking is scientific proof that can be repeated under strictly controlled laboratory conditions. The material scientific approach to psychic phenomena, including communication between this world and the next, disallows all anecdotal accounts as being invalid. So the fact that numerous highly qualified individuals gave sworn statements that they witnessed the 19th century medium Daniel Dunglass-Home levitating is discounted. On one occasion Lord Adare witnessed Daniel Dunglass-Home floating in and out of a window, he stated: 'Home swung out of a window in a horizontal position, he came back in again feet foremost and I could not see how he was supported'.

There have been a number of eminent scientists that have studied psychic phenomena and submitted papers supportive of the reality. One such was Sir William Crookes a member of The Royal Society, he is best known in scientific circles for his work on Cathode Rays and as the inventor of The Crookes Tube. One subject that Crookes examined in some detail was the aforementioned Daniel Dunglass-Home along with many other prominent Victorian mediums. When Crookes published his findings in 1874 there was a serious outcry in the scientific community and talk of depriving him of his membership of The Royal Society. That seems to have been par for the course ever since, if the scientific materialists do not see repeatable evidence then no matter how eminent and erudite the examiner may be the reports are derided and the results ignored.

The founder of The Skeptic Society Dr. Michael Shermer has taken his disbelief to an advanced level by recently setting himself the task of becoming a psychic in one day. The way he set about this was to study what he termed various 'Cold Reading' skills, that is this man believes that clairvoyants use practised trickery to deliberately fool their unwitting clients. The audacity of Michael Shermer led him to write a paper titled: 'Psychic For A Day: How I Learned Tarot Cards, Palm Reading, Astrology and Mediumship in 24 hours'. Let me offer you a sample from the article, this is how Shermer suggests he would gull his subjects into feeding back affirmative responses to his fishing expeditions: 1. Does this make sense to you. 2. Can you see why this might be the impression I am getting. 3. What might this link to in your life. 4. Do you connect with this? The man is obviously little more than a professional cynic who operates on the mistaken assumption that all clients of psychics are simpletons who would fall for such obvious nonsense.

The ability to communicate with those in the next dimension of life is not a trick, it is not a fraud and as anyone that ever witnessed the incredible mediumship of Gordon Higginson will know, it is at times beyond reasonable doubt. I once saw Higginson point to a member of a four hundred plus audience and tell the lady that before she set out for the theatre that evening she had made a telephone call to her sister, which she agreed she had, the he gave her the full telephone number which she accepted was absolutely correct. Let Michael Shermer explain that. I have worked with many professional psychics and produced hundreds of theatre shows in which clairvoyant and clairaudient powers were used to pass information to members of the audience. In 1992 I worked with James Byrne the Bolton based medium and produced his show at The London Palladium. I would say that had trickery been used by Byrne or by any of the other mediums and psychics I have worked with then I must have known about it. The truth is that Shermer and his Skeptic Society are barking up the wrong tree, there is no trickery involved with genuine psychics and mediums. The reason that these scientific materialists believe that it is all a confidence trick is that they simply can not otherwise explain it.

Is there anybody there? Yes of course there is and we will all make that wonderful inevitable journey through the moonlit door into the next dimension, it is just a matter of time. There is absolutely no reason for anyone to fear what we call death as there is no such thing. What there is amounts to travelling forward into another world leaving behind the physical body that has done its job. Ask yourself this question: Imagine your life journey is like a car ride, at birth you get into the vehicle and set off from say London, you drive through Birmingham aged 40 years, at Preston you are 60 years at Edinburgh you are 90, at Inverness you reach your destination, would you just sit there in the car? Of course not, destination reached you get out and move on and so it is with your physical body. Enjoy the ride.

CHAPTER THIRTY TWO

UNDERSTANDING SPIRIT

There is now a new way to enjoy radio programmes dedicated to spirit communication and Spiritualism this is through the World Wide Web using a computer or other compatible device such as an Apple Ipad etc. Many years ago, 1992 to be precise, when I first began to work professionally with Psychic-Mediums in the media there was no such thing as the internet as we know it today. Indeed the first time that myself and the Psychic-Medium James Byrne conducted a 'LIVE' on air radio psychic 'phone-in telephone show it made the national press as it was so controversial. We even had a thump of Born-Again Christians banging on Bibles waving banners in protest at the front of Red Rose Radio station in Preston, Lancashire. That was twenty three years ago. The embryonic WWW officially started on the 6th August 1991, which just happened to be my 42nd birthday, when Tim Berners-Lee posted a note in cyberspace using HTTP that is Hyper-Text-Transfer-Protocol. This is an exact copy of part of the first message ever posted: ''The WWW project was started to allow high energy physicists to share data, news, and documentation. We are very interested in spreading the web to other areas, and having gateway servers for other data. Collaborators welcome!'' This was effectively announcing that the message was available to all computer users throughout the world who were connected to a network. That was the birth date of the World Wide Web, same as the birthday of John G. Sutton 6th August. What started then as little more than an idea very quickly developed into something that really has changed the way the world communicates.

When I was a young boy we had mechanical wind-up clockwork gramophones that worked by spinning a hard composite grooved disc at a steady speed of 78 revolutions per minute or RPM and allowing a needle to read the sound waves impregnated into the disc by placing this on the revolving record and transmitting the sound received up through a tube into a large brass horn. That was the technology existing when I was born and I still have my favourite old 78rpm recording of Fats Waller singing 'My Very Good Friend The Milkman'. There was of course Radio through the BBC but the very idea of being able to broadcast messages, music, images even from individual houses across the world was virtually beyond the power of imagination. Indeed Dan Dare, a popular comic paper Spaceman, only had a wristwatch radio and that was Science Fiction in the 1950s.

On 10th January 2013 I was a special guest on the WWW Radio station Paramania Radio on the show Understanding Spirit hosted by the very gifted psychic-medium, exorcist and psychic-surgeon Mr. Alan Cox. Here is a brief resume of Alan and his amazing work that benefits so many people:

Alan Cox is a psychic investigator, clairvoyant, healer, psychic surgeon and radio personality with his own weekly show "Understanding Spirit" on www. paramaniaradio.com

In 1996 Alan was awakened to his spiritual path by a major event that happened to his partner Anne. Where they used to live in Wednesbury in the West Midlands unusual spirit activity started to occur. The main event that happened was when Alan was at work and Anne was home alone. Anne was pushed down the stairs top to bottom narrowly missing the telephone table at the foot of the stairs breaking her wrist. this event lead Alan to seek help which culminated in his spiritual awakening (the story is told in detail on Alan's website **www. calmingthoughts.com**

Alan's work, is two fold. He travels to clients' homes and/or businesses, work place to clear demonic/negative energies from there and also from the people themselves. He can also clear energies from a distance but prefers to be with the client in person. Alan has had remarkable results when healing and giving psychic surgery. this is Gods universal energy using Alan as a conduit to help people, not Alan himself. He has traveled to Arizona USA to help people in person as well as helping people in all four time zones in America. At a distance he has helped people worldwide, Canada, Jamaica, Mexico, Ireland, France, Singapoor, Austrailia, New Zealand, Malaisia, Germany, Switzerland as well as the UK. Alan respects and values his psychic connection and only uses it to help others. He can help people to find their true spiritual path. He can help connect people with their "Spirit Guides" so they can have the benefit of the guidance they can give. He can be contacted through his website or by email at alancox@calmingthoughts.com or by phone 07906 973289, or although based in England he has an American Skype phone number 717 798 9268 so anyone needing to contact Alan from the USA can use that number.

My interview on the Understanding Spirit programme with Alan lasted almost two hours and you can, if you so wish, hear a complete unedited version of this on Alan's excellent website CalmingThoughts. Com Readers of Psychic World may be pleased to hear me talk of many of the stories I have told in print here in this column over the last twenty two years or so that I have been writing the column. I speak about my times in HM Prisons encountering numerous discarnate entities, of the terrifying consequences of abusing spirit by using the wrong approach via an Ouija Board. I also tell of my near death experiences as a boy of 18 years and again as an adult whilst suffering the amputation of my right leg. You can hear me tell of my time working with the sixties pop singer PJ Proby when he recorded some of my songs. There is even one of my new poems 'Flowers' which Alan kindly played and I feel sure that you will enjoy that as the poem tells the story of a love that transcends time told through flowers. Just get onto the WWW type in CalmingThoughts.com and on the left side of the home page you will see a link to Alan's shows at Radio Podcasts. My interview is dated 10th January 2013. Send me an email let me know how you enjoyed it or better still tell Alan Cox he would love to hear from you and maybe listen in to future programmes as Alan always has interesting guests.

CHAPTER THIRTY THREE

MATERIALISATION MEDIUMS

Recently promoted to spirit our Deputy Editor Michael Colmer spent many years trying to have the unfair conviction of the Scottish materialisation medium Helen Duncan overturned by Royal Pardon. Michael, you be reading this and smiling I know as the battle you fought for Helen is not over but, to date this has not been won as even now over sixty years since Helen was wrongly convicted the powers that be are unwilling to accept that she was the victim of official persecution. They now have the bare faced audacity to state that it would not be in the public interest! Really? I personally believe that the argument presented for not granting a full pardon for Helen is good evidence that she is innocent. I believe that this Government, just like the Government of Winston Churchill in 1944, dare not admit that there are supernatural powers outside its ability to control. Big Brother has to be all powerful or how could we be subjected and subjugated by the system and make no mistake about it we all are subjects of Government.

In his seminal work 'The Trial' the Austrian-Hungarian author Franz Kafka (1883-1924) describes the persecution of Josef K. who is arrested by the secret police and placed on trial for an unspecified offence. The book tells the dark story of how Josef K. is continually faced with oppressive officialdom that totally denies him any ability to defend himself as the charges are never specified all they will say is that this is a very serious matter. So it would have been for poor Helen Duncan, physically assaulted by her arresting police officers whilst in trance she was seriously injured and subsequently died some five weeks after her arrest on unspecified charges. In his book Kafka describes how Josef K. is eventually worn down by the persecution as two mysterious men enter his apartment, lead him away and offer him a double edged butchers knife with which to kill himself, he declines so the two agents of the state hold him down whilst one stabs him through the heart. The last words of Josef K. describe how he has been killed 'Like a dog'. And that is exactly the way our Government dealt with poor Helen Duncan, they treated her worse than one would treat a dog. It is therefore, in my opinion, little wonder that even today the authorities can not admit they were wrong as that would be tantamount to an admission that if one gets on the wrong side of Big Brother then they will kill you. To admit that would not, so they say, be in the better interest of the public.

Let me look at the potential reasons why the Churchill Government of 1944 would perhaps have deemed the rather diminutive motherly figure of Helen Duncan to be a threat. It was during a séance in which Helen Duncan went into trance that the spirit of a dead seaman materialised wearing the cap bearing the name of his ship HMS Barham. The sailor had drowned when the ship was sunk by the enemy. At the time The War Office specifically denied that the ship HMS Barham had been sunk and the families of the crew believed that all were alive and well on a secret mission. So the evidence presented by the materialisation of the dead crew member of HMS Barham directly contradicted the official story which was, in blunt terms, a deliberate lie. It could be argued that this lie, this untruth, was being promulgated to protect the nation and put the enemy on the wrong foot. Whichever way one looks at it the lie was just that and Helen Duncan, in trance, had done no more than allow spirit to tell the truth. The truth though is, as a man said, the first casualty of war and poor Helen, being an innocent victim of the system, was subjected to persecution to prevent her from potentially presenting damaging evidence, albeit innocently, that may have offered injudicious aid to the enemy. So though Helen was not in herself a spy , she was an uncontrolled conduit between the spirit world and this offering insights into what had happened and what was to happen immediately ahead. As the invasion of France or D-Day was being planned the authorities must have decided they could not risk Helen's spirits disclosing information and so, on trumped up charges related to the antiquated Witchcraft Act of 1735 she was imprisoned. Now they say it is not in the better interest of the public to grant the woman they effectively murdered a pardon. Michael Colmer fought a hard fight for poor Helen, well done old friend and enjoy the promotion you earned so well.

I realise that my own personal efforts to tune in and materialise spirit are not as yet in the same league as the amazing Helen Duncan but of late I have been experiencing the materialisation of faces in and around my head, hair and shoulders. These images of spirit are capable of being captured on camera by my wife Mary who is herself a sensitive lady with mediumistic powers that she is very cautious of allowing. I include in this column a photograph taken by Mary of myself in the woodlands of the Lake District that shows quite clearly the face of a spirit materialising at the side of my head. There are a number of photographs taken around the time and another shows the same face in a somewhat different aspect proving beyond reasonable doubt that this is not a trick of the light but a genuine materialisation.

I personally have absolutely no doubt that the spirit world can and frequently does use mediums and psychics to materialise. Please if you dear reader have evidence then do contact me, email or call me and send me your photographic evidence. There are many strange things happening and about to happen in this rather difficult world now. We have right now all across the globe from nation to nation the greatest depression in living memory. There has been nothing like this since the 1930s and we all know what happened then, World War. I am not predicting a war BUT there is one certain way that history shows us ends all depressions, great conflagration, such as the Great Fire of London in 1666, the French Revolution of (1787-99) the first World War (1914-18) and WWII (1939-45). We live in interesting times.

CHAPTER THIRTY FOUR

SPIRIT COMMUNICATION: FACT OR FAITH?

The basis of the Spiritualist faith is communication between the incarnate and the discarnate. Such communication is most usually through a spirit-medium who has a developed gift be that clairaudience (hearing the voices) clairvoyance (seeing and also hearing) or clairsentience (sensing the information). As Spiritualists we accept that such communication is possible and when a medium passes on a message to us from our departed loved ones in the next world that message is truthfully given. However there are now and no doubt there always have been, tricksters, charlatans, out and out fakes that pretend to communicate but are really having a laugh. One only has to put the television on these days to see some fool in a dark house spooking up imaginary ghosts. The biggest offender of all the fake ghost hunting TV shows was Most Haunted which at one time featured a psychic who claimed to channel the spirits and pretended to go into a trance. On one notable occasion this prankster even managed to channel an imaginary, totally fictitious character called Kreed Kafer, invented by the resident parapsychologist to test his veracity. That is the name Kreed Kafer and a false story about this character were fed to the so-called psychic who swallowed the bait and pretended to channel him. You can see the result on the internet at YouTube.com there is the video showing this fraud doing a fake trance routine and putting on a stupid voice shouting 'KKKreeeed.....KKKKaaaaafer' Which as the parapsychologist knew when he designed this test was an anagram of DEREK FAKER. The faker being set up was of course Derek Acorah.

Such ridiculous nonsense as Most Haunted has had a deleterious affect upon Spiritualism and Psychic-Mediums in general as the public, who are hoodwinked by this bilge, believe that trance communication and ghosts appearing left right and centre are what actually happens during a clairvoyant consultation. It is not as if Spiritualism needs any more enemies, we surely have sufficient to deal with and I think now of the sceptics. I myself am sceptical, if someone I do not know tells me they are psychic and can communicate with my departed relations then it must be reasonable to expect a little proof? For example my father was a Police Inspector with the CID serving in the Greater Manchester force. He was what you might call a typical copper, big, tough, analytical, outspoken and honest. Now if a psychic-medium were receiving a message from my dad there is just no way he would want to tell me that I had just changed the curtains in my lounge or some other such mundane nonsense. There would have to be something serious, something verifiable in any message given to me before I could accept it really was from my father. But I know he is around me as I have seen him fully materialised many times. That is my proof. Spirit communication is therefore not a matter of faith for me, it is a matter of fact.

The Skeptic magazine is edited by Dr. Michael Shermer a brilliant and highly intelligent gentleman who does not believe for one minute that there can be communication with the dead. He and his colleague James Randi are of the firm opinion that psychic-mediums are nothing more than charlatans who are, in effect, defrauding the public. Randi makes many valid points in his lectures on the falsity of psychics and to a certain extent one can agree with him. For example if you were trying to tell someone your name would you perhaps consider giving them a clue by say whispering your initial as in 'My name starts with a J.' I know I wouldn't I would say, my name is John. So why would a spirit give only an initial? Such nonsense brings the whole matter of spirit communication into disrepute. Dr. Shermer lectures on the gullibility of people and how they can be quite easily tricked into believing they see and hear things when in fact they are deluding themselves. I can see where these two learned gentleman are coming from and agree that some of what we may perceive of as paranormal phenomena is little more than wishful thinking.

The UKs answer to Dr. Michael Shermer is perhaps Dr. Susan Blackmore who for many years conducted extensive research into the paranormal. Her scientific approach led her to conclude that communication with the discarnate was not a verifiable fact. These are her words: 'It was just over thirty years ago that I had the dramatic out-of-body experience that convinced me of the reality of psychic phenomena and launched me on a crusade to show those closed-minded scientists that consciousness could reach beyond the body and that death was not the end. Just a few years of careful experiments changed all that. I found no psychic phenomena – only wishful thinking, self-deception, experimental error and, occasionally, fraud. I became a sceptic.' Dr. Blackmore is no longer researching the paranormal.

Spiritualism is unique among faiths in that it provides, through its Church mediums, proof that there is life after death and the communication of spirit is essentially a fact. However, the level of what is considered proof varies from individual to individual. For me the idea that my late father would return to tell me that my curtains in the lounge had just been changed is not only not proof but an insult to my intelligence. Watching TV and observing some fool rolling about on the floor supposedly possessed by the spirit of Dick Turpin makes me doubt their sanity and one wonders what it is doing to the general public? I suspect that most people view such programmes as light entertainment but they actually do a great deal of harm to Spiritualism. Perhaps that is the real reason we are now seeing a vast proliferation in Psychic TV shows, to undermine the truth of spirit communication.

CHAPTER THIRTY FIVE

OUIJA BOARD HACKING SCANDAL!

There has been in the news lately a great deal written and reported about the interception of personal messages to celebrity individuals by investigative journalists working, in the main, for newspapers owned by Rupert Murdoch. That is THE SUN and THE NEWS OF THE WORLD. The term HACKING has been used to describe the methods deployed to gain unauthorised access to personal answermachine and voice-mail message systems. The Justice Leveson Inquiry is investigating this in great depth and some very seriously connected people have found themselves arrested and charged with related criminal offences. What I am able to disclose now is that one of Britain's best known so called celebrity psychics, Mr. D. Johnson also known as Derek Acorah, is claiming, in THE LIVERPOOL ECHO of 15th May, that the journalist Aaron Tinney from THE SUN newspaper hacked into his very own Ouija Board and accessed a message from Acorah's invisible guide 'Sam'. This message is rather disturbing as it purports to be about the location in the spirit world of the missing child Madeleine McCann who disappeared in Portugal some years ago. The outrageous nature of said message has brought a great deal of negative publicity for Acorah and he is blaming THE SUN for misrepresenting the facts. Aaron Tinney went on to list a few other facts pertaining to the Liverpool based Psychic: Acorah claims he had his first supernatural experience as a child when he was visited by his dead granddad. (he claims to have named himself after a dead relative but that has been shown to be utter nonsense) Acorah set himself up as a medium after failing to make the grade as a Liverpool footballer. He got his break in 2001 on TV's Most Haunted and became one of the UK's best known psychics. But in 2005 he was allegedly outed as a fraud by Most Haunted's psychologist Dr Ciaran O'Keeffe. While shooting at a haunted prison in Cornwall, O'Keeffe secretly invented a long-dead jailer called Kreed Kafer and talked about him while Acorah was in earshot. Acorah was later filmed becoming "possessed" by the fictional character. O'Keeffe then revealed the name Kreed Kafer was an anagram of "Derek Faker." Acorah was later sacked from the show. Will we see Derek and the transparent Sam at The Justice Levenson Inquiry?

In **THE DAILY TELEGRAPH** the journalist Tom Chivers on the 15th May 2012 wrote the following: 'Derek Acorah whether a charlatan or deluded should be ashamed over his Madeleine McCann nonsense. Madeleine McCann probably is dead. It's a sad thing to write down so starkly, but it's likely to be true. Derek Acorah, on the other hand, is definitely a callous self-publicist, and either deluded or a charlatan. The "psychic" (he's not a psychic, obviously) told The Sun that "I know her parents are convinced Maddie is alive and I'm really sorry – but the little one has been over in the spirit world for some time. I don't think it'll be long before she reincarnates. When children pass over who haven't had full lives I believe they choose the time to come back in the same form again – as another little girl.' Chivers continues: There is a strong case for everyone concerned to move on and to leave the McCanns to grieve in peace. But what there is not a case to do is tell a national newspaper that a visitor from the spirit world has come and told you that their daughter is dead.

Tom Chivers then goes further with his criticism extending his attack to include many more associated with spirit communication: 'I am honestly livid about this. The whole practice of "TV psychics" is disgraceful, preying on the gullible and the weak and the bereaved, telling them that their belated husband is happier beyond the veil, using cheap parlour tricks – cold reading, audience plants, even (allegedly, in the case of "Psychic" Sally Morgan) the blunt instrument of gathering information about potential participants before the show and having an accomplice relay it to the stage via a radio earphone.' Readers of Psychic World may recall I covered the story of Sally Morgan and her alleged use of relayed information previously. This latest gaff from yet another TV Psychic is again damaging all connected to spirit communication in general and Spiritualism specifically. It should be obvious to the public that the likes of stage and TV performers such as Acorah and Morgan are not even remotely associated with the Spiritualist Church but that is not the case. Especially when we have Acorah billing himself, believe this or not, as 'The Sexiest Man in Spiritualism'. Amazing. What next one wonders, maybe THE SAMANDELLS Derek and Sam get their kit off: Is There Any Body There?

The real problem underlying all this negative publicity that the likes of Acorah and Morgan are generating is that it reflects badly upon Spiritualism. When serious broadsheets, such as The Daily Telegraph start to condemn not just the dubious practices of the show business psychic publicity hunters but extend their attacks to include all of Spiritualism then all associated suffer as a direct result. There are far worse sins than just being ignorant, and insensitive, one thinks of the disgraceful scandal that continues to make news within the Roman Catholic Church and its proven track record of covering up the horrific abuse of children by ordained priests who were known to be paedophiles but with the help of Bishops were allowed to maintain their status with continuing access to young people. Many continued to abuse children for decades despite their predilection for such deviant practices being known to the Church authorities. Now that is a real scandal and it should cause great alarm to all connected with the Roman Catholic Church.

This sexual abuse of children by priests of the Christian religion is by no means just a recent phenomena. My own Uncle Mr. Alf Sutton who is now resident in Canada told me that as a boy of ten years he was approached by the priest at his local R.C. Church and offered sixpence to allow this middle aged man to remove his trousers and fondle his buttocks. Unlce Alf declined, he tells me, but he knew of others that accepted the money which in the 1930s was quite a lot for a little boy. The full truth and extent of the sexual abuse of children by ordained ministers of the R.C. religion will doubtless never be known. In fact one R.C. Bishop actually tried to put the blame on the young victims in a recent interview the Bishop of Teneriefe Bernado Alvarez said 'There are thirteen year old adolescents who are under age and who are perfectly in agreement with, and what is more, wanting it, and if you are careless they will even provoke you'. That is a typical statement of a paedophile.

In comparison to child abuse the posturing and posing of so called celebrity TV psychics who talk to invisible people and fake possession by fictitious characters pales into insignificance. But the press and the media seem to have made their minds up that all psychics must be frauds because the likes of Acorah continue to bring discredit to Spiritualism with their selfish and thoughtless shenanigans.

CHAPTER THIRTY SIX

DO THE FARIES BELIEVE IN YOU?

The usual question one asks on the subject of elemental creatures is this: do you believe in fairies.? The real question is do the fairies believe in you? I would consider myself to be a reasonably rational individual, yet I really do accept that elemental beings, such as goblins, elves, pixies, gnomes and fairies, the little people in fact do exist. It is my experience that they occupy a parallel dimension that exists alongside what we perceive of as being reality within the usually accepted parameters of, length, depth, and height. This dimension, call it the fourth dimension, is inextricably connected to our supposed reality, interwoven in fact and as real as the trees, the rocks and flowers that are a natural part of this world.

At the risk of seeming facetious I am going to detail just two of the elemental beings that may be familiar to you and briefly discuss origins and anecdotal accounts of encounters between said fantastical creatures and members of the human race.

Gnomes: The 16th century occultist, astrologer and alchemist Paracelsus (Phillipus Aureolus Theophrastus Bombastus von Hohenheim 1493-1541) expounded the theory that there existed within the earth a species of humanoid beings he called Gnomus and describes them as being approximately two spans in height. (a span is the distance between the tip of the thumb and the tip of the little finger when the hand is spread wide. So two spans would be around 16 to 18 inches). These beings were able, according to Paracelsus, to travel through the earth as easily as humans walk through air. This would mean, in essence, that the Gnomes were not constructed of flesh, blood and bone but of an etheric substance less substantial, at least as we perceive. There have been reports of gnome sightings on the isle of Gibralter where a certain sailor whilst partaking of a picnic with a young lady on a hill there had his sandwich stolen by a very naughty gnome. He reported that the little fellow had a pointed cap, a buckled belt and was carrying a small hammer. In mythology gnomes are associated with mines. The first movement of the musical work Pictures at an Exhibition by Mussorgsky (1839-1881)is titled The Gnome and the music creates an image of a the elemental being busy underground hammering away.

Fairies: There is a worldwide belief in fairies who are also known as The Good Folk or The Little People. In Italy they are called Fata, in Portugal Fada, in France Fee, In Greece Moirai. The fairy folk have been known throughout history and they were in ancient Roman times associated with fate and known collectively in Latin as Fatum. Clearly there have been accounts of fairy folk in many countries and various cultures dating back thousands of years so though we today in our materialistic world may consider such reports as nonsense there were times when serious consideration was given to the existence of elemental beings. There exists today numerous websites dedicated to reporting modern day contemporary sightings and encounters with fairies. One such site is Realitywalker.com created by the former medical research scientist Clive Hetherington who states that he does not just believe in other dimensional beings he knows they exist in the same way he knows that the computer he uses to access the internet exists. Here is a brief example of an encounter Clive had taken verbatim from his website:

By Clive Hetherington: My first encounter with a fairy was just off the local popular bridal way near where I used to live in County Durham between Rolands Gill and Medomsley. I had a period when I would jog about a mile or so up the track in an attempt to get fit. Often however, I never made the mile as I would either be dragged into the wood by some fun nature spirits wanting to play or by Herne to be led to some interesting energy areas. On one such occasion I was led through the undergrowth until I emerged by a stream. There was a small overhanging tree on the other side which seemed to have some sort of being sitting in its central branches about two meters from the ground. As I got closer it resolved into a white creature holding a long stick type thing which actually twinkled at one end – sorry but I just could not handle that this could be a magic wand. What really confused me was that it seemed quite big (about two feet tall (60cm)) and seemed eh! somewhat overweight. As I believed that fairys were very small – say no more than six inches tall (15cm) and slim this encounter caused me slight confusion. As did the fact that it actually seemed to have some sort of magic wand. Communication went something along the lines of; 'Are you a fairy?' – 'Yes I'm a fairy' – 'Eh!! – Are you sure?' – 'YES' 'Aren't you eh!! . . . too eh . . . big? . . for a fairy? . . . ' and is that a magic wand? . . . . . ' I don't think she was impressed with this exchange; she went a little sulky. So, a fat over sized fairy stretched my boundaries about fairies. She seemed to be lonely and wanted to keep to herself. I never asked if she could cast spells with her wand.

In my personal experience I have always known that there are what I see as semi-translucent beings that I identify as elementals. As a child I saw in the Pendle hills and woodlands close by my home village of Foulridge in Lancashire tiny beings that appeared on the branches and bows of trees and hedgerows, though they kept themselves to themselves. As a young adult I lost the ability to see these beings or fairies as many call them. It was only in later life, having experienced many physical traumas and encounters with death that I suddenly discovered that I could again innocently interact with the little people. I use a flute to play them a happy tune and in the wild woods of Cumbria where myself and my wife Mary visit throughout the Summer season into Autumn I have found many fantastical elementals. In fact I have now found a wonderful new way to explore the amazing and wonderful world of elemental beings through the power of digital photography. Indeed there is a website dedicated to displaying photographic images of the fairy folk this is on the world wide web available to all: fairytastic.ning.com You really should join this site if you are at all interested in seeing elemental beings because they are for real, the photographs on this site show you clearly, to me at least, that what we may miss with our naked eyes can be discerned by the powerful multi megapixel digital cameras of today. Test this for yourself. Go into a wood, twilight is best time, find a quiet dell, running water, a stream is best or even better a waterfall, sing a song, play a mouth-organ a guitar or whatever then take some photographs. At home on your computer photoshop programme enlarge these to 150%. You will, with an open mind, see the fairy folk as they are there within the foliage and mists of our woodland glades.

There is a slight problem I perceive for most adult sentient beings, that is the fairies do not believe in such people at all. You see, as crazy as this may appear, to the elementals we humans are as diaphanous as they are to us. That is why I always sing and play to them they love this and will come out to join in the fun. Remember to treat their homes with respect as indeed you must always treat fairy folk for they can be wonderful friends but terrible foes if one upsets them. I always say hello, please and thank you to the little people when I visit the woodlands for I know they are sensitive to our intrusions. I feel that now is the time for knowledge of the fairy people to be accepted. But most importantly it is essential that we respect their world then and only then will the fairies truly believe in us as friends.

You can check out the websites I have mentioned: www realitywalker com and www fairytastic.ning

CHAPTER THIRTY SEVEN

DISCARNATE TELEPATHIC COMMUNICATION

When telepathy occurs spontaneously in everyday life, often in some family or friendship situation, it is often greeted with some sort of surprised pleasure; as at the recognition of the sudden presence of some lesser telepathic god, who has descended fleetingly to earth and shown his ancient face: Joe Cooper in The Mystery of Telepathy published by Constable 1982. The problem with spontaneous telepathic communication is that all the evidence is anecdotal, it meets no scientific tests or standards and as such is dismissed as lacking reason. This is, in my opinion, because it simply is not explainable in scientific terms yet that surely does not mean that it does not exist. It has certainly presented in my life:

Within my own family there is what I believe to be a very credible, if anecdotal, account of discarnate communication dating back to The Great War 1914-1918. My great grandfather Charles Sutton and his family lived in the Lancashire town of Nelson and one son, William Alfred Sutton joined the army and was posted to France fighting on the front line at Flanders. His youngest brother Frederick was aged three years at the time and during one night woke and reported seeing his big brother William standing by his bed, there was a message given to little Fred who went into his parents bedroom and said 'Our Illie's dead' as young Fred could not pronounce the W in William. His parents thought this was nothing more than a bad dream their son was having and sent him off back to bed. The next day a telegram came from The War Department stating that William Alfred Sutton had been reported as missing in action and was believed to be dead. His body was never found.

I myself work as a professional clairvoyant and do, from time to time, have dreams that are of significance, that is they convey something meaningful. During early December of this year I woke one morning clearly recalling a horrible vision I had of seeing a young girl being pushed from a great height and falling down a mountain, in my dream I turned away to avoid viewing the terrible result. The next evening I was giving a psychic reading to a lady from Manchester and as I spoke to her I had a vision of terrible injuries and many months in hospital, I saw spinal problems and as I undertook my usual practice of automatic writing the pen wrote: Walk the walk will succeed. When I gave this to the lady she explained that it was all correct. She had recently been discharged from hospital where she had been treated for injuries to her spine and both her legs. She was slowly learning to walk again after months spent recovering from the results of a terrible fall. She told me she had been pushed off the top of a multi-story car park. When I asked where the car park was she said it was on the outskirts of Manchester overlooking distant hills. The question I now ask myself is this; was I shown her accident in my dream, and if I was then why? Perhaps she herself had sent me that dream vision telepathically as she knew beforehand that she was due to speak to me.

Also in December of this year I woke at approximately 3:15am to hear the sound of someone knocking loudly on the front door of the house. The thumping continued echoing through the building so I climbed into my wheelchair and propelled myself to the door to see who would be waking me at this strange time of the night. As I drew closer to the door the banging stopped and I then realised that it was impossible for anyone to actually be at that door as it was located immediately behind our seven foot high locked and bolted iron gates. There was no access to the door only to an electric bell located on the iron bars. That same evening my Uncle Alf who lives in Canada called me on the telephone to say that his son James Sutton, who had been very ill, passed to spirit and he had just been advised. I believe that James, to whom I had only spoken a few times, had called in on his way to paradise to say goodbye.

This kind of death visitation has happened to me many times in my life. In the year 1985 whilst my dear wife Mary and I were caring for my maternal grandfather Willie Walsh aged 78 there was another such occurrence. My great aunt Norah, the sister-in-law of my grandfather was seriously ill in Airdale Hospital near Skipton, Yorkshire. At around 5 a.m. one morning I was woken by the most tremendous knocking and thumping on our front door, we lived in a huge Victorian mansion at the time and it sounded like something from a Hammer Horror film. Jumping out of bed I threw back the curtains of the bedroom and looked down to the main entrance immediately below, as I did so the banging and clattering ceased, there was no one there and beyond, down the empty half lit street, there was absolutely no one, it was deserted. Just moments later, before I had time to get back into bed the telephone rang, it was the ward sister at Airdale Hospital to advise me that some few minutes before my great Aunty Norah Brown had died. It was then my sad duty to go immediately and advise her rather aged husband, my Great Uncle Jim Brown. I am sure that Aunty Norah was waking me on her way to meet her loved ones so that I could do what I had to do.

The late Joe Cooper, a great friend of mine, quotes from Society for Psychical Research Proceedings Vol. XXXIII the case of an apparition of a dead airman in the year 1918. One Lt. Larkin a Army Pilot (pre-dating the RAF) reported that his friend the pilot David McConnel was about to fly a Sopwith Camel from Scampton in Lincolnshire to Tadcaster in Yorkshire and back. He had remarked to Larkin that he would be returning in time for tea. Then he exited and flew off in his plane. Larkin state the following that occurred some hours later: I heard someone walking up the passage; the door opened with the usual noise and clatter which David always made ; I saw his 'Hello boy!' and I turned half round in my chair and saw him standing in the doorway; half in and half out of the room, holding the doorknob in his hand. He was dressed in his flying clothes, but was wearing his navel cap, there being nothing unusual in his appearance. His cap was pushed back on his head and he was smiling, as he always was when he came back into the room and greeted us. I remarked 'Hello, back already?' He replied 'Yes, got there all right. Had a good trip'...I was looking at him the whole time he was speaking. He said 'Well cherrio!' closed the door and went out'. McConnel had crashed at Tadcaster at about that time. He had, by some ghostly telepathic process, come back 'in time for tea'.

You can read more of the wonderful Joe Cooper's researched accounts in his book: The Mystery of Telepathy: Joe Cooper published by Constable ISDN 0 09 464170 6

CHAPTER THIRTY EIGHT

WHY HIDE THE TRUTH?

Throughout the world, in every community and since time immemorial there has always been a belief in life after death. The Egyptian Book of The Dead exists as proof that the belief in the afterlife existed thousands of years before Christianity. Predating even the Book of The Dead are the ancient 'Coffin Texts' the coffin texts emphasize the subterranean elements of the afterlife ruled by Osiris, in a place called the Duat. An Osirian afterlife is, according to the ancient Egyptians, offered to everyone. In ancient Greece the poet Homer described the underworld as being populated by the virtuous dead with various mythological characters present, such as Charon the ferryman that carried the discarnate souls across the river Styx to the kingdom of Hades. Philosophers such as Plato and the mystic Orphics and Pythagoreans include the concept of the judgement of the dead. Spirits were assigned to one of three realms: Elysium for the blessed, Tartarus for the damned, and Asphodel for the rest. Further, they believed in reincarnation and the transmigration of souls. This is all long before anyone thought of The Holy Trinity and the concept of heaven through belief. It is a relatively recent idea that only by accepting a certain ideology could ones soul transmigrate, leaving its incarnate corporeal body to enter the afterlife.

As well as a worldwide belief in life after death there has also always existed a belief that the spirits or souls of the dead can return and that these can be seen as ghosts. In The New Testament there is an account of the disciples of Jesus fearing they had seen a ghost: Matthew 14: 25-27: During the fourth watch of the night Jesus went out to them, walking on the sea. When the disciples saw him walking on the sea, they were terrified. "It's a Spirit," they said, and cried out in fear. But Jesus immediately said to them: "Take courage! It is I. Don't be afraid." If we accept The New Testament as the truth then there is good evidence that the disciples believed in ghosts.

In The old Testament the book of Samuel 28:7-20 king Saul said: 'Seek me a woman that hath a familiar spirit, that I may go to her, and inquire of her'. Saul was taken to see 'The Witch of Endor' and she brought forth from the afterlife the spirit of Samuel and the spirit said to Saul 'Why hast thou disquieted me, to bring me up?' The end result was that Saul received advice from the spirit of Samuel that he and all his kin would soon be dead. That is though not the point, the point is that in Biblical terms ghosts or spirits are accepted as being real and can communicate. As I said, throughout the world and since recorded history began there have been accounts of spirits.

The question that we as Spiritualists should perhaps be asking is this: Why do so many supposedly devoutly religious individuals deny the veracity of communication between the two worlds? There must be a reason, perhaps more than one, but I suggest that the main reason is that if it is accepted that survival is a natural phenomena then the need to subscribe to a religious belief to enter the afterlife disappears. The ancient Egyptians believed that all souls are eternal, animals too. The Greeks also believed that the underworld or afterlife was the ultimate destiny of all, though divided into sections based on worthiness not on belief. But what, you should be asking, has established religion to gain by denying the truth of life after death and most of all the communication of spirits? Why would any religion want to hide this truth?

I fully realise that anecdotal accounts are not what any academic would consider to be truly scientific research and I agree that personal experiences can cloud reasoned argument. However: Some few years ago a distant relation of mine who was a landlord, owning many properties in the North of England, became ill. Although he was of advanced years he had, till his diagnosis, always been a big, strong and very determined man who knew what he wanted and got it. He was a typical blunt, no messing, Northerner. This man had a son and this son had been a dutiful one, helped his father run the business and always cared for his mother etc. When the man became ill and was told that there was no effective treatment, instead of turning to his family for support he turned to religion. Within just a few weeks he went from being a real rugged rough and tough man's man who took no prisoners, to being a bible reading, church going, hymn singing religiously devout Christian. The priests were round his bedside as he weakened and his house was full of prayers, day and night. When he died and the lawyer read his will there was a shock for all his family as he had left all his properties to the church and not one to his son or any other family member.

It is perhaps a little known fact that one of the biggest land owners in the UK is the Church of England. This established church actually owns 0.3% of the UK land. I realise it may seem cynical in the extreme but could it perhaps be the case that established religion has a vested interest in denying the truth of life after death as a natural process? I mean if the churches announced that we all move on to the next world no matter what and that the destination there is based not on belief but on deeds, as you sow so shall you reap, how many would subscribe to a very restrictive belief system? Also if the church accepted the communication of spirits, which in fact the Bible as explained above actually does, why would people not seek guidance from a gifted psychic that offered proof of survival instead of an academic priest whose learning, however wide and varied, is of this earthly plane?

In times long past when humankind lived relatively primitively, before civilisation as we accept it existed, there was a belief in communication with the spirit world through the shaman. Organised religion denies that such natural pathways still exist. It is my argument that they do so not because they believe that they are the way, the truth and the light but because they have a vested interest in exercising control over people and their property.

CHAPTER THIRTY NINE

RITUAL FOR SPIRITUAL PROTECTION

PROTECTION AGAINST PSYCHIC ATTACK AND NEGATIVE ENERGY.

It may seem a very fanciful notion but there are people, seemingly ordinary people, who can influence your daily life by attacking you with their psychic powers. Such people are walking in the darkness of this material world and are using their God given gifts for their own personal gain and self-glorification or gratification. I know personally of so called 'psychic-mediums' who practice this abuse and utilise their esoteric knowledge and powers to further their own ends.

Let me give you an example of a simple, non-specialist, psychic attack. This happens often in everyday life and involves the discharge of negative energy, in the form of thoughts, aimed at you, your family and/or your home. For instance, you have a serious disagreement with a work colleague and they issue insults and maybe even threats against you. These negative thoughts exist in the etheric plane and form themselves into a kind of invisible dagger that, given opportunity, will tear into the very fabric of your life.

William Shakespeare, the great British poet and dramatist, wrote of such invisible negative forces in his infamous Scottish play. 'Is this a dagger I see before me' Act 2 sc. 1. And further he wrote 'There's daggers in men's smiles' Act 2 sc. 3. Shakespeare was recognising the fact that thoughts have substance and can kill or injure. If you wish another evil and give expression to your thoughts of wickedness then you are creating a negative energy force that has a strange power that is beyond the reasoning of mankind. That such a power exists is attested in mythology and legend dating back to time immemorial. It is from such expressions of negative thoughts that curses come. Serious psychic attacks are a form of curse issued against a person or persons by an individual with enhanced psychical powers and esoteric knowledge.

It is often said that if you do not believe in the mumbo jumbo of curses and such like then they can not, in any way, harm you. This is rather like saying that because you do not believe in rain you will therefore not get wet. Being the subject of a psychic attack can result in serious consequences. These could be quite distressing, perhaps even dangerous, if you are unaware that you or your home and family, is under such an attack.

Here is a list of occurrences that will noticeably increase during a period in which you or a resident family member are under psychic attack.
Accidents, falls, things being dropped, fires, etc. Sleeplessness. Waking to strange noises in the night. Loss of appetite. Feeling of sickness. Inability to concentrate. Unnatural sexual urges.Change of personality. Angry outbursts. Depression and feeling of worthlessness. Feeling of constant unease.

You may, of course, experience any or even all of the above without being the subject of psychic attack. But if you have noticed a serious increase in such unpleasant occurrences then you might consider conducting a ritual of self-protection that I term a 'Candle Rite'.

CONDUCTING
RITUAL
Simply follow this step by step guide to conducting a candle rite and you will protect yourself and others from any psychic attack.
EQUIPMENT: Four white candles. Three green candles. A white sheet. A bowl of water. A bowl of salt.
1.   Place the white sheet on a table or other flat surface.
2.   Sprinkle a little water over this sheet.
3.   Sprinkle a little salt over this sheet.

4. Place the four white candles in a straight line approximately twelve inches apart.
5. Place the three green candles in a straight line slightly in front of the white ones, they should be approximately six inches apart.
6. Sit in a high-backed chair facing the candles and light them.
7. You should be no more than 24 inches from the row of green candles, seated in an upright position facing them.
8. Now repeat aloud the following prayer of invocation:

Dear God I pray that you will protect me from harm, from evil and from all thoughts of wickedness that may be directed against myself or those that I love.

Dear God I pray that you will wrap my body and the bodies of my family and all who live in this house in the protective cloak of your eternal love.

Dear God please disperse the evil energy and thoughts that may have been directed against all those living within this house.

1. Repeat the above seven times, each time looking closely into the flames of the candles.
2. Having completed this ritual close with a prayer of your own choice. Or you may use the following:

Dear God thank you for hearing my prayers. Please forgive those that would trespass against members of my family and myself. Please bring peace and understanding to those who would spitefully use me. And allow me to live in the protection and love of your eternal light now and forevermore. You have now completed the ritual cleansing of your home and any negative energy that was present will be dispersed.

The above Candle Rite works because you are a child of God and are calling upon the hidden powers within and without your physical body to protect you. From the world beyond and also from the world within you are now protected.

In this present time of economic crisis we all need protection. I can commend the above to our readers, it works. (Extract from The Psychic World of Derek Acorah published by Piatkus and written by J.G. Sutton)

CHAPTER FORTY

ORBS: Alternative Explanations.

The relatively modern phenomena of white or semi-transparent orbs, that is circular shapes, captured by cameras and only visible when the photograph is processed, is a contentious issue. There are those who argue that orbs are in fact spirit lights or energy, in other words a form of ghost. The conflicting explanation is a scientific one arguing that digital cameras, especially the smaller compact cameras, when used with a flash that is located close to the lens, causes a form of retroflection from minute dust or rain particles that are, to the naked eye, only semi-visible. The technical photographic term used to describe such incidences of orbs is backscatter or near camera reflection.

I have seen many photographs that include orbs and some are more obviously backscatter than others, so doubt about the more prosaic explanation i.e. backscatter is raised. To the scientific mind the idea that orbs are intelligent energy or discarnate entities may appear ridiculous. To the student of psychic phenomena the purely technical concept of near camera reflection is perhaps insufficient for a number of reasons. Let me offer some examples of orbs that without doubt were not reflections in a camera lens because they were seen by the naked eye.

Some few years ago my wife and I purchased a 42" Hitachi Flat Screen TV and it was working wonderfully well until one evening I looked and saw at the far end of our main lounge an orb. This orb was misty white, about the size of a golf ball and it drifted slowly across the room, I tried to get my wife Mary to see this but she couldn't. I watched this orb as it moved forward to the near new TV set and in it went, right into the front of the screen and it vanished there obviously inside. At

169

that point the TV changed channels by itself, from one station to another. We had been in the middle of watching a programme so were not best pleased with this interruption but try as we might the TV would not stay on the channel we wanted. Then the TV began to issue speech in a foreign language that neither myself nor my wife could understand. The next day I called the suppliers and as it was under guarantee they agreed to have repair staff come and check it. Some days later the man arrived and fitted a new main circuit board, he switched it on looking quite pleased with his work and the TV switched itself from one channel to another and was broadcasting a weird language that sounded like many mixed together, a sort of polyglot. Astounded at this the repair man took it away and said they would work on it in the main workshop. Time passed and we heard nothing so I called the number he had left me and when I was connected the staff told me they could not get our TV to work. We were sent a credit note and bought another TV that stays on channel and broadcasts in English.

I recently undertook a psychic survey within the historic Shropshire towns of Ludlow and Shrewsbury. The Lion Hotel in the centre of Shrewsbury dates back to the 17th century and has had many illustrious guests including Charles Dickens, The Beatles and Charles Darwin. My room was on the second floor which is accessed by lift from the reception area. The floors of the corridors and rooms of The Lion Hotel are all made of oak, they creak as you walk along. Twisted wooden beams support the ceilings and light from the high windows illuminates the long hallways where shadows hide dark mysterious alcoves and many turnings. There are noticeable temperature variations down certain passages inside The Lion and one such cold spot I found between my room 205 and the lift. There was a clear fall of around five degrees and a gentle breeze from no identifiable source as all the windows were closed tight. Immediately before me was a long passageway, I saw there something move though the shape was indistinct, taking my Cannon Digital Camera I took a photograph hoping to capture an image of whatever had caught my eye. When at home I opened the file of that photograph on my PC and saw there a faint orb, within that orb I could see a ghostly face.

On returning to my room at The Lion, as I stood before the door I saw something shining silver on the rusty red patterned carpet. Reaching down I found a 25c coin from The Netherlands known as a kwartje or little quarter. The Netherlands currency is now The Euro they switched in year 2002 from The Guilder. The coin was dated 1957 and is in near mint condition. (on checking I discovered that such coins are actually made of silver and have value) There had been nothing on the floor when I came out of my room and I do look as being disabled I have to check carefully where I am walking. When I asked at reception if there were any foreign guests in the hotel I was advised that yes there were but not on the second floor and the room next to mine was empty. When I told the receptionist about the cold spot along the passageway and how I had encountered something there the lady told me that was where others before me had experienced an unseen presence. She said that during a previous psychic investigation the mediums conducting the search had stated that the long corridor from the lift on the second floor had a presence.

CHAPTER FORTY ONE

TODAY'S ROGUE MESSIAHS

False prophets, charlatans, self appointed messianic leaders and their like have, throughout history, misled the vulnerable into destruction and depravity. Colin Wilson has written an excellent examination of such fakers in his book 'Rogue Messiahs' in which he offers insights into some recent cases. One thing that many of these intellectually distorted so called spiritual leaders have in common is the misuse and abuse of The Bible, often using selected scripture to support their personal messages. The problem is that frequently the messages are not of the love thy neighbour nature but more often of hell fire and damnation for none believers. In this short essay I will be arguing that we should all be aware that rogue messiahs come in many guises and we can all be vulnerable to their misguided manipulations.

When we think of manic messianic leaders we may have in mind obviously twisted individuals such as the Rev. Jim Jones who was responsible for poisoning his followers at the self created village; Jonestown. Or David Koresh who sexually abused and degraded his initiates before many of them perished with him in the flames of his Waco, Texas ranch. Both these rouge messiahs used The Bible to justify their deranged behaviour. There are more like them in the world today using so called Holy Scriptures to bemuse, mesmerise and ultimately control their victims. As I write there has just been a modern day would be messiah convicted of a terrorist offence for preaching hatred on the streets of London. Trevor Brooks, also known as Abu Izzadeen was found guilty at Kingston Crown Court of supporting terrorism. He actually said 'Allah gave mujahideen chance to kill the American' whilst attempting to raise money to support attacks on British and USA troops in Afghanistan. However, he actually killed no one and the argument made in support of what he said is that coalition forces are actually killing people in Iraq and Afghanistan.

The use of the name of God, Allah, Jehovah etc. to justify war or jihad as some term it is common and really an accepted practice. Historically God's will etc. has been the excuse used by leaders to explain to the people who will actually be doing the fighting that their cause is just and right. Centuries ago Britain staged The Crusades, which were conducted, supposedly, to free the so called Holy Land from the infidels or none believers. The more likely truth is that it must have seemed quite a fantastic adventure to go plundering a foreign country and kill for the thrill of killing. It is happening today.

Recently there was a great commotion in the media about Prince Harry going with the Army to Afghanistan. I watched in astonishment as the rights and wrongs of this were debated on the SKY TV News channel and the presenter actually said 'Of course he should go, he'll have great fun'. Now that is the awful truth of it. There are people in positions of authority in this country and indeed I believe in all countries, believing that war is fun. War is in fact about death, about murdering, maiming and disabling human beings for gain. There is no other way to look at war, it is hell on earth and it can only be viewed as fun by the morally and intellectually bankrupt.

Today throughout the world there are self appointed rouge messiahs that are preaching to their followers that the murder of those that do not follow their very specific religious beliefs is God's will. Or Allah's will or Jehovah's will or whatever name they have. Nothing has changed in that respect as killing seems to be at the top of most divine beings wish list. That strikes me as strange as if God etc. made everything why would he want to destroy his creation? It can not be argued that it is because many of his children deny him and follow a false faith as there are countless places on this Earth that have never heard of Christianity or Judaism or even the Islamic faith for that matter. Somewhere in Iceland, Outer-Mongolia or perhaps even Timbuktoo there will exist someone who has no knowledge of religion. In fact there is someone you know who is exactly like that, they will however be just a few months old.

My argument is that it does not have to be a religious fanatic thumping a Bible or a copy of the Koran etc. to lead vulnerable people into committing acts of atrocity. It can be someone who appears on the surface to be perfectly rational who is in fact a rouge messiah. All that is required is that the people believe in them. Their followers then accept that what they say is the truth and they will act on it without question. Today's most dangerous rouge messiahs do exist but they may do so behind an acceptable façade of responsible respectability.

In the not too distant past one such rogue messiah was Hitler. I have lived in Germany and the people are wonderfully warm hearted and friendly. Yet one man, a messianic maniac, persuaded the good German people to commit the most heinous atrocities in the concentration camps such as Auschwitz or Belsen. In the UK during the Falklands conflict our navy sank an Argentine battleship called the Belgrano, many hundreds of innocent young Argentinian conscripts drowned and our then Prime Minister, Margaret Thatcher, welcomed the horror saying 'Rejoice, Rejoice' as if we the people of Britain should glory in this mass murder. Indeed The Sun 'newspaper' did just that with its infamous headline 'GOTCHA' above a photograph of the stricken ship. It made me feel physically sick.

We should always question our leaders, they have no divine rights, they are simply human beings doing what should be a professional job of work. When we stop thinking that our appointed Government might be wrong we are in trouble. Our Government has openly admitted it was wrong about WMD in Iraq, but they now tell us that getting rid of the so-called dictator Sadam Hussain was worth all the death and destruction caused by invading that sovereign land. As I write 48 people have just been blown apart at a funeral to the north of Baghdad. In all it is officially estimated that over 150,000 people have been killed in this war that our elected leaders started on a false pretext without reference to us. Our unthinking silence is our acquiescence. By doing and saying nothing we allow today's rogue messiahs to mislead us on the pathway to infamy endangering our immortal souls. It has happened before.

Rogue Messiahs by Colin Wilson is published by Hampton Roads ISBN 1-57174-175-5.

CHAPTER FORTY TWO

MESSAGES AND VISIONS OF THE UNUSUAL AND BIZARRE

As a practising professional psychic clairvoyant I work to one basic rule, I give what I get. That is I pass the information given to me by the spirits to my client as clearly and concisely as I possibly can and I do so no matter how weird that may be. When I say weird I mean really odd even bizarre so that I would, if I were processing the information on a purely logical basis, filter out the totally whacky. But that would spoil the fun wouldn't it. Let me give you some examples of the unusual messages I have received for clients, no names no pack drill as they say in The Army.

Mrs. A. is divorced mother of three young adult children living in a semi-detached house in the Clifton area of Salford, Greater Manchester UK. Whilst conducting a psychic reading for her I saw something most unusual. I had a vision of this middle aged lady walking round and round in circles and doing so time after time, but to a certain order. When I told her what I was being shown she explained that she had developed a habit of walking round her bedroom three times each morning before leaving the room. She did this every morning. The spirit of her late grandmother found this quite strange and wanted to assure this lady that she need not do this as all was going to be perfectly well.

Mrs.B. of Swinton was with me when I saw something strange concerning her feet, I could see a bed with covers and out of the bottom sticking clear of the clothes were her bare feet. I was able to hear the spirit of her mother telling me that she had pulled her big toe the other night. When I gave this odd insight to Mrs.B. she told me how she always slept with her feet out of bed and yes she had experienced the sensation of someone pulling at her toes. Now she knows who it is.

I was conducting a telephone consultation for a lady living in Knightsbridge in London, as I spoke to her I was told that she had just conceived a boy child and the father was linked to the Shakespeare play Hamlet. I both saw and heard this, seeing visions of a castle. When I gave what I had received she told me that yes she and her husband had indeed been attempting to have a child and that he had been born in Elsinore Castle in Denmark the son of parents related to the Royal Danish throne. Some months later this lady telephoned me again, she had been to her doctor who had confirmed that she was pregnant. That was some years ago and I now know that she, her husband and their son are doing well, now living in Copenhagen.

During my psychic readings I use Automatic Writing to allow my guides to channel evidence directly into words written down by the pen I hold loosely in my right hand. It was during one particularly hot summer's day a few years ago when I was reading for Mrs. C. of Chorley in Lancashire. The pen wrote about a diet this lady was on and then wrote down a weight, I believe it was 14 stone 6lbs. I read what had been written to Mrs.C. who looked a little uncomfortable with this information and asked me how could that possibly be known. The pen answered writing down 'I was watching in the bathroom'. The look on her face was quite something as she told me that she had weighed herself on the scales in the bathroom that very morning, her weight was indeed 14 stone 6lbs and she always stood on the scales directly out of the bath so she wanted to know who it was watching her. I got the impression she would be wearing her dressing gown next time she got weighed.

Miss D. is a young lady from Salford in Greater Manchester and she was most surprised to learn that her late grandfather was really enjoying the way she had been pulling her face into the mirror. I was then shown exactly how she did this, by gripping the sides of her cheeks and pulling whilst at the same time sticking her tongue out to touch her nose. I refrained from demonstrating. The funny thing was, she said, that she did this quite often and had no idea that anyone was aware of her actions. In actual fact face pulling is relatively common and I do see this from time to time. With Mrs. E. of Eccles in Greater Manchester there was shown to me something truly strange, I could see a vision of a large fat belly being pulled outwards and then slapped as it fell back into place and there was a loud slapping sound that went with this. When I tod the lady what I could see she laughed explaining that since her third child she had been unhappy with her inability to shift her rather round tummy and yes she often did exactly as I described. You know dear reader it takes a little courage to advise complete strangers that you can see them face pulling or belly wobbling, but I do so most sincerely as I am shown these strange things and the customer has a right to receive that which is given.

There are also tragic visions that I receive and dealing with these is a delicate matter. Suicide victims do come through in spirit to me and sometimes show how they died at their own hands. Images of dead bodies hanging behind doors or with severe self inflicted wounds etc. would no doubt seriously disturb most people but then I spent many years as a nurse working in HM Prisons where such horrible occurrences where unfortunately frequent. The one common denominator with suicide spirits is the recognition that this was a mistake and they want to apologise. The most difficult part of passing the message to the family member or friend sitting with me is the effect this can have. Some are extremely angry with the suicide spirit for inflicting the pain their action caused. Others are simply bemused and sad at the loss of a loved one and seek to know why. In my many years of dealing with spirit communication I have yet to encounter a discarnate suicide victim that really could offer any reasonable explanation. There simply is no good reason to kill oneself other than, possibly, as an act of voluntary euthanasia when facing a painful and incurable terminal illness.

I was recently asked by Mrs. G. of Walkden in Greater Manchester to attend her home and exorcise what she believed to be the ghost of her late husband and he had been a suicide victim. This man, in life, had seriously assaulted Mrs. G. breaking both her legs and puncturing her lung in one violent attack. She had eventually reached the point where she could take no more from him and had issued divorce proceedings. The day after he was served with the court papers her husband took a length of rope and hung himself. Since that day her home had been, she said, haunted. Noises in the night kept her awake, footsteps were heard when no one but she was in the house and the place was freezing cold even with the heating on. When I went in to the house I immediately sensed where the spirit was, in the lounge by the chair he had used almost daily in life. This was an arrogant spirit that did regret the suicide but blamed his wife. Now this spirit was not religious, Mrs. G. told me he was just a nasty piece of work and believed in nothing but his own imagined right to do what he wanted. So, using all the refined social skills I learned behind the walls of jails such as Wormwood Scrubs and Strangeways I set about dealing with this recalcitrant and troublesome spirit. My method is simple, they want trouble well here it comes. I just located the spirit, gave him the hard word and an option, out the house now or else. He took a bit of convincing as he did seem to think he was still alive, but eventually I got the ghost of Mrs G's husband out of her home. Then we ripped up his photograph and threw it in the dustbin. As for the deliverance to the white light of peace, well I did say a prayer for the lost soul.

One rule I have is to never predict death, that is rarely shown to me but even if it were I would use discretion in presenting such information in an acceptable way. I realise that there are psychics who do profess to provide insights into serious illness, one even had the bare faced audacity to tell a number of my staff that I had cancer of the brain and was terminally ill. That was some years ago so they were completely wrong.

Such charlatans get the profession of psychic consultant a bad name and in my opinion should be disbarred from practising.

CHAPTER FORTY THREE

GHOSTLY PETS

There are those that would deny that animals have souls like we human beings have. Quite why some people think that we are so unique is beyond me, we are animals too, human animals. We have souls in the same way that other living creatures have souls and the proof is to be found in the world of spirit.

One gentleman that has encountered the spirits of animals is Gerald of Sheffield in the county of Yorkshire U.K. One day Gerald was walking behind a lady at his local Bingo Hall when he saw a little Yorkshire Terrier dog following her, Yet this was no ordinary dog, it was glowing and shimmering like gold caught in the rays of the sun. Gerald watched in amazement as this little dog trotted just behind the lady. He felt he just had to say something and asked her if she knew there was a wonderful little dog with her. When Gerald described the dog to the lady she seemed quite surprised. 'Why' she said 'that can't possibly be, my little Yorkshire Terrier died three years ago'. It was then that Gerald knew he had seen the ghost of this lady's pet.

Just a few days later Gerald was visiting his local college. Whilst he was there Gerald noticed a cat sitting on a chair looking so contented and happy, as cats do when they are comfortable. Gerald mentioned this cat to one of the college staff and described it in some detail to them. At first the lecturer thought Gerald was joking 'You can't have seen that cat' he said 'it died two years ago'. But Gerald had seen the college cat, dead or not.

When Gerald's brother died he decided to join a Spiritualist Church to seek guidance and advice. The people at the Church were kind and helpful and told Gerald that his brother was now in the world of spirit and at peace. However, Gerald soon knew different. The very next day Gerlad was standing by the front window of his home when he felt that his brother, now deceased, was trying to contact him. As he looked out along the road, down which his brother had often walked, Gerald saw a beautiful shining bird flying towards him. This glorious bird flew right up to window and seemed to be smiling at him. For a split second Gerald was quite certain that this was the soul of his brother returning to say one last goodbye before flying off on its journey into eternity.

Since that day Gerald has had no doubts whatsover that animals have souls as we have. Indeed he subscribes to the idea that some spirits can return from the world beyond in the form of animals and birds as he believes his brother did. Gerald is not alone in such beliefs, there is an old belief that at the moment of physical death the souls of the good went into birds and that the souls of the bad went into other animals such as dogs.. Hence the saying 'he has gone to the dogs'.

It can be argued that the psyche of a dog is different from the psyche of a human being, but only in so much as one might argue that in a corporeal sense. I believe all living things are a part of the unseen collective consciousness of the universe. Our human souls are simply hosted by a different physical body than the souls of the creatures that we call animals. But we too are animals, human animals, Homo sapiens. The physical difference between a man and a monkey, in genetic terms, is generally agreed as being no more than one percent.

However that 1% puts us in control, or does it? Perhaps we are assuming too much when we consider ourselves to be the dominant species on the planet. Mankind is still evolving, whilst cockroaches have remained unchanged in hundreds of millions of years. These insects share our food for free, live in our homes without rent and visit even the most palatial of hotels at will and without a gold card. At the risk of seeming facetious, they can't be totally stupid, can they?

Many pet owners will tell you that their dog, cat or whatever is tuned in to them. Often we hear people say; 'I'm sure he/she knows every word I say'. In my book 'Psychic Pets' (Published by Bloomsbury) I gave numerous true accounts of animals that had displayed seemingly paranormal powers to help and comfort human beings. Recently I received a letter from a Mrs. R.A. Henderson of Stafford in which she told me that one of her pet dogs returned to her from beyond the grave with a message of love. As Spiritualists we accept the truth of communication from the spirit world, why should we deny that animals can and do return, bringing with them joy and hope of life eternal. Let me tell you Mrs. Henderson's incredible story. She owned two pet dogs, Timmy and Sally. Timmy passed to spirit and Mrs. H. was left to share her life with little Sally.

Sally was a black and tan long haired standard daschund and Mrs. H. owned her for twelve years. They were really close friends, especially since the passing of Timmy, and Sally seemed able to read her owner's thoughts.They were as close as a dog and a human being could be. Then, one unfortunate day shortly after Sally's 12th birthday, she escaped through a hole in the garden fence and was knocked down by a car. Sally died in Mrs. Henderson's arms. That very evening she was laid to rest in a quiet grave dug in a far corner of the garden in which she had played.

Mrs. Henderson was deeply saddened by the loss of her friend. They had shared so much love together. That night she could hardly rest, let alone sleep. So, sitting in her easy chair she took a sleeping pill. Then still restless and unable to sleep, she took another. That did the trick. It was about 5 a.m. when Mrs. H. woke, there was something pushing against her leg, a furry something was rubbing itself along her shin. Looking down Mrs. H. saw it was Timmy, or rather the spirit of her old dog Timmy who had passed to the next life some time before. As Mrs. H. stared in amazement at the materialised dog she received a form of communication. It was as though Timmy had returned to tell his former owner not to worry, he was looking after Sally from the world beyond. A sense of joy flooded through Mrs. Henderson as she realised that her friend was safe in his new home.

CHAPTER FORTY FOUR

ENERGY THERAPY

In Israel there lives a lady called Gerdi Altman, she practices Energy Therapy, healing and helping many people. She was recently interviewed by Luanne Hunt, this is her story: On the natural path to physical and emotional wholeness, there are bound to be a few bumps and bruises along way. With every treatment or remedy, there's a time of waiting and learning to make adjustments to one's behavior. Getting well without the use conventional medicine also causes us to exercise our faith muscle in ways that might be foreign or uncomfortable.

Holistic practitioner Gerdi Altman understands this delicate process and has guided countless people to optimum health through a natural therapy called Energy Tuning. Altman, who lives and practices in Israel, said she takes great interest in the well-being of her clients, helping them tune in to positive, life-transforming energy. She believes just about any physical or emotional issue can be corrected through Energy Tuning, a technique she developed in 2000. According to Altman, the technique has helped correct everything from migraine headaches to chronic fatigue to depression. It involves changing or rebalancing the energies within an individual's energy system to bring them to the correct frequencies.

"Basically, I'm the cleaner and the alarm that tells people what's going on inside their bodies," said Altman, who holds a diploma in medical dowsing recognized by the Institute of Complementary Medicine in the United Kingdom and accredited by Thames Valley University. "When I'm checking people, I loosen or get rid of the negative stuff and replace it with positive energy. It's like taking an X-ray of your energy, but I think it's a lot better because I can get a picture of everything that's going on within a person."

Through Energy Tuning, Altman said she is able to identify imbalances and blocks using a pendulum and various energy level tests. Once these blocks are located, she implements a clearing process that will remove the rubbish and allow good energy to come through. This is accomplished with various energy remedies, which Altman sends into the client's energy system. "The remedies used are always energy remedies and no substance is ever involved," said Altman. "For example, if the indication is that a certain herb would be beneficial, the energy of this herb and not the physical herb itself would be captured and adjusted in the correct way and sent across into the client's energy system. There are thousands of remedies to choose from."

When it comes to detecting, measuring, tracking and monitoring energies, Altman believes the pendulum is the perfect instrument. She said by recognizing and interpreting the movements of a pendulum correctly, energies in the human body can be observed with precision. Altman's pendulum is lightweight and made of clear crystal. These devices can be of various weights and made of wood, metal or other materials. Typically, they are suspended from a chain or a string. "Over the years, I've learned that the pendulum is extremely reliable," said Altman. "I can see from the strength of the swing, or spin, what's going on. There's no guessing, personal opinions, experimenting, trial-and-error or hit-or-miss situation. Through an energy link with the client, the pendulum will give the exact picture."

In order to get a clear snapshot of a person's health, Altman creates what she refers to as an energy link to them. She does this by asking them for their date and location of birth, as well as a strand of their hair. This information allows her to begin checking all the energy systems in their body to see which are running correctly and incorrectly. She said a person does not need to be present for the therapy and she works with patients via telephone and e-mail all around the world.

According to Altman, a course of energy clearing and balancing can take days, weeks or sometimes months. She said while chronic conditions such asthma and back pain may be more difficult to correct, less severe problems like the flu or eye irritations usually clear up quickly. All of Altman's treatments require follow-up sessions that differ in frequency depending on the individual's health issues.

Along with Energy Tuning sessions, Altman recommends a variety of holistic remedies to encourage healing, such as homeopathy, vitamins and minerals, Chinese herbs, Chakra balancing, aromatherapy and acupuncture, to name a few. Additionally, she educates her clients about the importance of proper nutrition. "Dietary advice gives an overview of the effects certain types of food have on your energy system," said Altman. "It is important to know in general but especially when going through a series of treatments so that the system gets the best possible care."

Catherine Edmonds-Hahn, a patient of Altman's, said she has benefited by Energy Tuning in myriad ways. Several years ago, the London resident sought Altman's help for extreme stress. After her husband's death and a major move, she said she was unable to think clearly and move forward in a positive direction.

"My life just seemed to come to a standstill and in desperation I turned to Gerdi," said Edmonds-Hahn. "Though the changes were slow, bit by bit the situation around me changed. I was calmer and more able to cope. Suddenly, good things started to happen."

Life has also gotten much better for Lucy Harrison of Ireland, who has been seeing Altman for seven years. Harrison said she had a debilitating eye condition that forced her to miss many days of work. She also had a difficult time coping with stress, especially when travelling.

After four years of treatments, her eyesight improved dramatically. She also began traveling to places such as Southeast Asia and India without feeling the least bit stressed.

"I credit the ongoing work with Gerdi for supporting me to regain my health and the possibilities that being healthy have now opened up to me," Harrison said.

For those on traditional medications or therapies, Altman said Energy Tuning will not interfere. She recommends that anyone undergoing medical treatment continue to follow their doctor's advice and let them know before starting any alternative program. "Energy Tuning is very effective but people have to be open to making changes in regards to the way they take care of their bodies," said Altman. "It takes time and effort to turn your situation around. But many of my clients get really motivated when other people start noticing the changes in them. When they tell me stories about how someone said they look much healthier, that gives me the biggest pleasure."

CHAPTER FORTY FIVE

THE ANGRY YEARS: Colin Wilson

This material world that we live in is, I believe, shaped in many ways not by the physical structures that surround us but by the intellectual parameters that form the spirit of our country. Some sixty or so years ago we were considered to be a Christian nation with the acceptance of God's divinity almost unquestioned. Our codes of conduct were shaped by those beliefs and the majority accepted 'The rich man in his castle, the poor man at the gate' in a land where all things were far from bright and beautiful. We did not know it then but the days of the old heavy industries, steel, coal, cotton and general manufacturing were numbered, as was the age of subservience. Within less than two decades of WWII society in Great Britain changed as the era of discontent dawned and people began to question authority. Something had to start this movement away from the previously accepted 'know your place lad' mentality of the working class. I believe that a major part of that something was the literary group known as 'The Angry Young Men'.

In the year 1956 a young playwright called John Osborne had his play 'Look Back In Anger' staged at The Royal Court Theatre on May 8th. It was generally panned by all the critics except one, Kenneth Tynan. Some critics said the play was like watching life at home. Osborne didn't know it then but he had written what was in effect the first 'kitchen sink drama' a forerunner of all the soap operas we have today like 'Coronation Street' and 'Eastenders'. The one critic that did like 'Look Back In Anger' Kenneth Tynan went overboard in his praise of the play calling it 'the best young play of its decade'. The Royal Court Theatre's press officer, George Fenton, disliked the play and said to Osborne 'I suppose you are an angry young man' and so the term was coined.

At the same time as Osborne found fame as a playwright Colin Wilson had his seminal work 'The Outsider' published by Victor Gollanz . The book was a publishing sensation rocketing the young Wilson to instant international success. The Outsider was critically well received as 'an enquiry into the nature of the sickness of mankind in the 20th century'. Soon Osborne and Wilson were being linked together and termed The Angry Young Men. But as Wilson says 'anger has to be directed against something and if you're angry about everything then you're not really angry'. One man that was really angry was the father of Wilson's young girlfriend, Joy. He had been shown an extract from what he believed to be a diary kept by Wilson in which he described various acts of deviant behavior (it was not in fact a diary but notes for a novel 'Ritual In The Dark') Fearing that Wilson was some bohemian beatnik set on debauchery with his darling daughter the man burst into his rooms brandishing a horsewhip shouting 'Right Wilson the game is up!' The next day Colin Wilson's literary career was in near ruins as the tabloid press ran lurid front-page features about the scandalous author and his wild lifestyle.

Soon Osborne and Wilson were joined by other writers, notably John Braine who wrote 'Room At The Top' about Joe Lampton a working class lad who fought his way to success by seducing the boss's daughter. Also Alan Sillitoe who wrote 'The Lonliness Of The Long Distance Runner' a gritty short story about a young borstal boy who defies the authoritarian regime by refusing to win a race against the local public school. This was subsequently a film starring Tom Courtney. The theme of all these writers was somewhat similar, working class anger against a system that seemed determined to restrict upward social mobility and keep the plebian masses in their place. These then were the Angry Young Men that through their literary talent helped to bring a change of attitude to post-war Britain. Their works enabled people to see that they were not merely subservient wage-slaves and could be anything they wanted to be if, as Wilson puts it, they had 'The Strength To Dream'.

Before we had The Angry Young Men we had the Jarrow hunger marches, striking Welsh miners faced British soldiers deployed by Winston Churchill who was himself a member of the aristocracy. There were twelve year old children labouring in the cotton mills of Lancashire whilst workers were paid starvation wages and survived in permanent fear of the boss man. What Wilson and his fellow writers taught us was that though we may be in chains we can sing like the sea and ultimately be free to be what God created us to be. Not just automatons programmed to dig coal, turn a lathe, weave cotton or stand in line on some soulless conveyor belt stitching soles onto shoes hour after hour after hour. Wilson did this kind of work but he knew that he was destined for far greater things so he abandoned his working class roots in Leicester and escaped to London where he spent all his time in The British Museum reading, researching and writing 'The Outsider'. What his genius achieved, along with the other 'Angry Young Men' and their like was to create a kind of intellectual sea change in this country that we call Great Britain.

As Spiritualists we accept that our short journey in corporeal form is to enable us to develop, learn our lessons and grow closer to the perfection and light of God the divine power. As prisoners of a system designed to control and subjugate us how could we achieve this? Sixty years ago we did what we were told by the masters, the bosses, the ruling class and generally we accepted these authority figures without question. Sixty years ago to think that one could step beyond the rich man's gate and take over the castle was tantamount to madness. Wilson, Osborne, Braine and Sillitoe broke down that metaphorical gate and showed us that far from being mere cap in hand mill-hands and workers we were free sentient beings capable of constructive thought. As Wilson says one has to be angry at something and he, along with his fellow young literary counterparts, were angry at a society that worshipped the protected elite and subjugated the poor. The Angry Young Men showed us that we have the individual capacity to rebel against the system and win. As Osborne says in Look Back In Anger the main character Jimmy Porter 'is hurt because everything is the same.' That is he was angry because he felt that the old class system, was oppressing him. But not for long as the angry young men opened the minds of the public to their possibilities and for the first time in centuries we dared to dream.

The Angry Years by Colin Wilson is published by Robson Books at 16.99p I am given an acknowledgement by CW in his book as I helped in the research.

ISBN 9-781861-059727

CHAPTER FORTY SIX

OUR EMOTIONAL PETS

Animals have emotions, of that I am absolutely convinced. Those of us that have lived alongside pets will know that they share our happiness and also our sadness. My own bulldog Grumbles used to recognize whenever I was feeling low and often would come and place her head on my knee and look up as if to say 'don't be sad, I am your friend'. It was a kind of telepathic link that we shared and I still miss that old dog.

Scientists term the attributing of human emotions to animals anthropomorphism which is a form of criticism, as if to believe that our pets have feelings like we do is mistaken or wrong. One book that challenges this is 'When Elephants Weep' by Jeffrey Moussaieff Masson and Susan McCarthy. I was given this book by Barry Cunningham the managing editor of Bloomsbury Children's Book and he suggested I read it as part of my research into the paranormal powers of animals when he commissioned me to write 'Psychic Pets'. I was deeply moved by many of the examples given by the authors and found the book truly inspirational. Here is a sample:

'A game warden in Tanzania was doing 'elephant control work' when he saw three female elephants and a half-grown male in tall grass. Since his job was to keep the elephant population down, he shot the three females-and slightly wounded the the half grown animal. To his dismay, he suddenly saw two elephant calves, who had been with the females but hidden in the long grass. He moved towards them, shouting and waving his hat, hoping to drive them back to the larger herd, where other elephants would adopt them. The wounded elephant was dazed and helpless and did not know which way to turn. Instead of fleeing, the orphaned calves pressed themselves against him and supported the wounded elephant away from further danger.'

The elephant calves, as described above, were acting in a manner that clearly indicated they were consciously helping their injured friend. Such action is contrary to what many scientists would have us believe about animals i.e. that they act instinctively. Surely the natural instincts of those two elephant calves would be to run away from the clear and present danger. But they did not do so, they acted to aid and protect their fellow creature, rather like a soldier may do on a battlefield. Such actions indicate that the elephants had feelings for without them they would surely have turned and run.

Freedom is one of the great joys of life that we will all have experienced at some time. Thinking back in my own life I recall the sheer exhilaration I used to feel waking on the first morning of the summer holidays knowing that there was no school and I could go playing in the fields with my friends. Animals also feel joy experiencing freedom as illustrated by this anecdote:

'In spring, when the chimpanzees at Arnhem Zoo are allowed out of their winter quarters for the first time, there is a scene of exultation as they scream and hoot, clasp and kiss one another, jump up and down pounding on each others backs. They are not free, but the additional space, the relatively greater freedom, thrills them. It looks as if it gives them joy'.

Anyone who has owned a dog and taken it for a run in a park will doubtless have witnessed something quite similar as the dog charges here, there and everywhere. That sense of freedom, clearly demonstrated by the dog's delight, is an emotion and is as real as our own feelings of joy at being free.

The great naturalist Charles Darwin in his book 'The Expression of the Emotions in Man and Animals' stated that emotional weeping was a 'special expression of man'. He did however note one exception reported to him by Sir E. Tennant that some Indian elephants, newly captured in Ceylon (now Sri Lanka) when tied up showed 'no other indication of suffering than the tears which suffused their eyes and flowed incessantly. One captured elephant sank to the ground uttering chocking cries, with tears trickling down his cheeks'. The emotion being expressed by the captured elephants was perhaps of frustration and sadness at the loss of liberty and segregation from their family. As human beings we too would likely shed tears in such a situation.

If we accept that animals have emotions and express them with their own particular physical attributes we should also accept that they are sentient creatures capable of making value judgements. That is animals posses the ability to act altruistically i.e. in a way that helps others but may endanger themselves, as in the example above with the elephant calves.

During the years that I have been working as a psychic author I have met many people who tell me that they have seen the spirits of their pets who are passed into the next world. We buried our pet bulldog Grumbles in a quiet corner of the garden where, in life, she used to rest in the shade and snore loudly. Last summer I was myself snoozing on the hammock that stands by that corner and as I began to wake from my nap I heard quite distinctly the familiar sound of Grumbles snoring away. Half asleep I looked up and saw, for one brief moment, that happy old friend flopped out paws before her head fast asleep. Then I remembered that she had gone and as I looked she disappeared into the shadows of the late summer afternoon.

Animals have souls, our pets, like us, do not die. The next world is as real to animals as it is to us and to think otherwise is just pure arrogance. We ourselves are animals, human animals and as such will take our natural place in the kingdom beyond this material plane that we call Earth. Elephants may indeed weep, as may we all, but in the next dimension our God will dry those tears as we become one with the eternal love that awaits all living creatures.

CHAPTER FORTY SEVEN

ATLANTIS AND THE KINGDOM OF THE NEANDERTHALS

Colin Wilson, the author of two previous books on the mystery of Atlantis, has recently written a new volume on that ancient lost land. His book, 'Atlantis and the Kingdom of the Neanderthals' is an enthralling read, offering many original insights and theories. Wilson starts his book with a preface detailing the experience of the anthropologist Michael Harner who, under the influence of a native Andes Indian drink called 'ayahuasca' saw what he believed to be the truth of humanities origins. In a form of induced hallucinogenic trance Harner 'saw' the whole land flooded as water gushed from the jaws of a huge crocodile. The water rose until it became a sea, then a galleon floated into view with bird headed creatures that reminded him of the ancient Egyptian tomb paintings. These creatures told him that they were the bringers of all life and lived within the bodies of every living thing on this planet. These bird-headed humans said that they were the true masters of humanity and that man was their servant. Wilson presents this as a possible vision of The Flood that destroyed the continent of Atlantis. However, the idea that bird-headed beings created humankind is perhaps, for most reasonable people, a difficult concept.

Then there is the question of Atlantis itself, as many believe the story of this lost continent to be nothing more than pure mythology. One argument discussed by Wilson in his book is that Atlantis may have been Antarctica. In support of this theory Wilson introduces the work of professor Charles Hapgood who declared that the earth's crust is subjected to periodic shifts that can cause continents to change their positions. Hapgood suggested that the continent of Antarctica shifted approximately twelve thousand years ago. This is no pie in the sky total nonsense as the foreward to Hapgood's book on the subject 'Earth's Shifting Crust' was written by none other than Albert Einstein. It was the scientist Rand Flem-Ath that took the hypothesis of Hapgood and applied it to the Atlantis question arriving at the potential conclusion that it may once have been the land that is now known as Antarctica.

Now the problem with that hypothesis is that it is generally accepted that civilization started in the Middle East about ten thousand years ago, approximately 8000 BC. It was whilst contemplating this anomaly that Flem-Ath received a letter from Hapgood stating that he had discovered evidence that dated civilization back far beyond the accepted date to a time before the last major shift of the earth's crust. When Flem-Ath wrote back requesting further details his letter was returned marked 'deceased'. Between writing his letter to Flem-Ath and his response Hapgood had walked in front of a motor vehicle and been killed. And so the search for the evidence hinted at by Hapgood began.

Attempting to gain proof that Hapgood had been right Flem-Ath conducted research into various religious sites around the world. It is a known fact that most religious sites are aligned to true north. What Flem-Ath found was that more than fifty such sites in Mexico were misaligned from true north. And that Mexico's most famous religious site 'Teotihucan', formerly a city as large as ancient Rome, had its 'Way of The Dead' 15.5 degrees off from true north. When Flem-Ath applied mathematics to this calculation it produced some remarkable implications. Assuming that this religious pathway was originally built running from south to true north, as all other religious sites usually are, then the land upon which it stands had shifted by 15.5 degrees and that shift happened when the earth's crust last significantly moved 12,000 years ago. In other terms, the 'Way of The Dead' had been constructed in a period of time before civilization was supposed to exist.

Hapgood himself had theories about Atlantis being Antarctica but had arrived at these by a different route than Flem-Ath. He had considered the ancient map of the Turkish Admiral Piri Reis, created in the year 1513. This map shows in some detail the coast of Antarctica with its bays and rivers. Nothing strange about that one might think this being a map to aid seafarers but at the time the map was drawn Antarctica, like today, was under hundreds of feet of solid ice. A geological expedition in 1949 used radar to penetrate the ice and show the land underneath, it exactly matched the Piri Reis map. Also core samples taken from the site showed the area to be 6000 years old i.e. 4000 years BC that is before the Sumerian civilization and it was the Sumerians that are generally believed to have invented writing. Yet the Peri Reis map, or evidence used to draw it, must pre date that period and a map would be useless without writing. This was yet a further clue Hapgood had discovered dating civilization back way beyond the currently excepted period of 8000 years BC.

Wilson's book captured my imagination with its many imaginative hypothesis and explanations that seem to prove, beyond what one might term reasonable doubt, that civilization existed perhaps as much as one hundred thousand years ago. That would be at the time of the Neanderthal man, before Cro-Magnon man. The generally accepted theory is that the Neanderthals were ape like and walked with a looping gait. Today the term is used to imply that someone is backward, slow or is a form of human dinosaur. However, it is a little known fact the brain size of Neanderthal man was substantially larger than that which pertains to homo-sapiens. Could it be, argues Wilson, that the Neanderthals were the occupants of Atlantis and that kingdom vanished when the earth's crust shifted?

Whilst Wilson's book does not provide all the answers it most certainly does raise a number of extremely interesting questions that have yet to be fully considered by many scientific disciplines that they involve. I highly recommend this book to anyone who likes a good mystery in the genre of The Da Vinci Code, for one thing Wilson does do, he makes you think.

CHAPTER FORTY EIGHT

GHOST HUNTING: FUN OR DANGEROUS?

Many of the old towns and cities of the UK now have professional Ghost Walks, that is guided tours around the locality offering stories and insights into reports of hauntings. The most famous of these are in the City of London where tourists are entertained by tales of headless queens and phantom monks that walk the ancient alleyways. Or the old Roman city of York where legions of soldiers still patrol walking on roads long buried beneath the modern streets. Many ancient houses and castles have ghost stories and no doubt some are based on factual accounts of experiences by credible witnesses. However many are little more than over embellished spooky tales told to capture the imagination of those with a few hours to spare. There is no harm in this that I can see other than when the tour guides encourage those paying for the service to take part in Ouija Board sessions attempting to summon departed spirits. Such practice is potentially very dangerous and should be seriously discouraged. No genuine psychic-medium would, in my opinion, encourage inexperienced, possibly young people to take part in a Ouija Board session.

I have first hand experience of what can happen when a group of untrained individuals experiment with Ouija. It was Germany in the late 1960s and in an Army barrack block a group of young soldiers were messing with an American made wooden Ouija Board. No one took the so-called game seriously and all thought it really funny when the message came through that the man in the room that had dared to mock this communicating spirit would be punished. The next morning the man whose room had been used came to complain that there had been extensive damage done to his bedroom, the metal cabinets had been smashed, tables broken and all the beds were scattered about the place like a hurricane had blown through. There was another problem, this was a military unit and the damage had to be reported. When the Sgt. Major in charge of the block was told he seemed unusually understanding. The block had, he said, during WWII been used as a prison and he advised that messing with the Ouija had potentially unleashed a troubled spirit. He ordered that room where this happened to be emptied and locked up. I can attest to the veracity of that story, you see I was one of those soldiers.

The rather ridiculous TV series 'Most Haunted' frequently featured the psychic investigators using a Ouija Board in an attempt to contact the spirits that were conspicuous by their absence. The televising of this dangerous practice should be condemned not supported by experienced professional psychics who really should know better. But then with the pressure of producing a TV show that had anything in it other than a dizzy blonde screaming every few minutes maybe they just agreed for effect. One truly appalling aspect of this TV show using the Ouija Board was the constant demanding of the presenters that the spirits show themselves and give some physical evidence of their presence. That is tantamount to asking for trouble and many who have tried this have found just that.

The Ghost Research Society based in Illinois USA is headed by Dale Kaczmarek who states that he believes the Ouija Board should under no circumstances be treated as a game. He says that in his experience the spirits that come through to communicate through the Ouija Board are on the lower astral plane and many will be lost souls having experienced difficult transitions following violent wasted lives. By opening a doorway for these negative discarnate spirits the users are offering free access into their lives and will potentially get what they are asking for especially if they request physical proof. Often such proof is the glass or whatever is used as an indicator will be violently moved or thrown. Sometimes nearby objects such as ornaments will be smashed, doors slammed shut and icy cold blasts of air experienced. These are not tricks, these are the disturbed and dangerous discarnate entities that have been offered an entry into this material world feeding on the psychic energy of those stupid enough to mess with the Ouija Board.

In the mid 1970s I lived for a brief time in Home Office quarters at the Cheetham Hill area of Manchester. Some four doors down from my house was a family of two teenage girls and their parents. Come summertime the parents went overseas for their holiday leaving the girls home, they were around 17 and 19 years of age so not youngsters. Early On the morning of the first Sunday I was walking to Strangeways Jail where I worked past the house and saw to my amazement all the windows were wide open, the front door was hanging off its hinges and of the girls there was no sign. I spoke to my wife about this and she agreed to keep a watch on the property whilst I went to work and reported the matter. That day the works department of the jail came out and boarded up the house. The girls had moved out and gone to stay with friends. When the parents came home they told me what had happened. It seems their two daughters had friends round on the Saturday night and were playing with a Ouija Board. Something had sent a message warning of death and destruction then all hell broke loose with a mirror falling off the wall, drawers opening and shutting, doors banging too and fro then a lound thundering booming noise echoed through the house and all in it ran into the street scared out of their wits. They abandoned the house. Needless to say the parents of the two girls were far from happy about this. Shortly afterwards the entire family moved away.

That was not the end of the haunting though, the man that lived in the house opposite mine came home one night shortly after this incident and in a drunken rage assaulted his wife and set about destroying his own home then was dragged by the police screaming and cursing to a secure van. I watched astounded as this huge crazy guy snapped the heavy metal handcuffs the police had fastened to his wrists, now that would have taken superhuman strength. Also some months later I myself was physically assaulted by another crazed jailer who objected to me advising him not to allow his dog to foul my front garden. For my troubles I received a broken ankle as he leaped onto my back as I turned to walk indoors. The whole area was filled with negative energy and I sincerely believe that those two silly young girls had opened the door to let whatever it was in to wreck havoc on their home and other people's lives, mine included.

Ghost Hunting with a trained and truly professional psychic-medium is one thing, it may be safe. Messing about with Ouija Boards and taunting discarnate beings that could be absolutely anything and potentially immensely evil is quite another and very dangerous.

CHAPTER FORTY NINE

WHY TROUBLES COME

Why me? Why do I always seem to get the sniffy end of the stick. What reason can there possibly be in my continuous experience of failure and loss. If it was not for bad luck I would have no luck at all...as the song goes. We will all feel like that at times, when things go wrong and the whole world seems to be against us. The truth, the real Spiritual Truth is that without bad luck, without problems there would be no progress. So why do troubles come into our lives? In the teachings of Silver Birch I believe we can find many answers to such questions:

From: Silver Birch: You have to suffer. You have to endure privation, perhaps ill-health, some crisis that will touch your soul, that spark of the divine, and begin to fan it into a beauteous flame. There is no other way. It is only in the darkness that you will find the light, only in ignorance that you will gain knowledge. Life must be a polarity, or if you like a duality, in which it is said action and reaction are equal and opposite.

Silver Birch is simply saying that without suffering there is no spiritual development, no lessons learned. We need a crisis to create an answer and we will find that answer there is no other way you can not face trouble and adversity without finding the strength to deal with it successfully. You will find a way.

You may think that is just a platitude, a way of fobbing off the injured, the sick, the lame, and the impoverished with some soft soap tosh to shut them up. But we will all suffer, each in our own very different ways. Even those that may appear to live precious protected lives experience anguish, doubt and often agonise about problems that we can not see. As a professional psychic I had for many years a very wealthy client that had all the money any one person could wish for. They had the use of a private plane, stayed in only the best hotels and were driven around by a chauffer in a huge Bentley. Anyone casually observing this young lady would have thought how wonderful it must be to enjoy such riches. But her wealth and social position were her prison. She suffered in a very unique way but she did suffer and many times I heard her cry out to be free of the trappings of wealth that locked her into a world where she could never be free.

From Silver Birch: You will not find spiritual truths when the sun is shining, if you are surrounded by riches, and wealth and possessions. You will not find spiritual truths when you have no problems. The catalyst will work only when you are in trouble.

Troubles come in many guises and we all must face what we have been given to learn the lessons that our eternal soul needs to learn. It would be useless, a wasted life, if we were born into riches, had a gloriously happy childhood, passed all the exams, won all the prizes, married the most beautiful partner, shared a delightful marriage, experienced the joy of children and saw them achieve absolutely everything they aimed for. What would one learn from such a life? That life is fun, life is brilliant and enjoyable. But what would have been accomplished in real spiritual terms?

From Silver Birch: It is not when the sun shines that the soul finds itself. It is not in a bed of roses that the soul comes into its own. It is in the hazards and challenges, the difficulties, the hurdles and the obstacles. These provide the only means by which the soul can realize its latent divinity. This is the story of every pilgrim on the road to spiritual knowledge. There has to be heartbreak, sorrow and suffering to appreciate fully the compensations that will follow. The individuals who will give service must be tried and tested, sometimes to their uttermost strength.

As Spiritualists I am sure we know that most, if not all of our effective mediums and spiritual leaders have suffered in their lives. There is something that comes from hardship, from facing the challenges of life and overcoming them that gives one the power to help others. Through the trauma of a terrible experience a soul will grow stronger. We can not die, there is no such thing as death and all must face their own trials and tribulations before they can progress. Death, physical death is not the end to suffering, it is just another experience on the way to understanding. Through the doorway marked death we will all travel and find there a peace that will be born out of comprehension. When we absolutely know that all we suffered in this incarnation had a purpose then we will be at ease with the experience. But first we have to face the fire. First we have to overcome.

From Silver Birch: In some religions they teach that there is survival for those who believe in certain doctrines and creeds. But survival has nothing to do with religion or with human beliefs, aspirations and hopes. Survival is an inflexible law, automatic in its operation.

As Silver Birch says the law of the universe is survival and we will only take with us from this world the sum of our knowledge gained through personal experience. I say that death is not the end to suffering, only spiritual oneness with the light of eternal love, that many call God, is the end to pain. Between now and then there is life, incarnate and discarnate, spiritual and material. I believe that you, me and all the rest of the people in the world would do well to accept that why troubles come is to teach us that which we need to learn. To the Proud: Insult and humility. To the Strong and Powerful: Weakness and despair. To the Rich: Poverty and indignity. To the Beautiful: Disfigurement and decay. To us all the troubles that come our way are sent to meet our needs, we need to suffer, we need to learn and we all need to accept that this is the law of the universe. But take heed dear reader, there is no universal law that states we must roll over and accept the kick in the reproductive organs that we are being given. Fight back, tooth and nail, fight all the way and never, no matter how tough the going gets, do you give in. Then you will learn what you need to learn. And what is more, you will make spiritual progress which is why you were born in the first place so stop moaning and get on with it.

CHAPTER FIFTY

HEALING POWERS HELP INVALID

In the year 2002 Mrs. Joan Bicknall of Fraserburgh in Scotland was injured in a minor car accident. The injuries that she sustained, though not life threatening, were sufficient to cause her body to rekindle her previous diagnosis of Multiple Sclerosis which quickly disabled Joan turning her from being an outgoing individual who enjoyed walks in the country, to a wheelchair bound invalid. By the year 2007 she had also suffered a stroke, was diagnosed with diabetes and her auto-imune system was closing down. The pain generated by Joan's illness was, by the start of 2007, so severe that she could not even sit quietly for more than a short time. At the age of just 59 years Joan was a virtual prisoner of her own incapacitated body and life seemed hardly worth living.

All her adult life Joan Bicknall had been a Spiritualist and when she became ill she naturally turned to the Church healers for help. The problem was that her home was over an hours drive away from her nearest Spiritualist Church at Aberdeen. But she did manage to get her husband to take her there and the healing she received was having an ameliorating effect on the extreme pain she was now suffering.

In the month of August 2007 the Lancashire healer and Spiritualist Mr. Bill Parker was on holiday in Scotland visiting his daughter-in-law and son. She knew of the problems that Joan Bicknall was experiencing and suggested to her father-in-law that he might be able to help by using his widely recognized healing powers. Bill, who is 78 years of age, immediately agreed and that afternoon he was driven over to Joan's home where he was invited to offer her help using his gift of healing powers. This is how Joan Bicknall described what happened next:

"I was already in some considerable pain when Bill Parker arrived, having had yet another night of near sleepless agony. To be honest I did not really think that anything he could do would be of much help but I agreed to let him try. So as I sat still in my armchair Bill placed his hands at either side of my head not quite touching and he told me he would now begin to give me healing. As I recall the time was around 2pm and I can normally sit in one position for no more than ten minutes. But as Bill moved his hands around me, all the while generating a sense of absolute calm and peacefulness, time seemed to stand still. Then as he extended his hand around my back, just inches away from my body, I felt an intense heat surge through me. Then he stopped and suddenly, as though waking from a dream, I was wide awake and looked at the clock on the nearby wall to see that over an hour had passed, yet it seemed like only minutes".

Before Bill Parker had been to heal Joan she had been unable to walk more than a few feet and had been using a wheelchair. Indeed so restricted was her mobility that her General Practitioner MD had requested that she be provided with an electronically operated wheelchair to give her some freedom of movement. That was before she saw Bill.

It was a little over a week after Bill's visit that Joan was looking out of her lounge window watching her husband Robin doing some tidy up work in the back garden. As she stood looking at him she noticed that her flowers that she had been so proud of in years gone by needed to be dead-headed. This is how Joan described what happened next: "I was so engrossed in looking at my plants that I forgot I was an invalid and couldn't walk. I just got this idea to go and prune the flowers and the next thing I was outside with a plastic bag and a pair of scissors snipping off the dead-heads of my beloved fuchsias. As I did this I was startled to hear the voice of my husband. "How did you get here?" he asked me and for a moment I didn't really know and said simply that I must have walked there. And I had done that, I had experienced no pain and alone, without aid I had come out of the house, down the garden path and walked to the fuchsia plants. It was like a miracle and for a while I stood astounded at my amazing adventure."

Since that time Joan Bicknall has experienced a continuing but gradual improvement in her health. Though she will never be cured, she has been told by the medical experts that the best she can expect is a period of remission, she is now able to get from A to B and is no longer confined to a wheelchair. So much did she improve that Joan went to see her GP and advised him she felt guilty at taking delivery of the promised electronic wheelchair but he told her that as it was an illness that progressed she would inevitably need this. But Joan has high hopes that it is not for a while yet as she is again starting to enjoy life and though she does have very bad days, when the pain is so intense that movement is impossible, she finds these are far less frequent and life has again become worth living.

This is what Joan Bicknall had to say about the healing she received from Bill Parker: "I have been a member of the Spiritualist Church all my life and as a young woman, when I lived in the county of Kent, I met and worked with many healers. I can say with all honesty that in all my life I have never encountered anyone that was able to bring so much healing power as Bill. I have been telling all my friends about him and look forward to receiving more healing from him when he next visits his daughter-in-law in Scotland. Sadly as I previously mentioned Bill passed to spirit, he was a most remarkable, gentle, kind and gifted man.

CHAPTER FIFTY ONE

INITIAL PSYCHIC EXPERIENCES

It is my belief and contention that we are all, to some degree, possessed of psychic ability. Rather like we can all, usually, kick a ball, though very few of us will become modern day Pele's. It is recognising and developing our gifts that is the key to connecting and the first signs that something is really happening to us varies from individual to individual. Some experience visions of spirits and communication at a young age and then it fades often returning in maturity. Some discover their connection in their middle years, sometimes in unique and very different ways. Here are some examples of the various ways people have found that they too really do have psychic facilities that can be developed.

The very gifted spirit-medium from Bolton James Byrne was subjected to serious physical abuse from his aggressive and frequently drunken father. James was often beaten and battered by his dad who, through the abuse of alcohol, obviously knew no better. It was during this period of his early life that James began to experience communication with spirit. His gift was clearly recognised by the spirit world as to his mother's front door came a Romany Gypsy lady who had a message for her, she told Mrs. Byrne that her son 'J' was a very special child and would grow up to be well known as a psychic. That prediction came true, in the year 1992 James Byrne starred in his very own show A PSYCHIC EXPERIENCE at the world famous London Palladium.

I myself as a child had numerous encounters with spirit the most amazing was when my parents would send me to bed early, around 6pm, during the summertime. I was confined to my bedroom and at age of six was too young to read fluently so I just lay on my bed wide awake and stared at the wallpaper. I recall there was a flower pattern and I attempted to count the individual roses until suddenly I was no longer a little boy in bed I travelled through time and space back to an ancient land where I became a grown man. This man was standing on a raised platform overlooking a river and immediately below me thousands of dark skinned men were heaving and dragging huge stones over desert sands. I was the architect or designer directing the proceedings and can clearly recall the amazing sense of power I held. Then, as quickly as I had travelled there I was back in my little boys body but exhausted and at the same time exhilarated by the amazing experience. When I told my parents they were very angry and forbade me to ever speak of this as it was the work of the devil. The stress of that, as night after night I flew back through some mysterious time-warp to ancient Egypt, then having to keep all this to myself, made me physically ill. I had to close it down to stop it. And so I did try, until many years later when I realised it was my destiny to communicate the truth.

There is a lady called June Dowling who recently contacted me to say she was starting to receive interaction from the spirit world. This is what June wrote of how she was discovering her gift: I experienced a strange buzzing in my head the same effect you get when you listen to music wearing headphones, I don't know why but I associated this sound with spirit So I called out, Who are you I know you there, but there was nothing so I called out again Who are you I want to see who you are! This time a man appeared but only from the waist up, he had long dark hair tied back in a pony tail and was wearing a blouse like shirt you know with puffed sleeves like what a pirate would have worn. I would say late thirty's and quite stern looking, so I said, who are you, what do you want ? He said, I am you and you are me but I loved you more in this world when you were a boy. He then took me on a journey and I felt as though I went out of the window like a burst of energy We were flying till we came to a red rock that was so big it would be impossible to climb. as I looked down everything below me was geometrically laid out, the plants, shrubs, flowers and trees everything was in pastel colours.

Then I saw a small foot bridge that connected one side to the other, I could see a large building on the other side, there were circles of light moving around and I was really excited because I knew I was going to see the akashic records, I was going to find out who I was and who I had been. Then suddenly I was awake on my bed. I had come so close, but had not seen the akashic records. However a door had been opened and I know now I am on an amzing journey of discovery. June Dowling continues to experience psychic phenomena and is gradually developing her gift.

CHAPTER FIFTY TWO

PARANORMAL POP STAR P. J. PROBY

I first saw the American born pop singer PJ Proby on the BBC Television show 'Around The Beatles' early in the year 1964. Proby was featured alongside John, Paul, George and Ringo with Long John Baldry and Cila Black. There was something about him that I recognised as I watched and heard him sing. Though at the time I was only 14 years of age I knew intuitively that I was seeing someone for the first time that would be in some way significant in my life. It was as if I had been gripped by invisible hands and shaken strongly. At the time I was interested in light opera, Puccini, Gilbert and Sullivan etc. more than pop music. Proby seemed to bridge the two in some mysterious way.

In early 1968 I actually met Proby for the first time, he was performing at The Garrick Theatre Club in the Lancashire town of Leigh. My father, Frank Sutton, was an Inspector in the CID there and knew the club owner so took me in and I was introduced to PJP in his dressing room. My dad clicked our photograph. But by this time Proby's star had fallen, outrageous antics on stage, splitting his trousers, being banned from all TV appearances and the major theatres had ruined his career. Proby had been declared bankrupt, evicted from his Chelsea flat and was now singing for his supper on the Northern club circuit. Yet his voice was absolutely brilliant almost operatic in its range and tonality as he sang 'Maria' and 'Somewhere' from West Side Story.

Years passed and in the mid 1980s I suffered the amputation of my right leg following an embolism that became gangrenous and suddenly I was on the edge of death. It was whilst hovering between this world and the next that I had a Near Death Experience. I could see my body in the hospital bed and walked away from it through the walls of the ward into what appeared to me to be an airport lounge. There I was surrounded by people that I did not know, though I felt completely at ease, in no way perturbed. Through high glass fronted walls I could see airplanes outside and this was obviously a departure area.

I recall sitting down and a female stewardess came forward and asked me to follow her. I was taken to a room at the far end of the departure lounge and inside was introduced to three people seated behind a long office desk. They were all male, middle aged and smiled at me in a gentle way as if to put me at ease. Then the gentleman in the centre said 'you do know that you are no longer in your body don't you?' For a brief moment I struggled with this thought but then replied that yes I did realise that. Then, one by one the three people began to ask me about my life and what I had done with it. We talked about my time as a soldier, as a nurse in the secure units within HM Prisons and how I was a husband and father. I told how I had cared for my grandparent, done all I could do and I explained that it was not my time to die as I had responsibilities, my wife and people needed me to help them. I clearly recall the three gentlemen looking at me and one said 'that is what everyone who comes in here says. so if you say you want to return tell us what you intend to do?' I knew then that this was the moment that would decide my fate.

The three kindly gentleman behind the office desk looked at me waiting for an answer. Thinking as quickly as I could I replied 'I would like to help adults with disabilities and learning difficulties' I looked and saw them smile 'do go on as we know there is something else that you could do' said the gentleman on my left. 'Yes, I will resurrect the 60s pop singer PJ Proby' I said, though why I said it at that time I did not know. That got a response though and I watched as the three talked briefly and then the man in the centre said 'we are very interested in that idea and may decide to send you back on a mission, but you must realise that you will be severely physically handicapped' I agreed then that I understood. 'Take a seat outside and we will discuss this further and let you know'. With that I left the room and sat down on a chair in the departure lounge waiting for their decision. I watched the others around go into the room I had just left and when they came out they walked through the lounge and onto a plane on the tarmac beyond the glass walls. Then I was alone, the only person left in the departure lounge. As I waited a voice came over the speaker system saying in a loud and commanding voice 'Would Mr. John Sutton please take his seat on the plane as we are waiting to depart'. I sat still, I was not going anywhere until I knew what the decision of the three gentlemen was and I wanted to know about my mission.

My wife Mary and brother Martin were by my side in the hospital when I regained consciousness. I vaguely recall asking my brother to take care of Mary as I was about to go to America on business, then I was again unconscious. The agony of those first few months following the amputation is hard to describe. I had developed a form of fungicide infection in my blood and was on kidney dialysis with total failure and given just days to live. My mother was flown over from Canada to attend my funeral and the consultant at the hospital told my wife that the chances of survival were less than twenty percent. The kidney specialist said I had but a few days as if my system did not show at least some signs of life then he would have to switch me off. Through all this I was intermittently awake and the pain was excruciating.

It took me a long time to get my strength back and I was a physical wreck when I left hospital weighing less than seven stone and confined to a wheelchair. The specialists told my wife I would never walk or work again. But I knew different, I just had to survive. The recollection of my interview in the departure lounge of the airport to infinity was not then clear in my consciousness but I was quietly certain that I was going to be a viable human being again. I just had to be. You know the toughest thing at the time was seeing people that had known me for years turning away rather than come and speak to me in my wheelchair and even when they did they spoke to my wife Mary and not to me, I was an invalid, a none person, but not for long.

In the year 1990 I was employed by Lancashire Social Services as a teacher/trainer of adults with learning difficulties at a day centre. I had retrained myself, been to college, taken a special-needs teaching certificate and was enjoying my job. It was April when one day my old school pal from Leigh, Kenny Greenhalgh, telephoned to say that he had heard something of potential interest to me. Kenny said that there was a pop singer we had both liked many years ago who was now living in the Lancashire town of Bolton. That singer was PJ Proby.

Following my discovery in April 1990 that the sixties pop singer PJ Proby was living in the town of Bolton, Lancashire, just a few miles from my home, I knew that the time for action had arrived. The memory of my interview in the airport lounge during my near death experience returned and suddenly I was aware that in some way I had to resurrect the career of that fallen star. Proby had been a big hit in the early sixties appearing with The Beatles and enjoying numerous top twenty pop chart hit records, such as 'Hold Me', 'Somewhere' and 'Maria'. However he had dropped out of sight during the last twenty years and was now a desperate down and out drunk existing on social services benefits and living as a free lodger in a small terraced house on a rather bleak back street. I had an idea to write a song for him, but would he still be able to sing that was the question.

I had written poetry all my adult life and knew that if I put my mind to it I could create a song about the life of Proby that would, with a little bit of luck and a lot of determination, maybe get him started again. At my typewriter I sat down and the idea came to me from the Shakespearian tragedy 'King Lear' which I had studied at 'A' level years before. The play tells the story of how King Lear throws away all of his kingdom, all his gifts, throws away everything and he says: When we are born, we cry, that we have come to this great stage of fools'. That was exactly what PJ Proby had done, thrown it all away. The words seemed to write themselves and I saw the song appear before me as if I were the instrument of a forceful intelligence from beyond. As I typed I kept hearing a discarnate voice calling my name from the empty room next door. 'John!......John!' it called, I looked but there was no one there, no one but myself and a song called 'Stage of Fools'.

When I had completed writing the song I had it made into a demo record by my friend Jeff Greenhalgh who once won on ITV's 'Stars In Their Eyes' playing the part of Paul McCartney. I sent the demo on a cassette to PJ Proby and when he heard this he called me from his lodgings in Bolton to say he was interested in singing it but wanted cash in his hand. We agreed terms over the telephone and on 27th June 1990 I collected PJ Proby from Bolton and drove him to a recording studio I had hired in Preston.

Proby was swilling Carlsberg Special Brew from a can sitting beside me as we headed down the M61 to Preston. He looked a real mess, prematurely aged with white hair and extremely thin with a grey unhealthy palor to his skin, he reeked of alcohol. As we approached the junction of the M61 and M6 the traffic came to a halt, we stopped in the middle lane and the outer lane was empty. We were there for around tem minutes not moving when in my side mirror I saw a white car approaching in the outer lane. I looked through the window and noted that it was a white American Stretched Limo with blacked out windows. As it drew alongside us I heard music coming from within from the car's stereo, the song playing was the 1964 recording of PJ Proby singing his big hit from West Side Story 'Somewhere'. The man himself was sitting beside me. As I stared in absolute amazement the limo continued ahead, though all else was standing still, until it seemed to just vanish into nothing. I turned to PJ Proby and asked him what he made of that: 'Never believe me if I tell 'em' he said. But I noticed he looked even paler than he had before.

When we finally arrived at the recording studio the sound engineer told me that there had been a serious car accident on the M6 with three people killed. That evening PJ Proby recorded his own first version of 'Stage of Fools' and he sang exactly as he had done so all those years ago, with the same deep tenor voice he had used to record 'Somewhere'. I knew then that I could make this work for him, he had the magic that was needed, he still had the voice. Proby really could sing.

In August of 1990 I decided to invest some more money in this project with PJ Proby and agreed with a studio in Chester-le-Street to record there. Again Proby demanded money up front, but he then refused to get into my brand new VW Golf as he said he would only go that distance if he got an helicopter. No get in car no money I said, he soon changed his mind and I got him to sign a contract then I paid him and he got into my car, we drove to The Holiday Inn at Newcastle.

The next morning at 09:30 I went to collect Proby from his room, it took a while for him to answer the door. Then when I went in he was back on the bed watching Tom and Jerry cartoons. I remonstrated with him, time was passing and we were due at the studio to start recording. I recall he was flopped out on the bed wearing his cowboy boots and Stetson hat 'Too early for me' he said and continued watching the TV. Suddenly the cartoons stopped and a News-Flash came on it was a local announcement stating that at Newcastle Airport there had just been an accident when a helicopter, a Jet Ranger, had collided with over head power lines killing both the pilot and the passenger. Proby jumped off the bed, pulled on his coat and said to me: 'Time to go to the studio John'. He gave me a really weird look as if he had been waiting for something to happen and now it had.

That incident really shook me up as I recalled that before we had set off the day before Proby had demanded that he needed a helicopter or he would not go. Now there had been a helicopter crash. What was also strange was the name of the helicopter it was a Jet Ranger and the collision had been with power lines. In 1960 when PJ Proby was signed to EMI in Hollywood USA his stage name was Jet Powers.

So far, in my quest to resurrect the faded career of sixties pop singer PJ Proby I had achieved a great deal with radio, press and television featuring what I termed 'The Greatest Comeback In The History Of Rock 'N' Roll'. The man still had his voice, he certainly could sing. His name was well known, albeit for many of the wrong reasons, such as ripping his pants on stage and getting banned in 1965 from all TV performances etc. Now, following the release of the CD Album 'THANKS' with PJ Proby in all the record shops in Europe the man himself began to display the kind of prima-donna behaviour for which he was infamous. He was also hitting the booze big time. I had signed him for a summer season to a Blackpool hotel called The Landsdowne and persuaded the owner to provide PJP with a house to live in during the term of the contract (PJP wrecked the place). The man lent Proby a Rolls Royce with a Mr. T. lookalike minder to drive him around and suddenly Jim Proby thought he was back in the major league. So sure of himself was PJP that he decided he no longer needed my help and instructed lawyers to issue proceedings against me to halt the sale and distribution of the recordings I had made and paid him for. When he told me what he had done, in the front lounge of my home, I physically assisted him out of the front door via a direct encounter with the wall. That was the last time we met, no wonder really!

At this time there began a new phase of my life. A long time friend (now sadly deceased) Pete Lally, had been on holiday recently to Gambia where, he told me, he had been into the jungle on a safari trip. He said that during this he had been into a tribal village where a witch-doctor had given him a message. Pete told me that this little old man in a mud hut, somewhere in a remote part of Gambia had told him that in England there lived a man that he knew named John, this man had a leg missing and the world of spirit had a serious message for him. Pete was told he must go and see John when he returned to the UK and advise him that the time was Now, the spirits needed him to consult with them. Pete Lally was the Managing Director of a contract flooring company, he was not at all familiar with mediums or psychics so when he came back from Gambia and told me this he did so with some degree of reluctance. I recall well how nervous Pete looked in telling me this weird story, but he said the witch-doctor was adamant that I had to consult with the spirit world.

It was shortly after the visit to me by Pete Lally that the Bolton born psychic-medium James Byrne came to my home and said that he had been directed by spirits to see me. James explained that he was a professional psychic and that his guides had sent him to see me as they had told him that John was to become his personal manager and take the message of life after death to the world. Within just a few months of meeting James he and I were on Lancashire's biggest independent radio station Red Rose in Preston and broadcasting what was promoted as the first fully audience interactive psychic 'phone in programme. At the time this was big news and made many of the national papers including a feature in 'The Sun'. Outside the radio studios there was a group of 'Born Again' Christians demonstrating against us. The Lancashire Evening Post ran the front page headline 'Devil Whorshipper Comes To Town'. At the theatres I promoted James Byrne at we experienced virtual attacks by banner waving Pentacostal religious fanatics who seemed determined to halt our presentations. Using my experience in promoting PJ Proby I quickly put this negative aspect to good use and sent all the press cuttings and a synopsis for a book to probably the biggest publishing house in the UK: HarperCollins.

In September of 1992 James Byrne was starring at The London Palladium. His biography 'The Psychic World Of James Byrne' had been co-written with me and published by HarperCollins. The James Whale Radio Show on National ITV featured myself and James Byrne conducting a live 'Psychic-Experiment' in which James transmitted his incredible paranormal powers over the air and viewers tuned in to these reporting their experiences. It was an incredible success and suddenly James Byrne was on his way to becoming the very best known psychic-medium in the UK.

In 1996 my literary agent Rosemary Bromley, the former representative of the late celebrity TV cook Mrs. Fanny

Craddock, arranged a commission for me with the London publishing house Bloomsbury Books. At their offices I met with Mr. Barry Cunningham, (famous for commissioning J K Rowling) the managing director, he explained the ethos of Bloomsbury advising that I would be working with an eminent Cambridge University Literature expert editor called Ingrid-von-Essen. I was then introduced to Ingrid who gently but very firmly explained that in the event that she considered my work to fall below the required standard then she would, without hesitation, reject it. The book I was commissioned to write was titled 'Psychic Pets'. It went on to be a major international bestseller and was featured by The Sunday Times Children's Book Club. It was also published in the USA by 'Beyond Words' and subsequently by 'Scholastic' the biggest publishers in the world. It took me onto the then highly popular TV show 'This Morning with Richard and Judy' and beyond to the world stage where Disney Corporation flew me to Florida to appear with their pet experts on 'The Animal Planet' channel. In New York USA I was flown in by FOX TV and featured on a special news feature with a live 'phone in link all across America. In the UK I was on BBC Radio 2, even on the 'Today' radio programme on BBC Radio 4 at 08:20 immediately before the prime minister. This was a simply incredible period of my life and all through it I was promoting the message that life was eternal and death but an illusion. Though I was doing it in a most unconventional and, I now believe, entertaining way, making it an acceptable message not at all spooky.

It was around this time, 1997, that the Liverpool born psychic Derek Acorah approached me asking if I would consider managing his career. He was then working from a one room rented office on Paradise Street in Liverpool city centre and had done no serious stage work, never been on the TV or radio. Within a period of months I had Derek on Red Rose Radio and had agreed terms with Granada TV for him to appear on the Granada Breeze channel as a stand up psychic performer. By 1999 I had Derek on stage and TV in Hollywood USA where I had done a deal with the director of the International Society for Paranormal Research to feature

Derek as one of their investigators. I also scripted an outline for Psychic Investigation film and arranged for Derek along with ISPR to film at the supposedly haunted museum Belgrave Hall in Leicestershire. In September of 1999 Piatkus Books Ltd. published 'The Psychic World Of Derek Acorah' co-written by me and that became a massive bestseller helping to push forward the career of Derek Acorah. Whatever one may say about Acorah, and I am a critic of some of the nonsense, he is funny.

Over thirty years have passed since I was amputated and underwent the near death experience in which I was interviewed by angels in the airport lounge that exists between this world and the next. I had been told then that the angels were to send me on a mission, though at the time they did not explain exactly what this would entail. I now know what that mission is. I have, since first encountering PJ Proby in the year 1990, gone on to promote the popularity of psychic studies. Any observer of the way the media have treated the paranormal and especially the truth of eternal life will have noted that during the past twenty or so years the subject has become more and more acceptable. I sincerely believe that in some small way my work has helped to do this. It may not yet be mission accomplished but I have tried and have dared to dream.

CHAPTER FIFTY THREE

O.B.E. OUT OF BODY EXPERIENCES

An Out Of Body Experience or OBE can be defined as an experience in which a person seems to perceive the world from a location outside the physical body. These experiences are often spontaneous and sometimes linked to shock. There was a famous cartoonist, whose name I will not disclose, in a bank in France when an armed robbery took place. The robbers opened fire shooting a shotgun into the ceiling and he, thinking he had sustained a hit, fell down and collapsed. During this period of unconsciousness the man found himself outside his body and in an airport lounge where he was surrounded by people that he did not know. He could see airplanes outside the lounge and noted that among the strangers around him was a lady dressed as a Nun. When he woke only moments had passed and he was alive and in the bank, unhurt and the robbers were exiting with their haul.

I myself have had numerous OBEs and one that was similar to the airport lounge experience. Another time I was seriously ill and found myself flying around the skies with a voice asking me where I wanted to go. After a brief visit to the Taj Mahal and the Eiffel Tower I decided to go see my beloved grandparents at their home in Foulridge, near Colne in Lancashire UK. But I never made it. I came to earth some distance away and was met by the most beautiful lady dressed all in shimmering white. She told me I now had a choice, to continue on and go to my grandparents home or return to my body. As she said this she held out her hand and a feeling of absolute peace and love flooded through me. I replied that I had better return to my body and as I held her hand I was instantly transported back to my 18 year old form and my fever had passed.

My friend Jeff from the Lancashire town of Leigh told me how he fell asleep in a chair in his lounge and, as he snoozed, discovered that he was walking down the hallway of his house. Suddenly he realized that he was not in his body and a terrible fear gripped him that he had in fact died and was now a ghost. At the moment, as he thought those thoughts, he woke with a start and found himself back within his physical form. Jeff told me that he had never really believed that Out Of Body Experiences were true before but that had changed his mind.

On the internet world-wide-web is a brilliant website called: paranormal.about.com and there you will find many first person accounts of paranormal experiences. Whilst researching this article I found this story by a lady called Nancy who tells of her own OBE:

In 1970 my son was about 4 years old. He had a habit of sleepwalking during the night. Our bedrooms were on the second floor and my son's bedroom was right next to the railing that led downstairs. He would usually sleepwalk early in the evening and my husband would put him over his shoulder and take him back upstairs and tuck him in. Our bedroom was just down the hallway.

One night I got up very fast and I rushed into my son's bedroom because I thought I heard him getting up and possibly going for a walk down the stairs. I was afraid he would trip and fall. I rushed into his room and I stood by his bed and I found that he was all tucked in. I wondered why I got up so fast. As I stood there, I looked down at myself and I found that all of me was a light gray mist! Even my night clothes were all gray. I was totally confused because this situation had never happened to me before. Then I thought that I had better get out to the hallway and as soon as I thought about doing that, my light gray body floated to the doorway. As I floated to the door, I could see my gray body, but I didn't seem to have any feet. As I stood there, I had a feeling that I could have gone through the wall to the right and have gone sight-seeing, or I could have made a turn to the left to go down the hallway where our bedroom was. I looked to my left and I could see my bedroom and there I was sitting up in bed with my head against the back of the bed. I was not moving at all.

At that point, I realized that my soul was not in my heavy body that was sitting up in bed. It was with me in my light gray misty body standing in the hallway. I knew my gray soul had to get back into my body, but I didn't know how I was going to do that. The next thing I did was that I floated down the hallway and I stood right next to the body that was sitting up in bed. The bottom of my night clothes and area where my feet would have been, came up and went into the top of the head of the body that was sitting up in bed. At that point, I realized that I was one person... body and soul. (paranormal.about.com)

I have myself recently experienced being out of my body. Myself and my wife Mary were on holiday in Spain and asleep in a hotel bedroom. It would be perhaps 2am when I opened my eyes to see that my wife's astral body was floating above her physical form alongside my own. I experienced an intense sense of absolute delight and exhilaration; I was free from that heavy body and could fly. Turning to my wife I tried to persuade her in her astral body to join me and escape. I pleaded with her to fly away with me but as soon as she realized that she was not in her body she shook her head and vanished. Then we both woke at once and whilst I had perfect recall she said only that she had experienced a very strange dream in which she had been floating. The question is, had she agreed to join me on my astral adventure would we have ever woken again in this material world?

THE SIXTH SENSE

The idea of watching a Bruce Willis movie that doesn't involve him saving the world wearing a dirty vest seems almost a contradiction in the terms of reference associated with this actor. Films such as 'Armageddon' and 'Die Hard' have carved a reputation for him as the almost stereotypical tough guy cast in the same mold as earlier screen heroes such as John Wayne and Clint Eastwood. However, in the film 'The Sixth Sense' Bruce Willis is both sensitive and compulsively convincing as the child psychologist with a mission. The story involves a young boy who sees spirits and can converse with them. Bruce Willis's character is called in to psychoanalyse the child when the boy's paranormal gifts extend to stigmatic lesions and poltergeist like phenomena occurs around him. The medical practitioners initially believe that the boy is being injured by his single parent mother, whilst the child himself is too afraid to discuss the truth of his psychic powers. The story is surely familiar to a number of readers of this journal, many mediums have had early encounters with the spirit world as children. No matter if you have had such experiences or have not, you simply must see this film.

There is a problem that psychic children face in trying to tell people that they can 'see' spirits and talk with them. Some are lucky enough to be raised by aware parents who know that there is another world that exists alongside the physical land in which we as incarnate beings live. Others are less fortunate and receive dire warnings that they are evil and must never talk about 'ghosts' as they are the devil in disguise trying to trick them into losing their immortal souls. Such medieval nonsense is little better than telling children that the 'Bogey Man' will get them if they are naughty. As adults we owe a duty of care to our children and responding to their honest accounts of interactions with spirits by issuing threats and intimidation is to fail in that duty.

As a child I myself saw visions of another world, a place where pyramids were being built in a far away land. To me, as a boy of five or six years of age, these visions were fantastic and exciting. To my parents they were the ramblings of a silly little boy who must never speak of such things. My mother and father were not being cruel, nor were they thoughtless in their actions in denying my truth, they simply did not know. Perhaps the religious beliefs of my parents coloured their perception of my strange stories of a country I visited from the twilight world of my bedroom. I soon learnt that telling people that there was a wonderful place far away that I went to through the wallpaper on my wall was not acceptable. In fear of being ridiculed, or worse, I ceased to speak of my visions and, in time, they vanished.

The Fleetwood based medium Margaret Eccles told me of her first encounter with the spirit world. She was just a child and had been left to care for her baby sister whilst their mother made the evening meal. As Margaret crayoned a picture in her colouring book her sister, who had been asleep on the couch, got up, tripped and fell into the coal fire, she was burnt to death. The next night, as young Margaret lay in bed crying, her sister's spirit returned to comfort her and say she was alive and well in the next world. When she told her mother the good news Margaret received a terrible shock, she was branded a liar and sent to stay with grandmother. The traumatic effect that the rejection of her truth had on young Margaret has never left her. To this day she can clearly recall the awful feeling of sadness that she experienced as her own mother denied the reality of her daughter's return.

There is a famous book on the subject of childhood mediumship, 'The Boy Who Saw True' is the published diary of a young man who had the ability to see and talk to both spirits and elemental beings, such as gnomes and fairies. In this book the boy is befriended by his private tutor, who listens to him and believes what the child tells him. Throughout the book there is an unwritten feeling that without the understanding and encouragement of the child's adult friend the sixth sense that the boy had would have been denied and would subsequently have vanished.

The well known author and broadcaster; Joe Cooper of Leeds, wrote the highly readable and erudite examination of two young cousins that had psychic powers. In his book 'The Case of the Cottingley Fairies' published by Simon & Schuster, Joe explores the possibility that whilst most of the photographs of fairy people taken by the two girls, Elsie and Frances, were fakes, there may well have been some truth in their claims. Joe Cooper is not a man to be fooled easily, his personal academic standing is beyond doubt and he is quite sure that the two girls did see fairies in Cottingley glen. Their attempts to prove the existence of these elemental beings to doubting adults led them to manufacture evidence. Joe Cooper was the man that solved the case of the Cottingley fairies, which he did by interviewing the two cousins and securing a confession. However, right to the last both Frances and Elsie insisted that there were fairies in Cottingley Glen. Joe's book is still available and is good evidence that there exists reasonable doubt that despite everything Elsie Wright and Frances Griffiths were, as children, gifted with a sixth sense. Which brings me back to the Bruce Willis film.

As adults we are immersed in the detail of living in this martial and increasingly materialistic world. So many of us forget that to be alive in a physical body is a gift to cherish. We are captives of the everyday problems of life in the age of high tech society, with its VCR remote controls, Digital TV, washing machines that require programming, instead of dolly tubs that required muscles, the technology traps us. With all the paraphernalia that goes with Year 2,000 living, we have little time for the innocence of our childhood. Often we block out the psychic messages that surrounded us in our youth. Shades of the prison house of materialism lock us into a tangible world of hard facts and scientific 'certainty'. Not so the children, they are open to use their psychic channels, their sixth sense, until we, with our authority and rules, close them down and turn them into 21st century technologically correct people, people who do not see spirits.

At the risk of repeating myself let me be clear, you must go and see 'The Sixth Sense' it is a wonderfully evocative and sensitive film that will, I believe, bring the joy of the truth of eternal life to countless millions of people. It is a film, a work of fiction, but it has within it that magical element that transcends the medium, bringing with it that unmistakable essence of truth. There is no death, only eternal and sometimes glorious life. Go and see 'The Sixth Sense' I promise you it will reinforce your beliefs not only in life after physical death but in the magic of cinema as a true work of art.

CHAPTER FIFTY FOUR

READ HOW WE DIED

Andrea was just a girl of 13 years when she had her first Psychic Experience. She recalls quite clearly that day, in the fishing port of Hull, Yorkshire. Whilst playing with some friends one asked her an innocent question about ghosts, instantly she replied 'we all exist forever in a parallel universe'. Astonished her friends asked what she was talking about, Andrea did not know.

For the moment she had felt as though some unseen being was speaking through her, using her vocal chords to answer her friends question about spirits and spooks. It felt, she remembers, as though she had been overshadowed by another presence. It certainly baffled her childhood pals who hadn't got a clue what a parallel universe might be

It was not until Andrea reached her late thirties that she would again encounter the paranormal. Her life had been one of reasonable materialistic success, she had run shops, owned a supermarket and had lived life to the full. Her leisure time was often taken up with playing Bridge, which she did to competition standard. Then she suffered a serious fall and damaged her sciatic nerve. For six months she was unable to walk and was, effectively, house bound. During her convalescence Andrea, for some reason unknown to herself, decided to read extensively about reincarnation and the spirit world. These were not subjects she would normally entertain. Her usual reading being confined to trade journals with the odd woman's magazine now and then. Quite why she decided to research the esoteric field of psychic matters at that point in her life, was outside her comprehension. But there is always a reason for everything, Andrea read many books and her interest developed.

There is a Spiritualist Church in Hull, on John Street. When Andrea was recovered from her fall she decided to go there and see if she could learn more about the subject she had been reading of. Following this, which was Andrea's first close encounter with Spiritualism, she went on to a The Psychic Centre in Hull where she witnessed a demonstration of trance mediumship by a gentleman called Frank Grieveson. That experience was destined to change her life. Her mind was opened to the reality of life beyond this earthly plane, she saw Mr Grieveson change from being a Yorkshire man talking with a pronounced accent to being the very likeness of an Oxford don who introduced himself as Peter Strickland.

Time passed and Andrea became closely involved in the development circle, she met Frank's son Alan there and eventually they were married. Together they continued to progress the power of their psychic gifts. Alan developed the same trance mediumship that Andrea had first seen demonstrated by his father Frank. Then Andrea began to 'see' clairvoyantly the aura of those around her, she could sense, intuitively, if something was wrong. Through Alan's trance mediumship came advice from the spirit of an old American Indian. This spirit taught Andrea how to read stones and clairvoyantly see other peoples past lives. Her psychic/spiritual gifts were really beginning to develop to the point where they could be used to benefit others.

It was during a period of trance mediumship, given by her husband Alan, that Andrea received a message from the spirit world telling her that she had to write. The discarnate spirit of Professor Strickland spoke through Alan Grieveson and said 'Will you write?' Andrea was unsure what was really meant by this but took up a pen and sat before a bundle of plain paper expecting she knew not what. She just felt that someone, some discarnate entity, wanted to write through her. She was more than a little uncertain but allowed it to happen. As she waited, expectantly, a voice came into her mind telling her about life in the next world. Andrea wrote down that which she was hearing and it made sense. It was rather like receiving dictation from an unseen executive, Andrea just transcribed the words she heard. Gradually the pages mounted into quite a collection of closely related accounts of how various spirits had found themselves in the next world. There were accident victims who told of the disbelief they felt at finding themselves outside their physical bodies, philanderers whose spirit lives were an impoverished isolated torment. One after another spirit after spirit came to speak to Andrea, they all had their own story to tell.

After many months of writing Andrea found she had amassed a large number of individual accounts given to her by the spirit people. It was then that Andrea received a message for herself, she was told to put her written works together and create a book 'Read How We Died'. This book was to enlighten the people of this earth and explain to them the many different experiences that await beyond the veil of physical death. Today Andrea Grieveson has these accounts published in a very readable book; 'Read How We Died' (Con-Psy Publications). She continues in her spiritual work helping and guiding others who seek to know just what lies beyond this often difficult world we live in. Andrea now lives in Ruabon, near Wrexham in North Wales where she continues to receive dictation from the spirit world .

Ann Heath's first memory of communication from the Spirit world was when she saw her Guardian Angel standing over her as she played children's games in her bedroom. "He was", she says, "as tall as the ceiling and dressed in a brilliant white robe. He never spoke, but his smile was so comforting and peaceful. I knew he was my Guardian Angel and watching over me. As a child of three, Ann attended the funeral of her younger sister, Patricia, who had passed with a childhood illness. However, there was no sense of loss for Ann. While she stood at the graveside, her sister was with her in Spirit, telling her how happy life was in the Spirit World and about her new Spirit friends. When Ann told her parents about this, they were upset and thought she was lying to them. As fundamentalist Christians, it was their belief that Patricia was now in "heaven in the arms of the Lord", and no further contact with her was possible.

Ann learned at an early age to say nothing about her Spirit friends who came to play with her. As she was going to sleep at night, they showed her visions of the past, ancient cities, temples and people, as well as worlds and dimensions not of Earth. To Ann it was like having a TV screen inside her head and history lessons not in books. During her school years, Ann was exposed to different religions and she compared them with what her Spirit Guides were teaching and showing her psychically. She felt sorrow for all the people who feared death because they believed in a blazing hell and eternal damnation. Her Spirit Guides taught her to have compassion for those whose spiritual world was so bleak and without the knowledge or experience of Spirit communication and vision. When she asked questions of the priests and ministers of the various churches, they either didn't know the answers or told her she must have blind faith in what they taught. She could not accept those man made limitations because she knew they denied her access to God, and her Spirit Band of Teachers and Friends.

Ann's Spirit Teachers guided her to books she needed to implement her spiritual understanding. They taught her about the spiritual and universal laws, such as: Life is eternal, forms change. Also: Life, in all its forms, is conscious. The Universe, as a physical manifestation from the Mind of God, is alive, aware and infinitely creative. It is Spiritual Evolution which impels us to discover our spiritual heritage as Beings of Unlimited Light, Love, and Beauty. As Descartes said, "I think, therefore I AM! Her childhood and adolescence was spent on a solitary spiritual path, depending on her Spirit Teachers for guidance.

The following years of marriage, family and work in the mundane world challenged her to use the truths which Spirit had taught her. She knew and was comforted that her Spirit Guides were always near to assist as she met the challenges of family and work. But she knew this was a time in which she had to test herself, use the teachings of her Spirit Guides, and depend on The Light within herself for her strength. Years passed. A marriage ended in divorce, her children grew into their own lives and Ann continued her studies at ever higher levels. Her spiritual and psychic abilities increased. One evening as she prepared for sleep, her Spirit Teacher appeared beside her bed and told her, "It is time." She was filled with joy because she knew it was time for her to begin the spiritual work she had come to do.

In time Ann was ordained as a Spiritualist minister and remarried, a wonderful pastor of a Spiritualist Church. Together they worked to teach others how to see and hear their own Spirit Band of Teachers, Guides, Angels, and Friends. By 1990, Ann had trained several students and ordained them as Spiritualist ministers, encouraging them to continue her work. For Ann it was time for her to return to work in the mundane world, to interact with people who did not share her spiritual opinions and gifts, learning more and sharing her knowledge, quite subtly, in a different setting.

In 1995, her Spirit Teacher said it was time for her to return to her spiritual work but in a different way. She was told to take up a pencil and paper. Her Teacher's firm but gentle voice said, "Relax, let me use your hand and we will draw a picture for you". Then a the Spirit Artist drew a portrait of Ann's Guardian Angel. Ann knew that the artistic ability exhibited was far beyond her own skills. Ann's new gift developed quickly as her Spirit Friends guided her to various places where she was enthusiastically accepted as "The Angel Lady" who drew people's Angels. One client was given a detailed drawing of a young woman in spirit who said she was the client's Guardian Angel and whom the client had never seen. The client took the portrait home to show her husband, who exclaimed, "That's my sister! She died before I met and married you!" Another wonderful proof of Spirit communication and that our loved ones in Spirit stay close to us to assist and protect us. Today Ann's work as "The Angel Artist" and a travelling Spiritualist minister, brings comfort and hope to many people. Her "Angel Portraits", as she calls them, seem to emit light and a beautiful spiritual vibration, showing that they are, indeed, gifts of love from the world of Spirit. Ann gives thanks daily to her Spirit Band of Teachers, Guides and Angels. She thanks them for their loving help as she works to increase God's Light and Divine Love on Earth and in the Universe.

CHAPTER FIFTY FIVE

CATHRINE COOKSON'S PHILOSOPHY

Catherine Cookson was one of the most prolific and best loved authors of the 20th century. Born into abject poverty in the Tyne and Wear area she was an illegitimate child who first thought her mother was her older sister. The early years of her life are recounted by her in the book 'Our Kate'. For those who believe that life is tough today this is required reading. Catherine's mother Kate worked sixteen hours a day caring for her own grandparents and the lodgers they took in to make ends meet. As a girl Catherine experienced actual deprivation of the kind that is almost unthinkable today. I refer to a lack of food, overcrowded housing, no internal sanitation and the ever present threat of 'The Workhouse' In this dawn of the 21st century deprivation is perhaps perceived as not having a colour TV set and a VCR. Gone are the days of people marching to London because their families were starving for want of food. But the vast improvements in our physical comforts have not been matched by any discernible increase in spirituality, quite the reverse in fact.

During the dark days of the depression in the 1930's, when Catherine Cookson was a young woman struggling to survive in the back street overcrowded houses of the North East of England, street crime (mugging) and burglary were comparatively rare. As I write the current crime figures for the UK show incidents of robbery and violence up 21%. I myself can clearly recall that my grandparents left the front door to their house open for friends to just walk in. They had no fear that some thug would enter their home and rob them. They lived within a community that may have been relatively poor by the standards of today but to them it seemed safe. The people of the fifteen streets of Foulridge, near Colne in Lancashire where I was born enjoyed in the 1940's and 50's, the last decades of decency. Since then the spiritual heart of our country has been eaten away, replaced by an avaricious consumer society where ownership of material goods and property is valued and compassion devalued.

In 1990 Catherine Cookson published a collection of poetry, prose and pictures that she said were intended to be understood by 'the people'. In this book titled 'Let Me Make Myself Plain' she sets out a simple view on the meaning of life gained from her hard experiences: 'All the while I was learning something, a philosophy you could say. I was learning that philosophy isn't the prerogative of the academic, the intellectual, all those supposedly knowledgeable people who blind you with the science of the mind. Philosophy is, as I saw it then and still do, the essence of the thinking of every ordinary man and woman. It is the sum total of what they have drained out of their living whether through sorrow or joy, satisfaction or frustration. I have come to my own particular philosophy by being educated in a hard school where lessons of poverty, shame, inferiority, fear and ill-health were hard to learn'.

Here are some examples of Catherine Cookson's poetic philosophy: On Friendship: 'Give me your hand to help me on my way/Give me your hand to get me through this day/Give me your hand to face up to life/Give me your hand to clasp in the night/When dreams bring fears more real than day/Give me your hand to let me know I am not alone/Don't wait for an anniversary to tell me that you care/Without your hand now, when that comes I may not be there.' In that verse of the poem Catherine sets out what she knows a true friend would do, give a hand in a time of need. Friendship is about that, it is about helping and supporting those that we call friend.

On Strife: 'Lord, beckon me to joy/My mind is weary/My body sick/Who can I employ/To ease my spirit/And lift my heart. And give me strength/To combat this strife/And the energy/To work at life/Lord, beckon me to joy. In those two verses Catherine Cookson recognises that there is a higher power that can, in conjunction with personal effort, help one to succeed in this work of life. She is saying, do not despair we are all at some time in our earthly existence in need of help and it will be there. All we have to do is believe and be the best that we can possibly be.

On Death: 'The greatest mystery in life is death/The greatest fear of life is death/The greatest sorrow in life is death/The greatest probe in life is for death....Again, why are we born/If not to learn how to die?' Catherine Cookson knew that the one thing that concerns all people above everything else is the mystery of death. Yet there is no mystery, we will all die. What most fear is dying alone, yet there can be no other way to die, we are all destined to make the ultimate transition between physical life within a corporeal body and the etheric realms where our soul lives on eternally. Here we may shed tears but in time our sorrows will melt into infinite understanding as the glory that is the Truth opens before our everlasting eyes.

We in the UK live today lives free of the threat of physical starvation. We have proper sanitation, a free health service, free schools and support from the welfare state should we require it. In the early years of Cathrine Cookson's life those conditions that we take as a basic right were restricted to the wealthy. Yet crime and violence have not decreased with the virtual extinction of real need. They have instead exploded into a massive problem that is dividing our society, terrorising our old people and degrading the fabric of daily life.

If those that offend against society, the thugs, street muggers, thieves, con-men, louts and bully boys only realised that they are inflicting damage upon their immortal souls by their actions they would perhaps be reluctant to proceed. The problem is that their values are confused by the immoral media, take a look at Channel 4 on a Thursday night after 10 p.m. Then the maze of consumer goods available in the shops is just inviting avarice. So many people seem locked into a debased value system that places material possessions above the spiritual. In the early days of Catherine Cookson there were no such things as DVD players, surround sound TV and the designer drug of choice would be Newcastle Brown Ale. Of course there was violence then, but not the mindless yob culture that seems almost the norm today. Is it drugs? Is it greed? It certainly is not need, at least not the real need experienced by 'Our Kate' and the millions of others like her that struggled through, working at life and not succumbing to the depraved behaviour so prevalent today. The solution is, I believe, spiritual truth. We need people, all people, to understand that life is not about materialism but about developing our eternal souls through meaningful experiences here on earth. We could all learn a great deal from the simple philosophy of Catherine Cookson.

'Let Me Make Myself Plain' By Catherine Cookson (Corgi Books) ISBN0552134074

CHAPTER FIFTY SIX

THE TEN COMMANDMENTS TODAY

In the news as I write is an account of a businessman in Essex who discovered one of his employees had stolen £845 from the company accounts by falsely issuing a cheque payable to himself. The businessman was infuriated and wrote out a sign saying I AM A THIEF I STOLE £845 AND AM ON MY WAY TO THE POLICE STATION. He then required the employee to wear this as he called the police. The end result was that the man who stole the money and admitted that he had done so was given a caution by the police and the employer, whose company had already lost £845, was sued by the thief resulting in damages and costs amounting to £13,000.00p The 8th of the Ten Commandments that were, according to Exodus Ch.20 handed down by God to Moses, is: You shall not steal. The result of doing so today is being told what a very naughty person one is and advised not to do it again. Then demand damges from the person or persons that apprehended you and grab some more money. That should do the trick eh! But let's not get ahead of ourselves, the 1st of the Ten Commandments is: You shall have no other gods before me. According to the aforementioned text in Exodus the brother of Moses, Aaron, melted down all the gold from the holy temple and created a Golden Calf that the people all worshipped whilst Moses was away up a mountain in Egypt receiving carved stone tablets. They were, it seems, having quite a wild time, dancing, drinking and doing what comes naturally until the Big Ten was presented by Moses who was not at all amused by the shiny calf and smashed said stone tablets to pieces, destroyed the golden idol and ordered the revellers to cease and desist having fun immediately. Today we are surrounded by glittering idols and the very idea of devoting ones life to the worship of God is perhaps considered unusual. I mean give today's youth the choice between a fifty inch flat screen HD TV with X-Box attached and some 18 Rated gut-blaster interactive internet linked serial killer game or three Hymns and a lecture about the Sermon on the Mount what chance does Jesus really have? Spiritualists do not, I feel, specifically subscribe to Christian beliefs but many, like myself, will have been raised in that gentle religious tradition. This being Great Britain we do have an established church headed by The Monarch. Most of us would, I feel, believe that the basic principles of Christianity, love thy neighbour, do unto others and you would have done unto you etc. are worthy. But as for abiding by the Ten Commandments, it just is not happening at all. I believe that this early 21st century society is in fact rapidly approaching a 180 degree about turn around. Here are some examples. (I have simplified the original text).

1.   **No other gods: Hollywood, TV, the mass media create instant idols. Ask any young adult who Susan Boyle is they will most likely know. Ask them the name of the prophet that brought the ten commandments to the people and you will get a blank stare.**

2.   Create no images: Even the Christians disobey this commandment, just pop into a Catholic church and look around at the statues. Look out your front window some sunny Sunday morning see the true believers cleaning their cars. All around us we have our idols, be they Jaguar E-Types or Statues.

3.   Do not take the name of God in vain: Profanity and abuse using all available expletives are bombarding us daily from TV programmes such as the excremental Mock The Week to family soap-operas such as Eastenders.

4.   Keep the Sabbath day Holy: Sunday trading now allows virtually all shops, supermarkets etc. to open. It is gone, the Sabbath, it's just another working day in effect, unless you are a banker then its clap hands Charlie and dip your bread.

5.   Honor your father and mother: In this post-industrial society we have seen the breakdown of the extended family. Support systems, children caring for aged parents, grandparents living in the same home, all that is of

yesterday as the Me Me Me generation expects the Nanny State to look after the aged.

6.   You shall not kill: Believe me if you have never seen an X-Box or Play-Station battle game then you have no idea how at odds that commandment is with such programmes that are in effect teaching our children that murder and killing are good and the way to win.

7.   You shall not commit adultery: Whilst many still do hold to this basic nuclear family principle a great deal more do not. On television we can see programmes that appear to actively encourage infidelity with titles such as Wife Swop. Log on to the internet and within a short space of time you will soon discover exactly how far the idea of fidelity has travelled. Search MILF and stand by to be astounded.

8.   You shall not steal: See para 1. above. Theft is still a crime but the punishments are such as to make it appear almost socially acceptable. If young, a thief may get an ASBO and become a local celebrity. Seriously.

9.   You shall not bear false witness: Basically lying on oath in court is perjury and one can get some serious jail time, as Lord Archer found out. But only if you are caught bang to rights.

10.   You shall not covert your neighbour's property: Margaret Thatcher ended all that with her Greed is Good policy as the era of the Yuppie was born in the early 1980s. Now it is all overtaking the Jones[1] forget just keeping up.

Spiritually and morally this country is fast becoming bankrupt. Just look around and like Moses on his return from the mountain you will see the images of today's idols: Aston-Martin cars, Ant & Dec, Rappers spouting filth, Simon Cowell Spice-Girl/Take-That wannabes and endless reality TV chancers. Now we have David Cameron's Big Society idea, this is totally and absolutely impossible as long as we have virtual ghettos divided on Race, Religion and Riches all operating selfishly in their own interests. I can see we are heading back to where it all began, in Egypt with a modern day Moses bringing some sense to the nonsense of today.

CHAPTER FIFTY SEVEN

THE GHOSTS OF STRANGEWAYS JAIL

I first entered Strangeways Jail in January 1975 when I was accepted by the Home Office as a trainee Prison Officer. During my first few days there I was shown around the old prison which was officially opened on the 25th June 1868. The name derives from the area upon which the jail was constructed, this being formally Strangeways parks and gardens. It was, until the abolition of capital punishment, used as a place of execution and one hundred convicted inmates were hanged there. The execution unit was still standing in 1975, at the end of 'B' wing and the condemned cell is located on 'B1 Landing' At the time appointed for the prisoner to be hung by the neck until dead, the hangman would attend with his assistant. The prisoner's hands were then securely fastened behind his back and he was led from that very cell to the gallows situated just a few yards away through a doorway at the end of B1 Landing. There the hangman, with gloved hands, placed a black cloth hood over the doomed man's head, quickly followed by the noose and he was hanged until dead. Death came to all the hangman's victims instantly.

Using the terrible tricks of his trade he knew how to snap the necks of those sentenced to die. As the rope gripped their throat there was no long lingering choke, just a spine breaking wrench as the hangman's knot twisted their necks violently to the left. It was a matter of pride to the Strangeways' hangman that his customers never complained. I clearly recall standing outside the door and feeling a distinct sense of unease. There was then and likely still is today a cold atmosphere around that spot and many say that it is haunted.

There is, according to accounts by long serving staff, a ghost associated with the condemned cell and the execution chamber. Staff on night duty have reported seeing a mysterious man in a dark suit carrying a small briefcase. He is always seen walking along 'B' wing from just outside the condemned cell towards the central control area. When they try to follow this dark suited man he vanishes just before the old iron staircase leading up to the main office. Some say that this is the ghost of the former hangman John Ellis who officiated at the hanging of many unfortunates during the 1920s and committed suicide in 1932.

The most probable explanation for this recurring vision of the past is atmospheric reproduction of an incident long past as though the walls themselves had recorded the incident and replay this whenever the conditions are right. This may be air temperature and humidity combining to trigger the repeating vision. So the ghost is not a ghost at all just a form of natural video recording that creates the image seen by staff. However, not all the ghosts of Strangeways are atmospheric recordings, there is one that actually interacts with staff and inmates. I have personally encountered this very unsettling entity.

There was, in the 1950s, at Strangeways a women's prison located within the twelve foot high boundary walls but in a separate series of wings. When I was serving as a Hospital Officer there in 1981 'I' Wing was a clinic and small unit for the treatment of young male offenders. The landing known as 'I 2' was used to hold inmates receiving clinical intervention, sometimes with psychotropic drugs. In the 1950s it was used to hold female prisoners awaiting execution and one such former occupant was the infamous Blackpool Poison killer Mrs. Merrifiled. Her spirit is still there and I, like many others, have seen it walking along 'I 2' landing then vanishing into what was long ago the condemned cell.

46 year old Louisa May Merrifield had been convicted of poisoning Mrs. Sarah Ricketts. Sarah Ricketts was a 79 year old, bedridden widow who lived in Blackpool. She had hired Louisa and her husband Alfred to look after her in March 1953 and soon made a new will leaving her bungalow to Louisa. Mrs. Ricketts had some rather strange dietary habits. Apparently, she was very fond of very sweet jams which she ate directly from the jar by the spoonful, washed down with rum or a bottle

of stout. Louisa, having got the will made in her favour, capitalised on these peculiar habits by adding Rodine, a phosphorus based rat poison, to the jam. Mrs. Ricketts' death was considered suspicious and so a post-mortem was carried out which quickly revealed the presence of the poison. A local chemists had recorded the sale of the Rodine to Louisa, but the police could not find the poison container which she had purchased, but felt that they had enough circumstantial evidence to charge both her and Alfred. She had talked openly of inheriting the bungalow and this also threw suspicion on her. The pair came to trial at Manchester Assizes on the 20th of July 1953. Alfred was acquitted, there being no real evidence that he was part of the plot, but Louisa was found guilty. She was duly hanged by Albert Pierrepoint on the morning of Friday, the 18th of September 1953.

The spirit I saw on 'I 2' landing at Strangeways Jail was short and wearing dark clothing it appeared semi-materialised, that is I did not mistake this for an incarnate human being, I immediately knew that this was a ghost. The vision lasted no more than five seconds or so as the very dark and shadowy image, perhaps no more than five foot in height, drifted past me creating a noticeable drop in temperature. Then the shape moved slowly to the closed door of a cell on 'I 2' landing and disappeared. When I opened the cell door to see how the young inmate within was he appeared even more disturbed than he had been when I had last attended to administer his medication. I will not forget his words to me 'who's that woman Boss?' he said 'she just walked in before you pointed at me and vanished'. When I later mentioned this to my more senior colleagues they laughed and one said 'that's old Mrs. Merrifield, she's been haunting this place since they hanged her years ago'.

The sightings of Mrs Merrifield's ghost seemed to increase around the early 1980s with a number of inmates of 'I Wing' telling me and other staff that they had seen a short woman dressed all in black walking about the landing. Some said they had asked her what she was doing in their cell and all said she had then disappeared. There may have been an explanation for this as at the time the works department of the prison were building some new office accommodation at the rear of what had been the old female cell blocks. During the digging of the foundations they had reported finding the remains of previously executed inmates who had been buried within the walls of Strangeways Jail in unconsecrated ground. Perhaps one of the bodies was that of the long dead hangman's victim Mrs. Merrifield.

CHAPTER FIFTY EIGHT

INSPIRATION AND AUTOMATIC WRITING

A lady named Jenny Gellatly sent Psychic World a letter from her home in New Zealand. Jenny wrote that she had begun experiencing a form of inspiration whilst in a partial or light trance state. During this period Jenny was prompted to write by a force she describes as being one of 'huge energy'. Whilst under the influence of this energy Jenny was told 'go get pen and paper'. The product of the first of these inspirational writing sessions contains the following paragraph;'Music brings joy, its form has a dimension beyond mankind's present knowledge. Sonnets of light and sound, which stir the soul, are my gift to you. Passion is to be found in sound, also suffering, joy, all the emotions. It is a gift of purity without measure in any other sphere. Tenderness cannot be conveyed so well as in sonatas, symphonies and arias. They breathe of the soul, you will know joy to listen'. Signed; Mozart.

In her letter Jenny describes herself as 'Mrs Average Housewife'. As a writer I can see that there is nothing average about the concepts considered in that paragraph. It is both inspired and, in its own way, inspirational. Jenny included many other examples of the messages communicated to her from the unseen energy that forms the words she writes. All are of a standard that would be outside the range of an untutored mind. Having read both Jenny's letter and her inspired writing I do believe that the latter came from a source beyond the physical plane. This source may or may not be the spirit of Wolfgang Amadeus Mozart, perhaps there is a New Zealand psychic researcher who would care to comment/investigate.

Andrea Grievson, the author of 'Read How We Died' (Con-Psy Publications) explains that she receives communication, regarding the passing into spirit of individual entities, in a similar manner. Andrea describes her work as being created through 'Automatic Writing'. When I spoke at length to Andrea on this subject she told me that during her dedicated writing sessions she feels as though the communicating spirit that directs her thoughts overshadows her entire being. These thoughts she then transcribes into the written word.

In his book 'A Guide For The Development Of Mediumship' Harry Edwards explains that automatic writing is 'Akin to trance speech, the difference being that the hand is used to transcribe the intuitive thought-flow, instead of speaking it'. I highly recommend this book to all Psychic World readers. Both myself and my dear wife Mary have developed and practised 'Automatic Writing', though our experiences differ considerably from the two examples described above. Our method is to simply hold an ordinary biro loosely between finger and thumb with the business end resting on a sheet of plain paper. There usually follows a tingling sensation in the hand holding the pen, rather like pins and needles. Then ideas form in the mind and the hand then seems to move of its own accord pushing and pulling the pen across the paper and forming words.

Deciding to test this phenomenon I asked my wife Mary to select and place an object in the ground out of my sight and I would then ask the communicating force or spirit to identify the object. This being done I sat quietly and meditated for a while before taking the pen to paper and asking the question 'What did my wife bury in the ground'. I felt my hand tingle but no words or thoughts formed in my mind, instead the pen drew three round objects close together. When I showed the drawing to my wife she agreed that this was quite correct, she had placed three penny pieces in the earth.

One afternoon, shortly after this experiment, a lady friend of ours was sitting with us in the garden and I was telling her about automatic writing. Being a total disbeliever she suggested that I give her the chance to test this phenomenon. So I took the pen, placed it on the paper and asked the lady what she wanted to know as proof, she asked me to ask the communicating force or spirit to state her weight, she had, she said, weighed herself that very morning. After a moments pause the pen wrote down a weight in stones and pounds, it was exactly correct. This shocked the lady, who shall remain nameless for my own health's sake. She then wanted to know what spirit had been watching her on the bathroom scales weighing herself naked. I decided against asking, but it certainly wasn't me.

A few months later Mary decided to try automatic writing, she followed the simple instructions and experienced the same tingling sensation in her hand. The pen wrote out the name of 'Mary Thomas' my wife's late grandmother. The content of my wife's message is of a personal nature, though in general terms it centred upon her late uncle Joseph Boydell Thomas of The Avenue, Leigh, Lancashire whom had left all his money, house and family heirlooms to his cleaning woman. As a test of the veracity of this communication Mary then asked for details concerning myself. The pen wrote 'Books sell all over the world'. Now that was in the year 1991, at the time I had no intention of being an author. The very idea was considered by me to be beyond belief. However in 1998 I had three books published in America, Canada, Australia and throughout the world. The communicating spirit or force had foreknowledge beyond the bounds of the possibilities current at the time. This, to me, is truly amazing.

If you are considering attempting 'Automatic Writing' I would suggest that you first of all take personal advice from a respected Spiritualist Medium. Your local Spiritualist Church will be pleased to provide you with a list of such mediums practising in your area. As in all matters concerning the direct communication of spirit it is better to be prepared and properly advised before you begin. Unlike spontaneous communication through visitation or manifestation, automatic writing is a long term psychic/mediumistic facility that may, with proper control, enable you to receive messages direct from discarnate entities. With such a power you must always exercise extreme caution and restraint.

CHAPTER FIFTY NINE

RETURNING FROM BEYOND

As Spiritualists we believe that at the point of physical death it is only our bodies that cease to live and we, the essence of what we are, our spirit, moves on to another dimension. Shakespeare wrote in Hamlet's soliloquy that no one comes back from the dead 'The dread of something after death, that undiscovered country from whose bourn no traveler returns'. Yet there are countless thousands of anecdotes about spirits of departed loved ones returning to comfort the living and announce the truth of everlasting life. Indeed it is the very basis of most religious beliefs that there exists, beyond the confines of this material world, a heaven or paradise where the souls of believers go. It is the belief of Spiritualists that not only believers but all, every living thing that dies, goes into the next dimension. We also believe that there exists a way back.

My late Aunt Edith was, all her life, a devout and committed member of the Roman Catholic Church. She attended each Sunday for Mass, her home contained many religious artifacts and she read the Bible daily. Aunt Edith had been married over fifty years when her husband became ill and died. I clearly recall attending the funeral at the Church and then the local cemetery in Nelson, Lancashire. Some few weeks later I received a call from Aunt Edith who told me that she had woken from her sleep in the middle of the night and there by the side of her bed stood her husband. She told me he looked younger than he had been and spoke to her of a wonderful land he lived in surrounded by friends and family, so she should not cry. He was, he told her, quite content and would be waiting for her when the time came, but that it was not yet. Aunt Edith told me this but was upset as when she had explained the visitation to her priest he had denounced this as a visit from the devil attempting to lead her away from the path of Jesus.

All credit to my dear Aunt, she told me that no matter what the priest said she knew it was her husband, she'd lived with him more than half a century.

In 'The Afterlife' by Jenny Randles and Peter Hough there are many personal anecdotes recounting visits from spirits returning to comfort or even heal the living. Here is an example taken from that book:

The famous singer and entertainer Tommy Steele was not always on stage, as a boy of just fifteen years of age he ran away to sea joining the Merchant Navy. However Tommy was not at sea for long, he developed a serious and life threatening illness, spinal meningitis. The hospital doctors feared that he would die, he was placed in a screened off bed and left to rest. Whilst there Tommy, who was semi-conscious, became aware of the laughter of a child in the room. Opening his eyes he saw on his bed a beautiful, brightly coloured ball just out of his reach. Thinking the ball belonged to the boy whose laughter he had heard Tommy struggled with all his remaining strength, reached out, picked up the ball and threw it over the screen in the direction of the laughter. Moments later the ball was thrown back and again landed on his bed. Not wishing to deprive the child of his ball Tommy again summoned all his energy and reached out for the ball and once more threw it back over the screen. By this time Tommy Steele was utterly exhausted but again the ball was thrown back landing on his bed and he made a really serious effort to reach it and throw it back. As he did this Tommy noticed that the feeling in his legs was returning. When the doctors next examined him they found, to their utter amazement, that instead of dying, as they had expected him to do, Tommy was getting better. When he was able to speak he told them that he had that little boy to thank for playing that game with the ball. That had given him the strength to fight on. But the doctors wondered what he was talking about and when they removed the screens Tommy could see that there was no one else in the room, there was no little boy nor had there ever been.

Tommy Steele's parents were delighted that their son was getting better and listened in wonder as he told them how his life had been saved by a boy that wasn't there playing ball with him. Then they asked him to describe the ball, which he did in some detail. Tommy's mother knew then who the boy was. Years before, when Tommy Steele was just a lad he had bought his three year old brother Rodney a ball for Christmas. That was to be the last present he was ever to receive for the poor child developed an illness and died shortly afterwards. There may be a number of explanations for what Tommy Steele experienced, such as an hallucination conjured up by his sub-conscious mind. But then could it not be that the spirit of his departed younger brother returned to save him.

In the year 1986 my Great Aunt Norah was ill and taken to hospital. I did visit her many times though the hospital was miles away in Yorkshire and at the time I lived in Flixton, Manchester. It was early one spring morning, around about 5am that I woke to the sound of loud banging on my front door. It was as if a giant were attempting to smash through the heavy Victorian oak panels, thump, thump, thumping away for at least half a minute. I jumped out of bed, ran to the window and looked down at the pathway and area directly before my front door, there was no one there. The path and indeed the street were completely empty. As I stood wondering how that could possibly be the telephone by the bed rang. When I answered it a nurse at the hospital where my Great Aunt Norah was being cared for told me that she had, just a few moments before, passed away. It is my belief that Aunty Norah had called at my home one last time to say goodbye as she made her journey into the world beyond.

You can get a copy of the highly readable and informative book 'The Afterlife' by Jenny Randles and Peter Hough from any good bookstore. The ISBN number is 0-7499-1804-7 and the publisher is Paitkus Books Ltd. I highly recommend this book to anyone interested in reading about life after death be they sceptic or believer this work will make them think.

CHAPTER SIXTY

OUIJA WARNING!

In the month of October in the year 1968 three young soldiers, John, Harry and Dave were serving in 39 Missile Regiment of Artillery with the British Army in Germany. Late one Friday night, in the barrack block, they decided to play with a Ouija board. The Ouija board is a wooden board with the letters of the alphabet, numbers 1 to 10 and the words Yes and No on it. The idea of this game is to try and contact spirits or ghosts who are said to communicate through the Ouija board by spelling out messages through a glass that moves to the letters. The three soldiers put their fingers on the upturned glass and asked the age old question 'Is there anybody there?' The answer and the messages came, but not the ones that the three soldiers expected.

Harry, whose room the three soldiers were using, soon got fed up with the Ouija board game. He thought the other two, John and Dave, were pushing the glass around the board and accused them of cheating. After a while he got changed and went to bed telling the others to get out. Harry even laughed at the idea that any spook was using the Ouija board to communicate. Then the glass began to move and spelt out this frightening message 'He will not laugh long, soon he will be sorry'. John told Harry, who just laughed even louder. 'Get out of my room and let me sleep' he said. It was long past midnight so John and Dave put the Ouija board away and went to their own rooms.

The next morning, being Saturday, John was trying to sleep in when he heard someone calling his name. It was just 7 a.m. when the angry voice of Harry woke him up. Harry insisted that someone had damaged his room. 'You better come and see the mess my room's in' he said. John reluctantly got out of bed and followed Harry down the cold tiled corridor to his room in the old barrack block. Inside Harry pointed to the scene of destruction, it was as though a bomb had hit the place. Harry's bed was upside down, his large metal locker was bent in the middle and all the contents scattered about the room. 'Who did this?' asked John, but Harry had no idea. 'It started just after you left me last night' he said 'I heard a weird laugh and then something began smashing my room to bits'. Harry had hidden under his blankets until dawn had broken.

In fear Harry refused to return to his room and moved out into another. But the terror did not end there. That very night John was woken at 2 a.m. by the most horrible loud clattering and banging. It sounded as though someone were dragging a huge metal locker over the corrugated tiled floor of the corridor. When John opened the door of his room to see what on earth was going on the noise stopped. Looking out into the dark corridor John saw only the silent shadows of night, nothing and no one moved. The really strange thing about the awful noise was that John's room mates had not heard a thing. Then the next night, Sunday night, it happened again.

It was pitch black in the barrack room and John was fast asleep. Suddenly an incredible booming noise woke him. It was 2 a.m. and John was frightened, the whole building seemed to be shaking from top to bottom. Jumping out of bed John ran over to the door and threw it open, though he dreaded what he might see. Then, just like the night before, the noise stopped. As John peered down the long corridor of the barrack block he saw the face of his friend Dave looking out from his room.

Dave walked down the shadowy dark corridor to John and together they set out to discover where the noise was coming from. As they came close to Harry's old room, now empty, they both felt a terrible cold surround them. Then, from inside the closed door, came a frightful hollow laugh. They turned and ran.

The next morning was Monday and John went to see the Sergeant Major in charge of the barrack block. He told this stern soldier exactly what had been happening and all about their silly games with the Ouija board on the Friday night. The Sergeant Major at once ordered that Harry's old room be cleared completely and locked up. 'You do know this old barrack block used to be a prison during the last war' the Sergeant Major said. Then he told John something that really scared him, 'those rooms you sleep in now were once cells holding evil criminals, perhaps the ghost of one of them returned through your stupid Ouija board'.

Reader, believe me Ouija boards are very dangerous and not to be played with. I know that for certain, you see I was that soldier.

CHAPTER SIXTY ONE

THERE'S A GHOST IN MY HOUSE!

Over the years that I have been associated with psychic studies and the paranormal I have on numerous occasions received telephone calls from people asking for help saying such things as 'There's a ghost in my house!'. These calls do not, as a general rule, come from the occupants of ancient castles but from ordinary people living in ordinary houses. The one thing these callers do have in common is the fact that they are experiencing paranormal activity in their homes and need advice and assistance.

I was recently asked to help by a family living in an 18th century cottage outside Fleetwood in Lancashire. When I asked the owners what phenomena they were experiencing they told me of cold spots and a sense of doom that seemed to hang in the air. They mentioned footsteps that had no physical source. The sound of furniture being moved in the night was another very frightening aspect that had really scared the eldest daughter who was now suffering from reactive depression. There had also been sightings of a ghostly figure on the stairs which had prompted them to call me because they now were convinced that the property was haunted.

When I arrived at the cottage the whole family were there ready to tell me their stories of how they had personally experienced the 'ghost'. The most disturbing factor was the deleterious effect that this was having on the eldest daughter, a young lady of approximately 16 years, who was quite clearly very scared by the phenomena. She told me that whilst in a certain area of the house she had started to feel sad, tears had welled up in her eyes and a sense of despair and hopelessness had overwhelmed her. She now said that following that experience she had been unable to shake off the feeling of depression and, as we spoke, she began to tremble with emotion. It was obvious to me that this young lady was an energy source for whatever entity was present in that cottage.

Following the discussion with the family I then conducted a room by room psychic search of the cottage and found, in the front bedroom, a cold spot that moved when I walked into it. The name 'Anne' was whispered to me and in the far corner of the room I saw the misty outline of figure that vanished as I approached. Suddenly I sensed that this was a former owner and occupier of this cottage who, now in spirit, had failed to make a full transition. The spirit was that of an old lady and she was now angry that the new owners had changed the interior of what she still thought of as her home.

The spirit of Anne had been responsible for creating the atmosphere of gloom and doom that was causing the young lady resident to react with a sense of depression. When I pointed out to the spirit that this was not acceptable and she should move on to her appointed place in the light of love and understanding that awaited her I immediately sensed a rejection. This lady was not for turning. However, using a forceful but compassionate manner I insisted that her time within this cottage was at an end and she should be content to leave the new family to live their lives in peace. Having explained this to the spirit I sensed a reluctant acceptance, as if the old lady herself was sighing in recognition of the facts and realising that she had to move on.

As I returned to the main room I looked again at the young lady who had been trembling with fear and saw that she was now smiling. 'It's stopped, the horrible feeling, it's gone'. And it had, the room that had before seemed dark and gloomy now had a new radiance as the daylight reached in illuminating corners that had previously been dark and unwelcoming.

Over the years I have received many calls from people who believe that they have a ghost in their house. The truth is often more prosaic with many supposed hauntings being more the product of a fertile imagination than supernatural phenomena. There are however cases where the caller is correct and a spirit entity is indeed present, as in the instance above. There are also poltergeist hauntings that are really difficult to resolve. These involve not the spirits of deceased people now alive in a discarnate form but entities that have never actually lived physical lives on earth. The poltergeist has many manifestations and some are incredibly disturbing. The term poltergeist comes from the German, it means noisy ghost. Some poltergeist hauntings involve not only noise but also physical movement of inanimate objects such as chairs, tables, lamps etc. They can be extremely frightening and put entire families in fear of living within their own homes.

I once had a ghost in my house. When I lived in London, at East Acton, my home was a three bedroom flat built on ground that had previously been a graveyard for the church that still stood some two hundred yards or so from the front door. One scorching July afternoon in 1976, the hottest on recent record, my wife Mary and I were in the main lounge by the balcony which looked out towards the distant dark stone walls of the old church. Mary was blow drying my hair having washed it following a home made short back and sides crop. The flat was silent, the air warm and still, outside even the birds were snoozing in the heat of that late summers day. Without warning the interior door leading in to the lounge burst open and a mighty blast of turbulent air blew through the room hitting my wife hard in the back knocking the hairdryer out of her hand and into my lap. Having blown past us the unseen entity smashed open the glass door leading onto the balcony and shattered a large heavy stoneware bread pot. There was nothing further, no indication as to what this invisible force was or who it had been assuming it was a spirit. Mary was shocked, I recall her looking in wonder at the broken bread pot and saying 'that used to be my mother's' The ghost busted it.

CHAPTER SIXTY TWO

A PSYCHIC EXPERIENCE: JOE COOPER

Joe Cooper's book `Modern Psychic Experiences" published by Robert Hale is a must read for all those interested in paranormal phenomena. Within this book are many well researched histories of individual encounters with the supernatural world. Joe Cooper"s scientific approach to these psychic experiences has produced a work that is certain to impress even the most hardened sceptic. Here is an example case-study which I have adapted from the pages of the book. It tells the story of how a young art student called Arthur was given a lift home by an elderly lady that lived in his village.

Arthur: `In the autumn of 1958 I had just started art-college in Birmingham and was thrilled to be there. I lived in a bed-sit during the week and went home to our village near Evesham at the weekends. The journey to the village on this occasion took about an hour by bus.

Joe: Were you tired making this journey?

Arthur: No, not at all. The evening was clear, the sky was blue, I was feeling elated, very happy and looking forward to the walk home.

Joe: Can you remember the exact date? Or the day of the week?

Arthur: One Friday afternoon in October, I think. I lived in a village called Iron Cross, which was part of a larger village, Salford Priors. This particular person who gave me the lift was Miss Slater. She was well off, lived in a big house, played the organ. She had lots and lots of cats. In fact she left all her money to a cat society.

Joe: What time was it?

Arthur: About half past six. I"d just got off the bus. I lived about three miles away. Salford Priors was about a mile further on. In those days everybody knew you and would stop and give you a lift automatically. Nobody was ever left waiting at bus stops. So I got off the bus and this car pulled up.

Joe: Was it directly behind the bus? Had it been following?
Arthur: Couldn"t say. When you get off a bus you"re not exactly
aware of what"s behind you. So this Miss Slatter pulled up.
Joe: How long was it since you had seen her?
Arthur: Oh-about a year. She was 65 or 70. The type of person
difficult to put an age to. She just indicated that that she
wanted me to get in, so I did.
Joe: What was your impression of the car?
Arthur: Oh, immaculate. It was big. About a 1947 Rover. A
Rover 90 maybe. It was an antique even in those days.
Midnight blue-nearly black, with blue leather upholstery.
Joe: How was she dressed?
Arthur: Tweedy costume, handknitted jumper. Very much the
country type. Stockings and brogues, hair pulled back in a bun.
She was very short in the leg and had cushions stuffed behind
her seat-cushions covered in hand crocheting.
Joe: What did you talk about?
Arthur: Oh, nothing much. How I was doing at college-can't
really remember. Nothing out of the ordinary. What a lovely
day it was-I was happy, thrilled with being at college.
Joe: And after three miles she dropped you at your home?
Arthur: Yes. I walked across the road and into the house. My
mother said `you"re home early" and I replied `Miss Slatter
gave me a lift". `And my mother looked at me very hard and
said `don't be silly, Miss Slatter's dead. She died last year".
Joe: How did you feel when she said that to you?
Arthur: I thought she"d got it wrong, that Miss Slatter wasn"t
dead. And my mother thought I"d mistaken somebody else for
Miss Slatter. Well I was intrigued. I thought I"d take the matter
further. I asked my mother what had happened to Miss
Slatter"s car and she told me it had been sold at the auction
after her death, along with household effects. My mother had
bought some dining chairs which were in our house, in our
dining room. I had to get to the bottom of this. I thought if it
was Miss Slatter and if it was that car, it was unusual you see,
there weren"t many large cars in the village. So I investigated.
I went to the auctioneers, Wrighton and Son in Evesham. They
told me that the car had been bought by a man called Mr.

Butcher who was a builder and he lived near Stratford-upon-Avon some twelve miles away. So I went to see him.

Joe: Had anyone previously told you about this?

Arthur: No. I thought the man would laugh at me but he was not laughing. He said `What can I do for you, young man" I said `Well, I feel rather foolish, but I"ve come about your car". His manner changed. He looked at me as if he was suspicious and became rather belligerent. He said `What do you want to know for?" and then he said `And how many of you were there.who was driving?. I said `there was a lady driving it" and told him the whole story.

Joe: What was his reaction?

Arthur: He was angry. He said I was making it all up. Then he calmed down and said `Well, you"ll not believe this either". He told me he had been in Stratford on Avon that Friday afternoon I was given the lift by Miss Slatter. He had parked his car, the big dark blue Rover, at the side of a road and he went shopping with his wife.

Joe: Did you actually see the car whilst you were at the builder"s yard?

Arthur: Yes, I saw it. The car was in the yard. He told me that when he came back from the shopping trip at about 4pm the car was gone. He thought it had been stolen.

Joe: Had he left it locked.

Arthur: Yes, he said the keys were in his pocket. They reported the car stolen to the police and went home by taxi. Later that same evening the police telephoned him to say that the car had been found parked exactly where it had been taken from. It was in the very same position and it was locked. The builder concluded that someone had taken it for a joy-ride and had just returned it.

Joe Cooper then investigated this case further and found that Miss Margaret Slatter had died age seventy three years from cerebral thrombosis and arteriosclerosis at Salford Priors on 19th April 1956. Joe found that this tallied with Arthur"s account but her appearance as a vigorous woman in her sixties links with returns by discarnates who often appear slightly younger than at death.

MODERN PSYCHIC EXPERIENCES by Joe Cooper is published by Robert Hale.

ISBN 0-7090-3830-5

This book is highly collectable and is currently fetching good money on ebay auctions.

CHAPTER SIXTY THREE

MAN OF MYSTERY: JOE COOPER

Joe Cooper was by training a scientist, holding various fully accredited university degrees he has previously lectured with The Open University. For many years Joe Cooper was a Tutor-Counsellor and taught countless hundreds of today's university teachers. He has had many books published, amongst these is his erudite examination of telepathic communication titled 'The Mystery of Telepathy'. It is a work of great erudition and produced something of a publishing sensation when it first came out in 1982, published by Constable and Company Ltd. Prior to this publication the serious publishing houses had virtually ignored the idea that there may be more mysteries in this world than are currently dreamt of in our philosophy. But Joe Cooper convinced them that it was now the time to dream the dreams of what had hitherto appeared impossible.

In his introduction to 'The Mystery of Telepathy' Joe Cooper writes: 'The importance of telepathy lies not so much in the novelty of the mysterious transfer of thought from one human to another as in its implication: for if it can be demonstrated conclusively that humans can communicate with one another outside the five senses, then it follows that there may be more to us than the known mind and body adjusted to the everyday world of time and space. It may mean that there are other and unknown parts of ourselves capable of making conscious impressions from time to time'.

What Joe Cooper is intimating is that if telepathy becomes an accepted scientific fact then this is a major signpost pointing towards proof that there is a non-material element to human beings which may well survive death. Thus telepathic communication should perhaps be the starting point for scientific investigation into the truth of survival.

In tribal societies there have always been shaman, or witch-doctors that are believed to have special powers to heal, foresee the future, conjure up spirits or cast spells for good or evil. There are numerous accounts by well respected travellers that give first hand accounts of such practices. In his book Joe Cooper offers many examples such as this from the pen of Laurence Van der Post writing about The Bushmen of The Kalahari Desert:

'Van der Post was told by an old Bushman that people were coming. He graphically describes standing in the hot sun with a few others, there was silence all around except for 'the day roaring like a furnace' in his ears. His conversation with an old interpreter ran as follows: 'Are you sure there are people coming this way?'...'Oh Yes! I feel them coming here!' He tapped a finger on the smooth yellow skin of his bare chest. 'Men and women in trouble coming this way'.

Such proved to be the case a few minutes later. A small group of men, women and children appeared, thirst-racked and starving. Having been separated from their tribe during famine conditions.

Joe Cooper also cites the autobiography; 'Magical Mission' of the aristocratic explorer George Sandwith. The public school educated Sandwith, who had served as an officer in WWII with the British Army, found himself in Ethiopia where he was given an Ikon and this aroused his previously inert psychic abilities. He goes on to describe how he was subsequently subjected to a psychic attack by a witch in a Fijian village he was visiting and how he used the Ikon to protect himself:

'One of the witches in the village was an enormous woman with a horrible hooked nose and little piggy eyes, she was sent to deal with me. As I was sat in the rest room reading a book something made me look up and I saw this ugly giantess staring at me. For a moment I held those devil's eyes with my own, then she looked down and walked away. At nightfall the attack began and George Sandwith prayed for help as he did so he heard a voice from his Ikon telling him to place this figure under his pillow, this he did and laid back to seek sleep.

The witch had attached shadowy cords to Sandwith's stomach and through these she was sucking away his very life energy and sending back fear. Sandwith recognised the attack method through his awakened psychic powers and with the help of his Ikon severed the invisible shadowy cords breaking the witch's spell. He survived and lived to recount this adventure in his autobiography.

Accepted western scientific thinking explains that there are, within tribal societies, close emotional bonds that no longer exist within the developed world. That is the tribe thinks and feels very much as one being. There is also the close ties of blood through breeding within tribal communities that creates an interconnectedness unseen in the Western world for many hundreds of years. This bond is exacerbated and enhanced by collective clan activity, such as hunting or agriculture with all involved thinking along similar lines thereby creating almost one mind. As we see with a flock of birds that seem to change direction in flight as if controlled by one thought. The scientific theory seems to me to be that when such a tribe collectively believes that one certain individual i.e. the shaman or witch-doctor has special powers then, because of the clan-mind reinforcing that belief they then, to all intents and purposes, actually do. That is the scientific argument.

What Joe Cooper argues is that the mystery of telepathy is not just a matter of misguided belief it actually exists and communication of original thought is possible between human beings using only the power of the mind acting independently of the five accepted senses of touch, smell, sight, hearing and taste.

The Mystery of Telepathy by Joe Cooper is published by Constable ISBN 0 09 464170 6. You may track a copy down on the internet at Amazon.co.uk prices vary to over £40.00p or order a copy from your local lending library.

Read The Obituary of THE Joe Cooper. My friend Joe died in August 2011

Joe Cooper obituary:

THE GUARDIAN.

He got the Cottingley fairy fakers to confess

Joe Cooper met the cousins in the 1970s and was far from sceptical about the existence of the 'little people' Public Domain

Martin Wainwright

Joe Cooper, who has died aged 87, was the jovial debunker of the celebratedCottingley fairy photographs (supposedly showing fairies captured on film in a Yorkshire garden in 1917). He remained a firm believer in unexplained phenomena to the end. In spite of finally prompting a confession of fakery by one of the two cousins who took the pictures, Cooper was far from sceptical about the existence of "little people" and thought that something genuinely unusual had happened in the West Riding village.

His engaging and sympathetic approach ended the long deception by the cousins, Frances Griffiths and Elsie Wright, who were in their 80s when Cooper's interview appeared in the magazine The Unexplained in 1983. They described to him how the "fairies" had been copied by Wright from a well-known children's book of the time, The Queen's Gift Book, and then held in place with hatpins.

Such trickery was widely assumed to have taken place by the time the interview appeared, in spite of the early endorsement of the images by photographic specialists and eminent figures, notably the writer Sir Arthur Conan Doyle. In a television discussion after Cooper's story had been published, Griffiths explained how she and Wright had seen a childish joke get wildly out of hand, because of people who "believed because they wanted to believe".

In a sense, this was true of Cooper, who combined an academic career with less conventional enthusiasms to which he devoted great zest. He promoted astrology and psychic investigation winningly, believing in Conan Doyle's summary of the fairies: "The recognition of their existence will jolt the material 20th-century mind out of its heavy ruts in the mud, and will make it admit that there is a glamour and mystery to life."

Cooper parted company with mainstream academia in research for his master's degree at Bradford University, which amassed data to suggest links between season of birth and eventual choice of occupation. One of his many other interests was playing the ukulele, and he performed his own astrological composition, Zing Zat Zodiac Zong, on TV after an interview with David Dimbleby in a series on the "beyond".

Cooper was born in Leeds, but the family moved early to Southampton and he was educated at Taunton school. During the second world war he served as a navigator in the RAF.

He tried various jobs after the war and had an early taste of the media when he appeared in a documentary made by the young Lindsay Anderson while working in a drawing office at Wakefield. He wrote material for Frankie Howerd and was an eager member of Leeds Art Centre in the 1950s, appearing in amateur dramatics with another cinema tyro, Peter O'Toole.

It was not until the end of the decade that he settled down to train as a teacher, moving on in the 1960s to become a lecturer in sociology at Bradford University (from where he retired in 1980). This led to wider involvement as the organiser of evening classes in psychic education in Yorkshire, and in the 1980s he wrote a column for the Guardian called Body and Soul.

Cooper met the Cottingley fairies cousins in the early 1970s and got to know them well. He later wrote a book, The Case of the Cottingley Fairies (1990), about the episode which played a part in the 1997 film Fairy Tale – a True Story.

He is survived by his son, David, and daughter, Jane.

• Henry Joseph Cooper, sociologist, born 3 February 1924; died 16 August 2011.

CHAPTER SIXTY FOUR

CHURCHILL: FATE AND DESTINY

As Spiritualists we believe that we are responsible for our own actions: The 7th Principle is: 'We affirm the moral responsibility of the individual, and that he makes his own happiness or unhappiness as he obeys or disobeys Nature's physical and spiritual laws.'

In this article I aim to examine the theory that there may be an external force that determines the outcome of our actions and that we are all aware of the nature of this intangible power. You may know it as luck.

Winston Churchill is best remembered as the leader of Great Britain during WWII when he was seen as the British Bulldog hero that inspired the nation with his brilliant speeches. But for the first part of WWII Britain lost virtually every single battle it fought, despite having Churchill as the Prime Minister. Was this bad luck? It is a little known fact that for the first sixty years of his life, despite being born into a highly placed and well connected family, Winston Churchill was a loser. It took him three attempts to pass the entrance examination to the Military Academy at Sandhurst, despite having had the benefit of a private education at Harrow, one of England's top schools. His position in society though was guaranteed by the fact that his family were highly respected and his father was a well placed career politician as well as being a member of the aristocracy, he was the 7[th]Duke of Marlborough. So in that way Winston Leonard Spencer Churchill was a very lucky young man. If ever a child had a silver spoon it was Winston.

Winston quickly rose up the ranks of the armed forces and then moved into politics. His early career was hardly successful, but he was connected so he survived. Most notable defeats in the early history of Churchill include the disastrous expedition to the Dardenelles, in which countless thousands of our troops were killed, he engineered this attack. In 1926 it was Churchill as The Chancellor of The Exchequer, who brought about the great depression which led to a general strike during which he said: "either the country will break the General Strike, or the General Strike will break the country." And he ordered British troops onto the streets to drive the striking miners back down the pits at the point of a bayonet.

In WWII, following the debacle of Dunkirk, we as a nation were on the very edge of defeat. We were losing on every front with German bomber-planes blowing our major cities and ports to smithereens. Above the green fields of England 'The Few' saved us from further attacks flying the famous Spitfires, but it was a near disaster. However, in 1942 following the North African Battle of El Alamein, in which the tanks of German General Rommel were defeated by the Desert Rats of Field Marshall Montgomery, Churchill's luck turned and from that point the British forces won every major encounter. That success led on to even greater success and it was, as Winston Churchill himself stated: "The Hinge of Fate". That is he believed that Britain's luck had changed and we were fated to go on to win. The success of El Alamein had broken the bad luck spell and, as history shows, the Axis Powers were ultimately defeated.

The Bible addresses the problem of fate: Ecclesiates 'And I looked and I saw under the sun that the race is not to the swift, nor the battle to the strong, nor yet counsel to the wise, nor yet riches to men of skill, nor yet favour to men of understanding, but time and chance happeneth to them all.' Time and Chance: As Del Boy might say in Only Fools and Horses, Who Dares Wins. One has to take a chance and if one does so often enough one must eventually win. Churchill won, in the end and recognised that his perseverance had opened the door to success as it swung on 'The Hinge of Fate'.

How then does luck, chance, fate and destiny relate to the 7th principle of Spiritualism? I believe that we have an absolute duty to our own selves to try and live our lives to the full extent of our potential. We need to be like Winston Churchill and take risks with our lives, be brave and refuse to be herded along in life like sheep. Think about this, The Bible talks about The Good Shepherd and his flock comparing The Lord Jesus to a shepherd and we the people to his flock. Think about this, it is the duty of the shepherd to control the sheep and their interests and the shepherd's interests are not one and the same. They are, in point of fact, diametrically opposed. Sheep get sheered of their wool, they get killed and eaten and the shepherd is responsible for ensuring that they accept that fate. So good or not the shepherd feeds on them! If you think that being a member of a flock is safe think about that. It is not lucky to be born a sheep. It is even less lucky to accept that metaphorical position and allow oneself to be controlled and clipped by the authorities, be they good or bad shepherds they are most certainly going to have the shirt off your back.

So how can you, if you feel unlucky and trapped by circumstances change your luck, how can you escape the flock and become a success? How can you make the hinge of fate swing open the doorway that can lead on to ultimate attainment? It was Napoleon Bonaparte that said 'Circumstances, I make the circumstances!' That is how you change your luck, you just keep on keeping on until the hinge of fate either swings open the door or you batter the damn thing down.

You owe it to yourself to make an attempt at living your life to the full, don't you? You do if you accept the 7th principle of Spiritualism. Accept your moral responsibility for your own happiness and be like Napoleon, make the circumstances that will enable you to achieve your goals. If, like me and unlike Winston Churchill, you were not born lucky with a silver spoon in your mouth then you might have to try harder. But think of the fun you will have when you finally win and you really will do BUT only if you try hard enough and never, not ever give in.

CHAPTER SIXTY FIVE

VISIONS, VOICES AND DREAMS

Throughout history there have been those who could, apparently, predict the future. Indeed in Greece prediction was officially recognised and practised in a temple at Delphi where the Oracle was a succession of females called Pythia. There were fees charged for the services of the prophetess who gave predictive messages to great historical names such as King Croesus and Alexander The Great. Cities and even countries would send officials to seek advice from the Oracle at Delphi. The method used by the Pythia involved a form of trance brought on by the inhalation of gasses that emitted from within the rocks upon which the temple was built. Whilst in trance the Pythia received communication and visions of the future. Of the Greek poet Homer the Pythia said 'He shall be deathless and ageless for ever' and so his name and work is. Though perhaps Homer thought he would physically live forever.

The problem with many predictive messages, voices and visions, seems to be in recognising their meaning. Priests did the interpretation of the messages given by the Oracle at Delphi. These were often obscure and even after interpretation the meaning was not brilliantly clear. It is so today with the visions dreams and voices that many of us experience requiring clarification. Simply recognising that one has experienced communication from the spirit world is difficult enough as the messages initially come in unfamiliar ways. Interpretation of the message is even more problematical.
Hearing voices when there is no obvious source can be quite disconcerting, at least at first. Yet for clairaudient mediums hearing discarnate voices is normal. However that is not the case for the vast majority of us. Yet there are occasions when many do hear such voices, often this is in time of trouble. Perhaps only a single word is heard, or maybe a name.

Whatever it is once you have experienced the phenomena there should be no doubt in your mind that it is real, unless you question your senses. I personally have heard an unseen spirit presence calling my name. I don't think I'm mad, though others may have a different opinion. I believe that the voice I hear calling my name is warning me. Certainly in times of trouble and strife I have noticed the phenomena presenting itself. During one period, as I was writing the lyrics to a song for the singer P.J. Proby, I heard an unseen spirit shouting my name, 'John!'.....'John!' it called to me. My wife was in the main lounge and at first I thought it was she calling of me. However, when I went into the room to see what Mary wanted she assured me that no one had called my name. But they had, I heard it and I should have taken heed and left the trouser splitting Texan well alone.

A gentleman named Gerald Mills of Sheffield wrote to me telling how he had received a warning from the world of spirit. Mr Mills told me he had been in Bow Street Spiritualist Church one Tuesday afternoon and the medium there had given him a message 'don't fight'. Now Mr Mills assures me he is not the aggressive type and would not normally engage in fisticuffs. So, when he heard this short message, he wondered what it might mean. Unfortunately for Mr Mills he was soon to find out.

It was approximately 7.30 that same evening and Gerald Mills saw a strange man prowling about near his home, which is located in a cul-de-sac. Wondering what this stranger wanted Gerald walked out of his house and asked him. 'I'm lost' the man told him and, being a gentleman, Gerald offered to direct him. However, this man was not lost, he was a thief. Suddenly Gerald became aware of a spirit presence that told him to hurry back indoors. But the thief was faster than Gerald and ran into his home and started to search the house for money. Remembering the words of warning he had received from the Spiritualist church medium Gerald did not try to physically prevent the thief from stealing his wife's money. Instead he wisely called for help from his neighbour whose two ex-Army sons grabbed the stranger and handed him over to the police. Gerald Mills is certain that he received a timely warning from the world of spirit that may have saved his life. If he had physically tried to stop the thief from stealing he might have suffered injury so 'don't fight' was good advice indeed.

I have, over the years, toured the UK with a number of professional mediums presenting demonstrations at theatres from Aberdeen to The London Palladium. At one venue in East Kilbride, Scotland the medium on stage gave a message of warning to a lady in the audience. 'Make sure you have secured you car it's in danger of being stolen'. The lady thought this quite amusing and was not in the least concerned. However when she left the theatre and went to the car park, there her car wasn't. It had been stolen even as the medium on stage gave her the warning. Great proof of communication, but just a little too late to be of help.

Sometimes the warning of danger from the spirit world comes as a dream whilst the recipient is asleep. It is a matter of record that immediately prior to the terrible 1966 Aberfan tragedy, in which 128 children and 16 adults lost their lives, a number of individuals, had premonitions of the disaster. One of these was a Mrs Grace Engleton of Sidcup, Kent. She had a dream on the 14th October, seven days before the tragedy, in which she saw 'a valley with a big building filled with children. Mountains of coal and water rushing down the valley, burying the building.' There is good testimony that this dream foretold the future disaster as Mrs Engleton had told a number of people about it, including her neighbour Mrs Rollings who confirmed this in writing.

The question is how do we recognise the warnings we receive as Visions, Voices and Dreams? The book stores are full of titles such as 'Interpret Your Dreams' or '10,000 Dreams and Their Meanings'. Keeping a dream diary is one way of developing ones own ability to interpret dreams. Perhaps also keeping note of all other psychic phenomena would assist in an individual's ability to make some sense out of the seemingly inexplicable occurrences that may, in fact, be messages from the world beyond. In the recent past in the U.S.A. a gentleman called Robert Nelson set up a Central Premonitions Bureau. This bureau recorded thousands of predictions and premonitions including many that came true, such as the Chappaquiddick incident involving Senator Ted Kennedy, in which a lady died. A woman in Pennsylvania who wrote to Mr Nelson prior to the fact, foresaw this incident in a dream.

Dreams, visons and voices that show us in many different ways images of the future are warnings yet they are not usually effective, that is generally no one pays attention. Perhaps we should.

CHAPTER SIXTY SIX

POETRY OF THE SOUL

Throughout mankind's history there have been poets, from the mythological Greek muses to the punk rock/rappers of today, human beings have sought to express their innermost feelings in verse. Virgil, the pre-Christian Roman poet said 'I sing of arms and the man', surely that is what all poets do, sing their songs, create the poetry of the soul, their soul, the collective soul.

It says in the Bible St. Matthew ch.7 v.20 'By their fruits shall ye know them'. When poets write and create verse they are offering up for public examination an image in words of their soul. Read the poems they write and see within those lines an insight into the true nature of the poet. It is a dangerous thing to publish ones work, it leaves the writer open to criticism, exposed to ridicule and, as anyone who has ever written will know, there is no shortage of critics. Yet without poetry, without art and music we are surely lost souls, just stumbling along in the stygian darkness of this material world. Poetry is the spiritual song of our soul, at its highest point it touches the very essence of our existence, in every sense.

Consider the power of the poem to tell us the truth in a simple and understandable way. Read William Wordsworth's ode; Intimations on Immortality: 'Our birth is but a sleep and a forgetting/The soul that rises with us, our life's star/ Hath had elsewhere its setting/ And cometh from afar'. Wordsworth is telling us that we reincarnate, his poem goes on to say that we bring with us into this world all the glorious and inglorious karmic influences that our souls have acquired in lifetimes past, when it had elsewhere its setting. We have our exits and we have our entrances, as a man said.

How much more life has a poem than a powerful sermon given by even the most gifted priest or orator? Why does poetry live

on when rhetoric so often dies? I believe it is because great poetry has the ability to reach our emotions, touch our souls and fire the imagination by offering us a truth we always knew was there but had failed to see. Poetry lifts the veil from our eyes in a way no other form of communication can, not even music.

I can clearly recall reading 'The Listeners' by Walter de la Mare and wondering at the imagery within those lines; 'Is there anybody there?' said the Traveller, knocking at the moonlit door'. We are all travellers and each one of us is asking that question 'Is there anybody there?' Yet it takes a poet like de la Mare to make us realise that we are not alone in that search for an answer.

How many countless millions of people have used the phrases of the great poets without knowing their origin? In truth they do not need to know, for encapsulated within these timeless lines is a power of expression that gives the very words themselves an existence of their own. I think of lines such as 'Stone walls do not a prison make'. Indeed they do not, Nelson Mandela said that during his decades in jail in South Africa his soul enjoyed a freedom unknown to the gaolers who locked him up. We create our own prisons in this material world and Richard Lovelace (1618-58) in ' To Althea From Prison' expresses this with a clarity of vision that has lasted centuries. If our souls, if our minds are free then no cell, no prison, nothing in the world can hold us captive.

It is my belief that by reading poetry we can all gain an insight into the nature of the human condition. As travellers along life's often long and winding road we need that insight to believe that there really is a meaning to our frequently difficult journeys. Of course not every poem addresses the nature or meaning of life, but all great poetry has life, it is meaningful and enriches our souls. I think it is not enough to say to people 'have faith', have hope, have knowledge, comprehend yes, but faith, blind faith is of little use except to those who are persuading you to accept their unsubstantiated teachings. In great poetry there is hope, understanding, truth and knowledge.

In despair we may lose faith, hope can fade like the light of a once glorious day, descending into the twilight and subsequent darkness of a desperate night. Poetry can release us from fear, open our eyes to the possible potentials of everlasting life, teaching us that we are not the first to have knocked upon some moonlit door asking the eternal question 'Is there anybody there?'

CHAPTER SIXTY SEVEN

HAUNTED LANCASHIRE

I was born in the Lancashire village of Foulridge, close by Pendle Hill, infamous for its association with witches. Like most families in the 1950's mine did not encourage the idea that there were ghosts and spirits that could be 'seen' by the sensitive ones we call mediums. In fact within my family I was actively discouraged from speaking of the visions and spirit encounters I had experienced. But there were ghosts in Foulridge and I recall hearing my grandmother Eva Walsh telling of the time her father had been terrified by the mysterious unseen spirit of a long dead navigator alongside the local stretch of the Leeds to Liverpool canal.

It seems that around the year 1930 Fred Walsh, a weaver in the local mills, was walking back from Barnoldswick to Foulridge along the tow path of the old canal. By the time he had walked three miles or so and could see the faint lights of Foulridge flickering in the distance it was gone midnight. Fred was a strapping big chap and afraid of nothing he could get hold of, but as he passed the last bridge before the mile tunnel on the canal he heard something he could not quite comprehend. From immediately behind him there came the sound of chains rattling as though they were being dragged along the ground. Turning and staring into the moonlit mists drifting off the canal he saw only the rough shale path reflecting the silver beams of that far away moon. But the sound grew louder and closer. There was a stillness in the air and all around the atmosphere seemed to cool. The chains rattled louder now and Fred stood transfixed in terror unable to move. Rattling and clanging the invisible chains slowly passed alongside Fred and disappeared into the misty Lancashire night. When they had gone he ran all the way home. According to my grandmother he didn't sleep too well for weeks after that encounter with the unknown.

There are many tales of ghosts in Lancashire which may or may not have a foundation in fact. One supposedly haunted location is Samlesbury Old Hall situated some five miles or so north-east of Preston. According to legend there is in this hall a spirit called the 'White Lady' who has been seen wandering both within the grounds and also along the main highway to Blackburn which runs by the side. A number of motorists claimed to have picked out a filmy white shape in their headlights late at night. Also some Air Force personnel from the nearby air-base at Wharton have described seeing the 'White Lady' drifting across the road heading into the ancient hall.

Samlesbury Hall was built around 1322 by Gilbert de Southworth who was a staunch Catholic. The family occupied the hall for generations and remained true to their faith during the reformation when the Catholic priests faced persecution. Legend has it that it the 'White Lady' is Dorothy the daughter of Sir John Southworth. Dorothy was a Catholic and it seems she fell in love with a member of the Houghton family of Houghton Tower, they were Protestants. Because of the religious differences Dorothy and her lover were refused permission to marry and decided to elope. This plan was discovered by Dorothy's older brother who lay in wait for her lover from Hoghton Tower and killed the man as she watched in terror.

According to the legend following the murder of her lover she lived as a recluse in Samlesbury Hall eventually dying in a local convent. Some say that along with the vision of the 'White Lady' they have heard the sounds of weeping and wailing. Could it be that the spirit of Dorothy Southworth is still haunting Samlesbury Hall mourning the long ago loss of her lover? There are those that do believe so. If you ever find yourself in Preston or thereabouts why not call in to Samlesbury Hall, it is open to the public. Who knows, you too may encounter the mysterious 'White Lady'.

One could write copious amounts detailing the legends and myths of haunted Lancashire filling books if one wanted to.

Dark tales of long dead lovers and ghostly horsemen galloping into lightning storms and thunder-clouded purple midnights abound, but what is the truth? Are there really such things as spirits that have spent countless ages wandering this earthly plane in utter despair wearying for whatever sad situation blighted their physical lives? As Spiritualists we must question such ideas and I personally do not believe that a discarnate entity would waste its time spooking people or hanging around some deserted patch waiting in vain forevermore.

Consider this, put yourself in the place of Dorothy Southworth, you have just passed into spirit and are now a discarnate being called into the light of eternal love having endured a truly miserable incarnation on earth. You have a choice to move on and enter the kingdom of peace or pop back to the ancient old hall where you watched your own brother murder the man you love. Would you seriously waste your time wandering round minus your physical body moaning and wailing about something that is past or would you get on with your new life in spirit and put that encounter with the stupidity of humankind down to bitter experience? I know what I would do!

So if we assume that spirits have some degree of common sense and do not haunt in the traditional sense what then of those visions of ghosts, white-ladys etc. They most certainly are **NOT** discarnate spirits. They are, I believe, no more than a form of video/audio recording captured in the atmosphere in the same way the actual video and audio records are captured on magnetic or digital tape. These recordings playback when the atmospheric conditions are right. This may be why sightings of 'ghosts' are often reported during storms as the natural electrical discharge and dampness acts as an enabling charge and pathway triggering the playback. The original scenes that are seen may have been recorded as they were themselves highly emotionally charged (as in the commission of a murder) thereby creating the power required to record on the atmosphere, the stones, bricks and buildings trapping

forevermore the incidents that then playback down the centuries.

That being the case there is nothing to fear from the mumblings, moanings and chain rattling visions of the past. They are simply a record of times long gone captured on natures Video Recorders playing back the same old scene century after century, rather like Dad's Army repeats on TV. Makes more sense than the idea that some love struck spirit is hanging round a dusty old hall waiting for a lover that will never appear, don't you agree?

CHAPTER SIXTY EIGHT

THE SPIRITUAL ESSENCE OF HOME

The spiritual heart of any country is, I believe, to be found not only in its history and traditions but also essentially in its indigenous population. Folk-lore and local legends passed from generation to generation may serve to mold the peoples minds, but is there perhaps something more, something unknowable that works a mysterious magic on those that are born and live within a given area? Could the mystery really be a Jungian collective subconscious specific to location that permeates the atmosphere and environment creating a spiritual essence that we call home? For we all do recognize where home is, like a magnet swings to the north we aim for the land of our birth where we feel we belong.

My own home is in the county of Lancashire, situated in the North West of England, some two hundred miles from London. It was once a huge area with major cities such as Manchester and Liverpool within its boundaries. Those boundaries changed dramatically in the early 1960s reducing the Red Rose County to less than half its size. Today, Lancashire is more a state of mind, but it still exists, the boundary changes have effectively altered nothing.

Charles Nevin, a author and journalist, born in St. Helens, set out to discover the spirit, the heart and soul of the county in his book 'Lancashire; where women die of love'. The title is a quotation from Balzac the great French novelist. Nevin's journey of discovery started in a boarding house in Blackpool, noted for fresh air and fun, where he found that the archetypal landlady, all rules and regulations, lived on. 'I asked Mrs. Harris what had happened to the battleaxe Blackpool landlady of legend. 'A myth!' she replied. Just then someone arrived. 'I hope he's not come in for his breakfast, because it's cold'. Said Mrs. Harris. Clearly the current incumbent failed to recognize that she was the new edition, the very epitome of the myth she so disparaged.

On the outskirts of Wigan, a town insulted by George Orwell in his book 'The Road To Wigan Pier', Nevin found that some there believed it connected with King Arthur. There is, in fact, a theme park called Camelot at Standish just down the road from the pier, which really does exist, it's a jetty on the canal once used by the barges bringing coal etc. to the mills. Camelot boasts 'jousting knights battling for good against evil'. Seeking the source of this idea Nevin contacted the original owner of Camelot, Mr. John Rigby. Rigby explained that the concept came from a discussion he had with a professor from Manchester who had told him of the legend of King Arthur's battle at Wigan close by the river Douglas which flows through the town. When Nevin asked at the local post office if anyone knew about this the postmaster replied 'maybe that would explain why they're always fighting round her.

Lancashire has produced many famous comedians and the county is noted for its whimsical sense of humour. Nevin lists some well known names, George Formby, Gracie Fields, Frank Randle, Tommy Handley, Les Dawson, Ken Dodd, Eric Morecambe, Victoria Wood, Peter Kay, Steve Coogan and Stan Laurel all were born in Lancashire. There exists in Ulverston, Cumbria (ex-Lancs.) a museum to the memory of Laurel and Hardy, Stan, the thin one from the comedy films, was born there. When Nevin visted this museum he found it to be a 'joyous jumble, a heady hymn to clutter and benign disorder. In short, exactly like Stan and Ollie themselves, another fine mess.' One exhibit, believe it or not, is the toilet seat that belonged to Stan Laurel. Ulverston has another claim to fame, it is the place where pole-vaulting was invented. According to local legend the farmers used poles to leap over ditches.

Reading Nevin's book on Lancashire caused me to ponder on the nature of the place, not as a geographical location, but as a way of being. The people Nevin describes, such as the Wigan taxi driver who when asked if he can drive him to a certain public house replies 'If I have to' encapsulate the essential attitude of Lancashire. The comment made by said taxi driver being a whimsical opinion on the selected destination and not on the task itself. Being a Lancastrian I recognized the style as being typical, as though the man was faintly amused at the thought of someone wanting to visit that particular pub.

Each area, each county of the UK seems to have its very own attitude or mindset. The folk of Yorkshire, the county adjoining Lancashire, have a totally different approach to life. There is a famous rhyme about people from Yorkshire: 'You must hear all; you must say nothing. You must sup all; you must pay nothing. And if ever you do anything for nothing, do it for yourself.' Despite the close proximity of Yorkshire to Lancashire there is a noticeable difference in the nature of the population. In Lancashire people are friendly, helpful, generous, funny and obviously amused at life in general. This is not so in many other areas of the UK. For example, without wishing to cast aspersions, can you imagine a London taxi driver light heartedly alluding to the undesirable nature of an establishment to which his fare requests to be driven, or a postmaster in Cheltenham commenting adversely about the pugilistic predilections of local residents?

So what is it within a given location that creates recognizable character traits? Charles Nevin's book appears to conclude that it is generational, attitude passed down over the ages from father to son. That is, without doubt, a major factor, but I also believe that the very ground itself holds folk memories and that these are assimilated into the being of residents via a form of subtle psychometric infusion. The result being a kind of collective sub-conscious base upon which the individual character develops producing unique minds supported by the same intangible infrastructure. There is, as they say, no place like home and is it not strange that deep within us we each instinctively know where it is?

Lancashire, Where Woman Die of Love. By Charles Nevin Published by Mainstream Publishing ISBN 1-84018-871-5

CHAPTER SIXTY NINE

I REALLY LIKED SPIKE MILLIGAN (1918-2002)

Spike Milligan makes me laugh, his work is timeless and is as funny today as it was when first written. His 'An Audience With Spike', on ITV illustrated what a comic genius the man was. Anyone over the age of 40 will most likely have happy memories of BBC Radio's 'The Goon Show' in which Spike along with Peter Sellers, Harry Seacombe and for a time the noted Spiritualist; Michael Bentine, entertained us. So why am I writing about a comedian in Psychic World? You may well ask. Well I believe that laughter is a gift from God that uplifts the spirit, and anyone who has made as many people giggle as dear old Mr. Milligan is fulfilling a fundamental spiritual need within us all. Consider this from Spike's novel Puckoon:

The Irish Catholic priest Father Rudden is trying to raise funds for the restoration of the church. In desperation he has told his congregation that he will perform a miracle and ask The Lord to make fire fall from heaven. The church pews are packed with expectant parishioners as the priest speaks; 'I COMMAND FIRE TO FALL FROM HEAVEN!' The sibilant voice of the verger comes wafting hysterically from the loft. 'Just a minute Father, the cat's peed on the matches!'.

Why do we find that funny? Well it is in itself an amusing scene, then there is the obvious analogy to be drawn between that little sketch and mediumship. The general public expect miracles all the time from mediums and psychics. If the established church and the priests that serve it had to prove their abilities in the same way that mediums do, then I suspect many would discover that the proverbial pussy had wet their wherewithal.

I once heard a medium deliver a message to a lady in a public demonstration that was worthy of the pen of Spike Milligan. In her late 60's this dear woman accepted the name given and said it was her late husband whom she had buried over ten years ago. The entire audience sat spellbound as detail after detail issued from the medium concerning the late gentleman. Then, as a parting shot, this little gem came through; 'He wants to know why you didn't bury him with his false teeth in?' The lady looked shocked 'I just forgot to give them to the undertaker' she replied 'I've still got them in the bathroom cabinet at home!'. That brought the house down as you can imagine.

There is something about laughter that enriches our souls, quite why it is rarely heard in places of worship is beyond me. However personal experience tells me that many priests consider a good chuckle in church to be totally inappropriate. Within church circles there are often exaggerated codes of conduct that define acceptable and unacceptable behaviour. As a boy of just 8 years I was a member of Saint Margaret's Church choir in Prestwich, Manchester. Our choir master was a man of great personal dignity who encouraged his choirboys to follow the fine, gentlemanly example he set. However, boys will be boys, as he found out.

It came the time for the annual choir trip, this being a day excursion to some beauty spot, the choir master selected the seaside town of Southport. We all wore our best school uniforms, caps, shirt, tie and blazer. My mother looked so proud of me as she stood waving us off on the platform of the railway station.

The highlight of the day for me was when I won a bottle of scent on a hoopla stall at the fairground. Unfortunately the cap broke and the contents emptied into my pocket, it was powerful smelling stuff. Then, on the way home on the train, one of the bigger boys grabbed my school cap and, for a joke, flung it out of the window. You can imagine this concerned me as my mother had purchased that cap only the week before. So I returned the compliment and flung his cap through the same window that had accepted mine. It was no easy task! In the process I lost my tie, but gained a black eye. By this time the choir master was in hysterics, pleading with us to stop fighting. Well I didn't start it.

I shall never forget climbing off the train at Prestwich station. My shirt was filthy, I had no cap, no tie, various bruises and I smelt like Zsa Zsa Gabor's poodle. The look of abject horror on my father's face is with me to this day. Mother just glared at me. We drove home in stony silence, with the car windows wide open. Without supper I was dispatched to bed, in absolute disgrace. Some days later a letter arrived from Saint Margaret's church, quite what it said I was never told, but my parents looked at me in a very suspicious way. Needless to say, my days as a choirboy were over. Looking back on that experience I can smile, but at the time I was made to understand that I had brought some kind of shame upon my family's good name. It seems that boys can be boys, but not on choir trips.

There are, within certain congregations, social positions marked by various accepted indicators. These form a kind of pecking order, best Sunday clothes, new hat, top pew etc. Quite how this brings one closer to God I don't know, some obviously think it does. But have a good look at these people, I see so many miserable looking individuals who are supposedly deeply religious, surely the one thing the search for spiritual truth should bring is happiness. Yet many wear their devotions to their God like a dark cloak that smothers the joy one should feel in living this wonderful life. I am certain the good Lord doesn't want us to walk in fear, living neat little orderly lives, controlled by sets of sombre religious and social rules. If everyone conformed imagine how dreary our existence would be. Give me an audience with Spike Milligan please, but spare me the new cap, someone is sure to throw it out of a window and I've been through all that once.

CHAPTER SEVENTY

SILENT NIGHT

People often ask me how one might set about becoming a published author. The answer is reasonably simple, start writing and sending off your work to magazines, publishers, agents etc. With regard to having a book published one way to do this is to get a copy of The Writers and Artists Yearbook and look through the lists to find a publisher or literary agent that has a list in which your work might fit. For example there would be no point in sending your MS on the paranormal to Mills and Boon. Having found what you consider to be the right publisher or agent send in first a covering letter asking if they would be interested in reading your work. You should include a single page synopsis and an SAE. Also include a very brief biography of yourself listing your published work to date. That is what I did in 1990 when I sent a letter to the editors at one of the world's biggest publishers HarperCollins. They replied, I sent them an outline of the book, they liked this, sent for me and within three months I had a commission to write the book which they subsequently published. That book was titled: 'The Psychic World Of James Byrne'.

My first success as a writer was winning The Lancashire Evening Post short story competition in 1989. This is the ghost story that started my career as a published author.

SILENT NIGHT

The deep leaden grey sky darkened as soft snow fell in flakes on this cold Christmas Eve. Alone in her neat and tidy front room, toasting her toes before a flaming log fire, sat Miss Felicity. Her fingers ruffled the fur of Marmaduke, the comfortable cat.

The Westminster clock chimed eight. "Soon be time for bed" she murmured, disturbed from her half-sleep by the familiar tones. Felicity gazed towards the table and her eyes rested on the now yellowing photograph of her long lost lover. Then her mind drifted back to that Christmas Eve many years ago when her Edward had stood by that very table and promised that they would be married when he returned from the war. But he never returned. She thought of the simple stark message from the War Office, "Missing in action, presumed dead". Felicity brushed away a tear. "So many years, so many years" she whispered and shuffled into her pink pom-pom slippers. Outside the frost froze the flakes of snow into a hard white carpet. An unearthly silence settled about the little house as she quietly prepared for bed.

Undaunted by the bitter cold, the all-male choir of St Mary the Virgin's church gathered in the congregational hall. Dressed in their warmest clothes with gloves, knitted hats and thick socks the singers carolled forth into the frosty street, determined to bring the spirit of Christmas to one and all. "Keep those lanterns up lads" shouted Harry, the keen as mustard choirmaster, his breath misting in the winter's night.

Inside her snug bedroom Miss Felicity curled cosy in a deep soft eider-downed bed. Drifting slowly into dreamless sleep she heard, far, far away in the distance, the faint sounds of the approaching carol singers. "Christmas alone" she sighed, thinking of times long past, when her life held promise, and Edward.

"Come on lads, let's sing Silent Night it's always a favourite. Harry cajoled his carollers who by this time were beginning to feel the chill of this frozen Christmas Eve. Slowly they began walking along the road leading to Miss Felicity's home. The house stood slightly sheltered behind snow-hung conifers dimly lit by a solitary street lamp.

"Mind if I join you for this one?" The voice came from a tall young man in a long brown overcoat with bright brass buttons. Harry was startled; the stranger had appeared, so it seemed, from thin air. "Must have been the snow deadening his footsteps" he thought. "Yes why not, spirit of Christmas and all that, hope you've got a good voice." Harry led the group to a halt almost directly beneath the bedroom window of Miss

Felicity's house. They formed themselves into their practised pattern with the tall stranger standing at the rear. He sang along with them in a deep, dark haunting voice: " Silent night, Holy night, All is calm, All is bright".

Miss Felicity was awake at once. They were singing her favourite carol. Happy memories flooded back from a time long, long ago when she was a young woman. Felicity filled with emotion, thinking of those distant days and what might have been. Pushing back the heavy eiderdown she shuffled to the window and drew back the deep red velvet curtains. Staring out into the bleak night she saw, in the semi-darkness below, the glow of the carol singers' lanterns. "Holy infant so tender and mild"

Her heart seemed to leap into her mouth, there at the back of the group of carollers he stood. Yet it could not be him, tall, strong, sure of himself dressed in his Army greatcoat, bright brass buttons reflecting the lanterns' yellow light. "Sleep in heavenly peace, Sleep in heavenly peace"

With an agility that denied her years Felicity hurried downstairs and flung the front door wide open. "Edward!......Edward!" she cried, but the carol singers had gone. She could see, for a brief moment, the indistinct outline of the group as it turned away disappearing into the swirling winter mist. Careless of the cold, she walked out to where the carollers had stood, singing of a Holy night long, long ago. In the dim light cast by the lone street lamp Felicity saw something twinkling, something yellow on the crisp white carpet of snow. Her thin fingers reached down and picked up a single brass button.

"You're quite a good singer" Harry said to the stranger as the choir strolled back to the congregational hall. "Have you ever thought of joining a choral society?" he asked. But answer came there none, from the still silent night.

CHAPTER SEVENTY ONE

INSPIRATION-V-PERSPIRATION

Thomas Edison once said that genius is one percent inspiration, ninety-nine percent perspiration. Now I make no claims in the genius department, though my wife, close family and friends do think I have a great gift for getting into trouble. However, I do believe that many of the worlds great works of literature and music are inspired. If this were not so how could they inspire others. I am thinking of such works as Samuel Taylor Coleridge's Kubla Khan 'In Xanadu did Kubla Khan a stately pleasure dome decree etc'. Coleridge had been resting in an easy chair and woke from a light sleep with that poem running through his mind. Taking a pen Coleridge wrote down an outline of the verse he already had spinning inside his brain, he did not sweat blood creating it. Kubla Khan and the damsel with a dulcimer came to him whilst he slept.

Paul McCartney of The Beatles tells the story of how he woke early one morning with the music and words of 'Yesterday' playing in his head. He immediately copied these down and one of the most frequently recorded songs of all time was born. Was that inspiration or perspiration?

Now there is a saying that God helps those who first help themselves and I sincerely believe this to be true. This initial phase is the real perspiration, the groundwork that goes in before inspiration can be interpreted with any meaning. Imagine being on the telephone to someone and trying to tell them to write down your name and address. It must have happened to us all at some time. Right; you say, 'John Sutton' and they say, 'Hang on I haven't got a pen' or 'There's no paper here can you call back' or 'You what! did you say Mutton?'. In other words if the intended recipient of the message is not prepared to receive it then no matter how hard the sender tries it will not get through.

That is a very simplified explanation of information being lost through lack of good preparation. In the instances given above, of Coleridge and McCartney, the recipients were both masters of their craft. They had the ability to receive and react to the inspiration they received and had gained this through long years of development. As a writer I awake with ideas running through my head, often at 2am I will jump out of bed, switch on the Word Process programme on my computer and write the outline down.

Now imagine if I had no computer, no sophisticated word process programme, no note pad even or pen, no tape recorder, nothing and had never attempted to teach myself to write creatively. What would I do with the inspired ideas whizzing round inside my mind? The answer is I would most probably turn over and go back to sleep.

Now those in the next world who bring us to inspiration know who is able. It would be useless to give Paul McCartney visions of building a bridge to France, he most probably wouldn't have a clue about engineering, but this is known to the spirit world. They know who to approach, who is available. Our duty is to make ourselves available through preparing and mastering our God given gifts. Be that as engineers, architects or creative artists.

The idea that great writers, composers, poets and musicians sit down and invent their work without inspiration is, to me at least, unthinkable. OK I too have heard the dross that today passes for pop music and I am sure we all recognise that this is low grade rubbish designed to give young people something to throw into their parents dustbins. No serious person considers the work of product groups, that are created by major record labels, as more than cheap preteen pop-culture garbage. There is nothing inspired or inspiring in a gang of fast fading floozies flopping their undistinguished attributes about on junk TV. That kind of bilge is 100 percent perspiration and zero percent inspiration.

When we think of inspiration we should look to works such as those of Wolfgang Amadeus Mozart. As a child of 7 years he

was writing symphonies for full orchestras. His lifes work was so extensive; 50 symphonies, 27 piano concertos, 37 violin sonatas, operas such as The Magic Flute and Cosi Fan Tutte etc. that it took a man of some high intelligence,one Ludwig von Kochel, to even list it. Listen to Mozart to hear genius if you doubt that it exists. How other than by inspiration could this mere child have created such a collection of undoubted classical masterpieces. He was dead and buried by the age of 35.

We will all, no doubt, have heard of children who seem to have some unexplained ability. We often hear parents say 'Well I don't know where he/she gets it from'. If it is not inherited, and who can possibly think that genetics is solely responsible, then the source must be from elsewhere. The argument is an old one, 'Nature or Nurture'. Is the child/ adult a product of genetic programming or of their environment?

Carl Gustav Jung suggested that there exists a collective unconscious body of knowledge that is multicultural and available to all who know how to open the door. Is it possible that our great geniuses have the ability to ease back the veil and see into the vast reservoir of facts, figures and imagination that Jung suggests exists in another unseen dimension. Perhaps in dreams those of great creative genius enter this kingdom of collected thoughts and deed seeking and finding inspiration that they then translate using their professional skills. Remember Mozart's father was himself a musician of wide acclaim and would have taught his son from birth. Thus the door was half open, all that was required was for young Wolfgang to step through into the world of inspiration, was he lead there by those in the spirit world who recognised his potential?

It is my belief that we can all take that step into the unseen land of learning, where we will discover the inspiration we should be seeking to live creative and enriched lives here on earth. Gifted children can make that transition, they are too young to realise that they are walking with angels. We as adults shrink from the absolute blinding power of true knowledge, preferring the half truth, the accepted and the acceptable. We are, in effect, programmed to be ordinary. To be like everyone else is, after all, a very safe bet.

It is my personal belief that those who try to work creatively will, in time and through years of hard work and perspiration, be lead into the world of inspiration by the God who loves them. As I said at the very beginning of this feature, I believe that God will only help those who help themselves. It's never too late, Cathrine Cookson, the author of hundreds of quite spiritually uplifting books, was over forty years of age when she was first published. That lady was an inspiration to us all.

CHAPTER SEVENTY TWO

SUFFER THE LITTLE CHILDREN

BBC TV's brilliant and brave Panorama series recently featured a documentary examining the incidence of the sexual abuse of children within the religious group known as The Jehovah's Witnesses. This harrowing programme offered up first hand testimony indicting the 'Elders' and leaders of this supposedly Christian faith in covering up and effectively condoning the sexual exploitation of both girls and boys. Numerous individuals spoke on camera of the ordeals that they had suffered not only at the hands of their abusers but also when they officially complained to the senior officials of their Jehovah's Witness Kingdom Hall, as their places of meeting are called. Some described years of physical molestation suffered in silence because the 'Elders' to whom they reported the offenders refused to accept their statements. Police Officers on both sides of the Atlantic were interviewed and gave tellingly similar accounts of their experiences in attempting to prosecute sex-offenders within the Jehovah's Witnesses. It seemed, to the Police Officers involved, that the 'Elders' were effectively obstructing justice and protecting the Witnesses that abused children.

Religious cults are notorious as breeding grounds for sexual perverts who seem to thrive within such exclusive groups, like pernicious weeds upon a dunghill. There have been many such minority movements in the past that have at their very core the rottenest, vilest and most corrupt individuals. For example in the mid-1970's there was the horror of 'Reverend' Jim Jones and his 'People's Temple'. Jones gathered about him a group of seemingly well-educated people whom he indoctrinated into believing that he, the 'Reverend' Jim Jones, was communicating the word of God. All who heard Jones speak, and by many accounts he spoke for hours upon end, were told that they were hearing the voice of The Almighty God. So when Jones began giving obviously deranged orders to his followers they simply obeyed without question because this, they thought, was the will of God incarnate in the physical body of Jones.

The 'Reverend' Jim Jones was not just a control-freak who demanded absolute obedience to his commands he was also a sexual deviant who abused men, women and children. At one point Jones handed out pre-printed forms that asked the question: 'Do you want to have sex with Father' father being Jones. Shortly after receiving numerous positive responses Jones instructed his followers that sexual relations were banned except with him, that is ALL such relationships whether in marriage or not. Jones's own sexual activities increased with him openly indulging in homosexual encounters with male members of The People's Temple.

The strange thing about this kind of abuse is that those who succumb to it are frequently educated and otherwise seemingly sane individuals. However, once within a cult such as Jones's the escape routes are limited. The horrific end of The People's Temple is well documented; Jones took his followers to Guyana where he had a compound that he called 'Jonestown' located in what he euphemistically named 'The Promised Land'. There his abuses continued until in 1978 the USA Government ordered an investigation. Jones had the leader of this enquiry, Leo Ryan, shot and killed as he attempted to board his plane back to America. Following this murder Jones ordered all members of The Peoples Temple to drink fruit juice laced with cyanide. Armed guards enforced this and even the babies had the poison squirted into their tiny mouths. By the end of Saturday, November 14th 1978 over nine hundred of Jones's followers, including the man himself, were dead. All because they believed that the 'Reverend' Jim Jones was God.

Jones is far from being the only messianic maniac to die amongst his converts. During the early 1990's one David

Koresh announced to all who would listen that he was 'King David' and also 'The Son of God'. Surprisingly quite a number of people not only listened but also believed. Koresh began his new career as a rogue messiah at the age of twenty-seven by seducing Lois Roden the sixty eight year old female leader of The Davidian Christian sect. He told her that he had received 'divine' guidance and she was to be the mother of his child. With the sect leader as his mistress Koresh quickly assumed control and convinced the members that he was, in effect, God incarnate.

Koresh then proceeded to use the Davidian sect members as his personal chattels and took his pick of the pretty young children as sexual partners. First he 'married' Rachel Jones, a fourteen-year-old girl and then seduced Karen Doyle her friend of similar age. Koresh stated that he had been divinely guided to 'give his seed' to these children. One of his younger conquests was a twelve-year old girl called Michele. Koresh claimed that God had shown him a passage in The Bible from the Song of Solomon about a girl with no breasts and this he took as a sign that he was to take this pre-pubescent child as his 'wife'. Koresh actually impregnated twenty-two of his young female followers.

David Koresh's abuse of children did not stop with the gratification of his sexual urges; he was also physically abusive towards innocent young people. In one particularly horrible incident Koresh demanded that Cyrus his own three-year old son acknowledge another sect member as his true mother, she wasn't. When Cyrus refused, as any child would, Koresh removed the boy's clothing and beat him naked in public for twenty minutes then forced this baby to sleep in a rat infested garage. When the child still declined to agree that the wrong lady was his mother Koresh starved him for two days.

The Davidian sect ruled by David Koresh came to a bloody end on the 19th April 1993 when USA forces stormed their headquarters in Waco, Texas. Fire swept the buildings and Koresh, along with all but nine of his followers who escaped, was found dead. When the authorities searched the burnt out remains they discovered that many of the corpses were lying face down in the ashes, the typical position of fire victims, but others had been either shot or poisoned. The survivors said that Koresh had decided they would all men, women and little children, commit suicide.

It seems obvious to Spiritualists that individual human beings have absolutely no authority, divine or otherwise, to proclaim that they are God incarnate. Nor do sects or cults, be they Christian or otherwise, have any authority to interfere in the Personal Responsibility that we all have to our own immortal soul. As a man said, 'to thine own self be true and it must follow, as the night the day, you can then be false to no man.' In other words, deep inside, we know what is right and what is wrong. The hard part is being strong enough to stand up and speak the truth when all around are bowing their heads.

CHAPTER SEVENTY THREE

THE POWER OF WORDS

It was Edward George Bulwer-Lytton (1803-73) who wrote 'Beneath the rule of men entirely great/The pen is mightier than the sword'. Words do indeed have an authority that can be used for good or for evil and they work a mysterious magic when manipulated by a master. I recently received a book from a lady named Annie Dale titled: 'From the 26 Letters of The Alphabet'. Reading through this book made me ponder on the power that has been unleashed from just 26 letters A to Z. Think of the use of racist or religious terms used to incite hatred and violence against others of different persuasions or ethnic origins. Or consider the truth spoken from the innocent mouth of a young child. We all use words, be they spoken or written they help to create our reality and enable us to construct what we believe to be plans and possibilities. Within Annie's book I found the following question: 'If you could select just seven words to express the meaning of your life what would those words be?' Here are some suggestions taken from Annie's book:

LIVE. LOVE. ASPIRE. READ. SERVE. LAUGH. UNDERSTAND: Wonderful words, the most powerful of these is, in my mind, understand. Seeking understanding, as the late Lord Runcie Archbishop of Canterbury did throughout his life, is undoubtedly a worthy pursuit. However, true understanding can only come from the consideration of all viewpoints, as the Archbishop pointed out when he asked us to pray for the families of Argentine soldiers killed in the Falklands conflict. To understand a situation from one side only is not to understand it at all. I'm certain many of us will recall with horror the tabloid headline that followed the sinking of the Argentine ship The Belgrano: 'GOTCHA!' 900 young men died as they were sailing away from the scene of conflict and we are invited to applaud. Or the jingoistic gibberish spouted by the then Prime Minister Margaret Thatcher as she condescendingly advised all to 'Rejoice! Rejoice!' when she declared that we had 'won the war'. Words spoken in public by public figures such as Thatcher or Churchill often echo down the ages affecting all our lives. It is a great pity that those words are all too often associated with war, death and destruction.

Annie Dale: 'Every word a man writes, every act in which he indulges, every word he utters, serves as inescapable evidence of the nature of that which is embedded in his heart'. In other words, by their fruit shall you know them. We are all aware of people who seem to bring a sense of joy into any human interaction. Good humour and a ready wit often help reduce tension in even the most difficult of situations. But not everyone has a sense of fun as I found out some years ago.

I think of the time I was working as a Hospital Officer inside the secure ward of H.M. Prison Manchester also known as Strangeways. The inmates on the ward included many that had committed terrible offences that would eventually lead to them serving life sentences. One patient had deliberately set alight to his own home in an attempt to convince the local council that their neighbours were persecuting his family. In the resulting fire his two daughters suffered 90% burns and subsequently died. I was caring for this socially inadequate and distraught individual when the Governor and his Chief Discipline Officer entered on a tour of inspection. Quite why I will perhaps never know but the Governor decided to inspect the ward floor and found there a slight residue of the fixative used to secure the tiles fitted some years previously. I was called away from my nursing duties and this was pointed out to me, I was asked to explain why it was still present. One can perhaps imagine that five-year old glue marks on the floor of a very busy prison hospital ward were not my top priority. So, I called for the inmate that cleaned the ward, introduced him by name and number to the most senior governor in the entire prison and left them to get on with it. The patients on the ward thought this hilarious but for some unknown reason the

Governor and Chief Discipline Officer were not amused. I don't work there any more.

.

In the year 1990 Strangeways jail in Manchester was almost totally destroyed by rioting inmates. Somewhere along the way to that destruction the prisoners had lost their ability to see the funny side of doing 'porridge' in a vindictive Victorian slum.

It is important to maintain a sense of humour in this life and the power of words help us to do just that. In Annie's book she offers some wonderful advice 'Memories and happenings we write in the book of life, each one a page or chapter printed on the mind. We cannot erase the sorrow or edit out the tears, or undo the wrongs we may have done. And we can never relive the years, but we can write new chapters in our book of life.'

As we go through our earthly lives how many of us must wish we could rewrite certain passages in our own book of life, we cannot. Indeed our personal destiny may already be written and our lives preordained. If this is so then how much more important it is to maintain a healthy perspective on life and proceed with grace and good humour. For myself I believe that we enjoy free will to explore the possibilities of this world and all that is within it. However the ultimate destiny of each and every one of us is surely known before our birth. We may be as Shakespeare said 'But players on this great stage of fools'. If this is the case then I want to know who wrote my part!

Annie Dale includes in her book these gentle but powerful words: 'Within the wealth of words lies dynamic power. Rich and poor alike may use this abundant 'gold' For in a word we may discover what Proverbs implies in 'A word fitly spoken is like apples of gold in pictures of silver' Proverbs XXV XI.' Written countless hundreds of years ago those words echo down the centuries creating positive images that live forever. Unlike the dark rumblings of war such words of love bring understanding and joy to our lives. It is for such beauty that we should all Rejoice! Rejoice! and not for the misguided mutterings of those who deal in death, destruction and authoritarian abuse.

You can write to Annie Dale Ph.D at 'The Haven' 5 Links Avenue, Mablethorpe, Lincs. LN12 10L Her book is available so if you do want a copy an appropriate donation would be appreciated I'm sure. Why not tell Annie your own seven words that define your life.

CHAPTER SEVENTY FOUR

POSSESSION AND THE POSSESSED

There are those, such as Dr Susan Blackmore, that deny the existence of discarnate entities believing that the mind and the body are as one. Therefore, they argue, there can be no such thing as spirits and, per se, no such thing as possession. However, there are others, equally well qualified, such as Psychologist Dr Keith Hearne, who believe that the body is the host of the mind (or spirit) and that it is possible for discarnate entities to enter the physical being of an individual and become the dominant personality. When this happens it may be termed possession. But is possession fact or fantasy?

In 'The Spirits Book' Allan Kardec outlines his understanding of the possible influence discarnate entities may have upon individuals. In this book he writes: 'Do spirits influence our thoughts and actions? Their influence upon (human beings) is greater than you suppose, for it is very often they who direct both'. In other words Kardec is stating that we may all, at times, be susceptible to the influence of discarnate spirits. Some people may even become possessed by a spirit or spirits.

Probably the most famous case of possession occurred in the year 1663 when the parish priest Urbain Grandier of Loudun in France was accused of bewitching nuns and causing them to be possessed by demons. This case involved young women, nuns, in a local convent who, according to accounts, 'screamed blasphemies and threw themselves onto the floor writhing around whilst displaying their private parts'. The nuns claimed to be possessed and these claims were investigated by two church appointed exorcists Fr. Lactance and Fr. Tranquille. The inquisitors tortured Urbain Grandier and despite his continued protestations of innocence he was subsequently tried, found guilty and burned at the stake. The Mother Superior of the convent at Loudun, Soeur Jeanne des Agnes states in her autobiography that she herself enjoyed the sexual feelings caused within her by the demons. One theory re this case is that the nuns suffered from mass hysteria brought on by the presence of the promiscuous priest Grandier who had been intimate with a number of them. However, within one month of the execution of Grandier, Fr. Lactance, who had tortured him, became possessed himself and died insane. Some few years later his co-inquisitor Fr. Tranquille also suffered possession, fell writhing on to the floor uttering blasphemies and died. The above case was the subject of a film 'The Devils' which starred Oliver Reed as Urbain Grandier.

.

The American psychic investigator Max Freedom Long believed that 'possession' resulted when discarnate spirits entered the body of a human being. Investigating the native magicians or Kahunas (keepers of the secret) in Hawaii, Long found that according to their religion (Huna) man has three 'selves' 1. The Low Self: the emotional and unconscious mind. 2. The Middle Self: our personal consciousness 3. The High Self: our superconscious mind that has the ability to see the future. They believed that after death the three selves separated and that it was the Middle Self that had the potential to become a ghost. Allan Kardec wrote in 'The Spirits Book': 'People who die suddenly, or are unprepared for death by reason of wasted lives, are often unaware that they are dead, and become homeless wanderers on the earth, attracted by human beings of like mind sharing their lives and experiences'. Such wandering spirits, or ghosts, see this material world but being without a body are unable to interact with it. They may still harbour all the desires that they had whilst physically incarnate and seeking gratification find a host i.e. a body and enter into it taking over possession. Thus the host body becomes possessed.

Psychologist Dr Keith Hearne answers the question: What are we to make of cases of possession? In the real world, in real therapy, there is no doubt that clients sometimes actually do seem to have discarnate entities within them. They often simply manifest spontaneously. Therapists can't ignore them, so there has to be a protocol for dealing with such situations. The entities that are usually encountered seem to be the spirits of human beings who, upon dying, for various reasons failed to go into the Light (universally reported by resuscitated persons and referred to in many ancient texts including the Tibetan Book of the Dead) and instead re-attached to a living person. They exist as spiritual parasites in a human host.

If spirit releasing therapy did not exist it would have to be invented – but of course such treatment has a very long history. In ancient times the notion of earthbound spirits causing psychological and physical problems in people was perfectly accepted. There are many references to the phenomenon in the Bible for example. About a quarter of the healing of Jesus involved releasing spirits.'

Trance Mediums allow themselves to become the temporary host of discarnate spirits that speak through them. One of the most famous trance mediums of all time was Mrs Leonore Piper whose spirit control Phinuit would regularly take possession of her body passing messages through her. The verifiable facts passed to the observers, such as Professor James Hyslop president of The American Society for Psychical Research, proved beyond reasonable doubt that this possession of Mrs Piper was a reality. But what happens when the possessed are unwilling hosts?

Psychologist Dr Keith Hearne explains the procedure for spirit releasing:
'There are several stages in the modern therapeutic method for spirit attachment. After the spirit has identified itself, simple questions via the client will determine the circumstances surrounding the attachment. Usually it happened when the host person was vulnerable – physically or mentally. "When did you attach ?" will reveal the occasion – often to the host's amazement. The therapist gets the entity to comprehend that it has violated the host's space and unfairly influenced their life. Eventually, this logical approach undermines their rationale for staying. They are made to see that they are 'stuck' in their spiritual advancement and need to

progress to the Light, where they can meet again with their peers and loved ones. Such realisations and the re-awakened instinct to go into the Light are enough to precipitate leaving.'

The truth of possession of human beings by discarnate spirits is a contentious issue. However there is a vast case history that seems to substantiate the belief that discarnate entities can take over possession of an unwilling host body and professionals such as Dr Keith Hearne testify to the reality of this phenomenon. You can contact Dr Hearne by telephoning his clinic: The European College 01784 479930 or by email: training@european-college.co.uk

CHAPTER SEVENTY FIVE

SPIRIT COMMUNICATION: FACT OR FAITH?

The basis of the Spiritualist faith is communication between the incarnate and the discarnate. Such communication is most usually through a spirit-medium who has a developed gift be that clairaudience (hearing the voices) clairvoyance (seeing and also hearing) or clairsentience (sensing the information). As Spiritualists we accept that such communication is possible and when a medium passes on a message to us from our departed loved ones in the next world that message is truthfully given. However there are now and no doubt there always have been, tricksters, charlatans, out and out fakes that pretend to communicate but are really having a laugh. One only has to put the television on these days to see some fool in a dark house spooking up imaginary ghosts. The biggest offender of all the fake ghost hunting TV shows was Most Haunted which at one time featured a psychic who claimed to channel the spirits and pretended to go into a trance. On one notable occasion this prankster even managed to channel an imaginary, totally fictitious character called Kreed Kafer, invented by the resident parapsychologist to test his veracity. That is the name Kreed Kafer and a false story about this character were fed to the so-called psychic who swallowed the bait and pretended to channel him. You can see the result on the internet at YouTube.com there is the video showing this fraud doing a fake trance routine and putting on a stupid voice shouting 'KKKreeeed.....KKKKaaaaafer' Which as the parapsychologist knew when he designed this test was an anagram of DEREK FAKER. The faker being set up was of course Derek Acorah.

Such ridiculous nonsense as Most Haunted has had a deleterious affect upon Spiritualism and Psychic-Mediums in general as the public, who are hoodwinked by this unmitigated bilge, believe that trance communication and ghosts appearing left right and centre are what actually happens during a clairvoyant consultation. It is not as if Spiritualism needs any more enemies, we surely have sufficient to deal with and I think now of the sceptics. I myself am sceptical, if someone I do not know tells me they are psychic and can communicate with my departed relations then it must be reasonable to expect a little proof? For example my father was a Police Inspector with the CID serving in the Greater Manchester force. He was what you might call a typical copper, big, tough, analytical, outspoken and honest. Now if a psychic-medium were receiving a message from my dad there is just no way he would want to tell me that I had just bought a new jacket or some other such mundane nonsense. There would have to be something serious, something verifiable in any message given to me before I could accept it really was from my father. But I know he is around me as I have seen him fully materialised many times. That is my proof. Spirit communication is therefore not a matter of faith for me, it is a matter of fact.

The Skeptic magazine is edited by Dr. Michael Shermer a brilliant and highly intelligent gentleman who does not believe for one minute that there can be communication with the dead. He and his colleague James Randi are of the firm opinion that psychic-mediums are nothing more than charlatans who are, in effect, defrauding the public. Randi makes many valid points in his lectures on the falsity of psychics and to a certain extent one can agree with him. For example if you were trying to tell someone your name would you perhaps consider giving them a clue by say whispering your initial as in 'My name starts with a J.' I know I wouldn't I would say, my name is John. So why would a spirit give only an initial? Such nonsense brings the whole matter of spirit communication into disrepute. Dr. Shermer lectures on the gullibility of people and how they can be quite easily tricked into believing they see and hear things when in fact they are deluding themselves. I can see where these two learned gentleman are coming from and agree that some of what we may perceive of as paranormal phenomena is little more than wishful thinking.

The UKs answer to Dr. Michael Shermer is perhaps Dr. Susan Blackmore who for many years conducted extensive research into the paranormal. Her scientific approach led her to conclude that communication with the discarnate was not a verifiable fact. These are her words: 'It was just over thirty years ago that I had the dramatic out-of-body experience that convinced me of the reality of psychic phenomena and launched me on a crusade to show those closed-minded scientists that consciousness could reach beyond the body and that death was not the end. Just a few years of careful experiments changed all that. I found no psychic phenomena – only wishful thinking, self-deception, experimental error and, occasionally, fraud. I became a sceptic.' Dr. Blackmore is no longer researching the paranormal.

Spiritualism is unique among faiths in that it provides, through its Church mediums, proof that there is life after death and the communication of spirit is essentially a fact. However, the level of what is considered proof varies from individual to individual. For me the idea that my late father would return to tell me that my curtains in the lounge had just been changed is not only not proof but an insult to my intelligence. Watching TV and observing some fool rolling about on the floor supposedly possessed by the spirit of Dick Turpin makes me doubt their sanity and one wonders what it is doing to the general public? I suspect that most people view such programmes as light entertainment but they actually do a great deal of harm to Spiritualism. Perhaps that is the real reason we are now seeing a vast proliferation in Psychic TV shows, to undermine the truth of spirit communication.

There is a video clip of Gordon Higginson on YouTube from the 1990s, Gordon was the President of Spiritualists National Union and was a simply brilliant medium. I personally saw him live at Manchester University in 1992 and he was accurate to the extent that he could give telephone numbers. With Gordon

Higginson mediumship was not a matter of faith, he proved it beyond reasonable doubt.

CHAPTER SEVENTY SIX

SUTTY DOG RETURNS

In the year 1997 my book PSYCHIC PETS was published by Bloomsbury Books and in it was featured a story about a little Scottish Terrier called Sutty Dog. The dog was in fact the pet of my daughter Dulcie Jane and the two were very close. Sutty Dog actually would sleep in Dulcie's room and followed her round the house. They played together in the back garden and for years the two were best of pals. Time passed and Dulcie became a young woman, she still did play with her Sutty Dog but, as young women will, she began making other friends.

As Dulcie began bringing her new friends home we all noticed how protective little Sutty Dog was of her pal. As soon as anyone new came into the house Sutty Dog would run to Dulcie's side as if guarding her and growl then bark at the strangers if they got too close to her pal. Then, one fine summer's day Dulcie told us all that she was bringing a young man to meet us and she said he was called Robert. My wife Mary and I kind of new that this young man was not just a friend but we said nothing and as for Sutty Dog, well we fully expected she would give Robert a proper barking at if he got too close to Dulcie.

It was, as I recall, late on a Sunday afternoon that Dulcie arrived home with Rob Dowrick by her side. Sutty Dog ran up to her and jumped up licking Dulcie's hand and then, to our absolute astonishment, she did the same to Rob. It was as if she knew he was to be trusted with Dulcie. After that Sutty Dog and Rob were pals too and we always said that it was Sutty that had picked the boyfriend. She had woofed like a wild thing at all the others so in a way she had.

Later the following year Dulcie Jane and Robert Dowrick were married and Sutty Dog was there to wish them a happy honeymoon as they set off from our home to fly to Tenerife. Dulcie and Rob sent a card from their honeymoon to Sutty Dog their pal and I can still see that inquisitive look on her face as I showed it to her.

Following the publication of Psychic Pets I was asked to appear on numerous TV shows promoting the book. Dulcie let me take Sutty Dog along as she was one of the star pets featured in her story: Sutty Dog and Dulcie Jane. The Dog That Picked The Boyfriend. It was with Sutty Dog that I enjoyed over thirty minutes of prime time TV on Richard and Judy's THIS MORNING, we had great fun together.

Sadly, as time passed Sutty Dog became older and gradually confused. Her health finally failed and one dark day the decision had to be made to place our friend beyond the pain of a physical reality that had become too much to bear. I called for the vet and asked my wife if she would prepare a grave in the garden near to where Sutty Dog had enjoyed so many happy hours playing with her pal Dulcie Jane and our other pet Grumbles the bulldog. I was sitting with Sutty Dog talking to her about the time we were once almost famous together and she sat still, looking up absolutely trusting me. It was an extremely difficult moment as we spent her last few minutes waiting for the vet to arrive. As we did so I heard a call from the garden, it was my wife Mary shouting to me saying that I should come and look and help a bird that had been injured. I went outside and saw there a blackbird standing still on the flags near the ground where the open grave stood waiting for Sutty Dog. I noticed the bird seemed unafraid of me which is most unusual for a wild creature. But it was clear that it was not injured.

After the vet had completed his duty and I held the now lifeless body of my little pal Sutty Dog I handed her to Mary who took her out and placed her into the grave. Gently we covered her in the earth and then stood quietly recalling the many happy days we had all shared and the time, not so long ago, when she had welcomed Rob Dowrick our fine young son-in-law and father of our wonderful grandson Aaron into our home. Then, much to our astonishment, the blackbird that Mary had thought was injured hopped across the ground and

stood at the edge of Sutty Dog's grave. It was within just a few feet of us and looked directly at me, paused and as I watched in amazement the bird flew straight up into the sky and disappeared into the blue. It was as if the bird had come to collect the soul of our friend Sutty Dog.

Some few weeks ago my wife Mary told me I needed an haircut as my long gray locks were, she said 'a right mess'. To show me what she meant Mary took a photograph of me sitting at my computer to let me see how long my hair had grown. When I opened the picture file on my computer both Mary and I were startled to see that instead of seeing my messed up hair we were seeing Sutty Dog she had materialised in my hair.

CHAPTER SEVENTY SEVEN

THE END IS NEAR!

Doom and gloom time soon as the world, as we know it, is about to end. Well they have been saying that for a long time, but seriously this time even Tony Blair is preaching the gospel of despair and he recently converted to Roman Catholicism so maybe he knows something you and I don't. This is all a bit spooky, scary even when you consider that Blair is not alone among the world's leading politicians in predicting a sticky end for us all unless...well unless we pay more taxes is what it all boils down to. Or am I being cynical?

Once upon a time, a long, long time ago there was a Mesoamerican civilisation called The Mayan. According to the latest peddlers of fear the Mayan calendar ends at the year 2012. Don't panic! These ancient, though highly developed people, were not just builders of fine cities where astronomy and mathematics were studied and taught, they also practised human sacrifice specialising in the removal of the hearts of young children who would be held down by the priests whilst having their most vital organ ripped from their chests to placate the gods. Different gods than ours, but way back then they needed their blood sacrifice and gods, false, make believe or not, tend to get what the priests tell the people they want. Today we are being told that sacrifices have to be made or the world will end. 55 days to find the solution Tony Blair said, so not long now folks!

According to the sages on the world-wide-web at sunrise on December 21, 2012 for the first time in 26,000 years the Sun raises to conjunct the intersection of the Milky Way and the plane of the ecliptic. This cosmic cross is considered to be an embodiment of the Sacred Tree, The Tree of Life a tree remembered in all the world's spiritual traditions. At this point in time we all cease to exist, or that is the latest theory.

In the USA there is a man called Al Gore who, somewhat optimistically, ran for President against the man who was counting the votes, one George W. Bush. Al Gore has made quite a name for himself predicting doom and gloom ahead unless we all cease using carbon based fuel etc. That is you and I stop using all this fuel, Al Gore needs it as he has a private jet plane, numerous huge Hummer style off the road vehicles and a massive swimming pool all consuming fuel. But we are being told by him that it all has to stop, at least for us. It's either that or Armageddon according to good old Al. But I just do not believe him. He's having a laugh!

The green movement do have a point; we all in the developed Western Civilisation consume vast amounts of the natural resources of the world. However, it is a fundamental law of physics that energy can not be dissipated it exists perpetually. Albert Einstein's theory of relativity shows that energy can be converted to mass (rest mass) and mass converted to energy. Therefore, neither mass nor pure energy are conserved separately, as it was understood in pre-relativistic physics. Today, conservation of energy refers to the conservation of the total mass-energy, which includes energy of the rest mass. Therefore, in an isolated system, mass and 'pure energy' can be converted to one another, but the total amount of energy (which includes the energy of the mass of the system) remains constant. So what is the problem?

We as spirits within a physical human body are a form of energy and we will all in time move out of the incarnate form and become discarnate beings, i.e. spirits. There appears to me to be a misunderstanding amongst many believers in life after death and this concerns the nature of the form we take in the next dimension. In time I am certain that the scientific world will prove that our physical forms, our human bodies, are powered by an energy source that we today call the spirit. As this spirit is a form of energy it will one day be possible for scientists to detect this within living organisms and identify it as being that which makes us alive. The misunderstanding that I perceive is this: Spirit is energy and that energy is life, the life that uses that energy is The Soul and that is where the problem is as I see it. When speaking of life after death we are discussing natural phenomena, as Einstein identified, energy cannot die, it can only transfer form. The question that then creates the conundrum is what directs that energy that we call Spirit? The answer is The Soul and it is the soul that is what we really are not just energy, in whatever form that energy is expressed. So the physical body is not that important to our Soul, our Soul uses the energy of the Spirit.

If we, as Spiritualists, accept that the power force within our physical bodies is the Spirit and that this Spirit will continue to exist long after the physical body has been destroyed then what is all the fuss about the end of the world? We are all heading for the ultimate physical exit anyway and not a one of us alive today incarnate in even the best physical body will be doing much good in a hundred years time. But our spirits will be. Eternity awaits so why not stop all the gloomies and get along with having some fun.

At many Spiritualist meetings the service starts with hymns, why not with some even jollier songs; Knees Up Mother Brown etc. and have a laugh. The world we are all to enter sooner or later is no holy shrine of silence and meditation it is bustling with life and energy. We are that energy. We are life and as souls on a pathway to paradise the body we are currently locked into is only a temporary vessel in which we are given the opportunity to experience many things and to learn from those experiences, both good and bad, happy and sad.

The Mayan calendar may well end in 2012 but one thing that will never end is you and I. We will all live into infinity and beyond as Spirit is energy and energy is eternal. Accept this, get your old Mrs. Mills LPs onto the record player and start dancing. In all cultures, everyone that there has ever been, including the Mayan, the people danced. Forget the end of the world and concentrate on enjoying yourself. After all, you're a long time living!

CHAPTER SEVENTY EIGHT

GHOSTS ON TV

On Thursday 15th November 2001 BBC TV screened a programme titled 'The Secret Life of Ghosts and Werewolves'. The title effectively captured the essence of this hodgepodge of unrelated 'paranormal' subject matter. The makers of this mysterious amalgam of bizarre 'facts' decided to reduce the communication of spirits to a discussion on magnetic fields and sound waves. The ubiquitous Dr Wiseman was featured explaining his psychological theories that invariably discount the presence of discarnate entities. Also amongst the participants in this collection of unrelated clips was Dr Susan Blackmore, seen strapped into a form of Ganzfeld sensory deprivation equipment under the auspices of the Canadian scientist Michael Persinger. (They were attempting to replicate the experience of alien abduction) Mind you Dr Blackmore doesn't really require a blindfold, she has been examining spirits and Spiritualism for years with both eyes seemingly closed.

The problem with programmes such as 'Ghosts and Werewolves' is that it potentially creates within the mind of the viewing public a sense that the subject matter is related. As Spiritualists we should feel deeply insulted that this religion is being held up to ridicule on national TV. Imagine the outcry if the notion that the actual body of Christ plays no part in the service of Holy Communion within the Catholic Church and was discussed by the likes of Wiseman and Blackmore in a similar fashion. Would the BBC screen a programme titled 'Transubstantiation and Cannibalism'? I seriously doubt it. The religious leaders of the Islamic faith would certainly not sit back and smile at a TV broadcast that suggested their beliefs were linked to feral children or murderers. The word fatwa springs to mind at the mere thought of such a thing being televised. Yet the BBC did link the communication of spirits, the essence of the Spiritualist religion, with unrelated sensationalist subject matter such as the 'Monkey Man' of

India. And if that isn't an insult to Spiritualism then I wonder what is?

At the risk of labouring the point our current Home Secretary is discussing introducing into legislation an Act that would create an offence of inciting religious hatred. It will be interesting to see if the likes of Blackmore and Wiseman along with their cronies at the BBC can be called to answer for their seemingly protracted attacks upon the Spiritualist religion and its basic tenets. Why are these obviously intelligent people and the authorities that fund and support them so interested in degrading the idea that life after death is a fact? Could it be that Michael Roll is correct in his assumptions and that they are part of some conspiracy to prevent the truth of eternal life being accepted by the general public? It seems unlikely that respected academics would knowingly involve themselves in such matters but something is going on as proof is being not only denied but subjected to ridicule. This may be denied but inclusion in TV programmes such as 'The Secret Lives of Ghosts and Werewolves' is hardly likely the enhance the reputation of Ph.D level commentators on the subject of paranormal research. (Dr. Blackmore when asked re this stated that she knew nothing of the 'Ghosts and Werewolves' programme and the section featuring her with the Ganzfeld experiment was taken from a serious documentary for the 'Horizon' TV series).

'Ghosts' on TV and Spirit Mediums are frequently portrayed in a negative light. Even the psychics that do appear are most often presented as being odd or as mere show business performers. In the BBC TV programme 'Ghosts and Werewolves' there was no mention whatsoever of Mediums or Psychics. So it seems that either Spiritualism is held up for ridicule or it is effectively ignored.

Any Spiritualist invited to take part in a TV chat show or documentary should be aware that it is highly likely that the producer/director will have a hidden agenda. I speak from personal experience and have been present in numerous television studios as the pre-arranged loud mouth pseudo-sceptic shouts abuse at the guest Psychic or Medium. These so-called sceptics are little more than ill-informed, low-paid actors posing as disbelievers to create an argument so that the TV producers have a 'show'. I have yet to see one of these doubters shouting insults at the token clergyman that is also a usual addition to the proceedings. Now that would create a show: 'Are YOU! Telling ME that this guy not only came back from the dead having been nailed to a cross for three days? BUT then HE also pushed a huge boulder away from the cave HE was buried in? Not only that But HE then FLOATED up to HEAVEN!!. I want some of what you've been on MATE!' Imagine the outcry if that happened? Yet Spiritualists receive that kind of insult time after time when they appear on TV.

It is a sad fact that Spiritualism is portrayed in such a down-market way by television. There was even a recent advertisement for Toffee Crisp that featured a mock up of a séance with a wrapper floating down as if the spirit had eaten the confectionary. It is hard to imagine the Christian equivalent but:

Scene. Inside the confessional:

Lady:'I have sinned......I have been eating to many sweet things......forgive me'

An empty Toffee Crisp wrapper is pushed through the closed curtain.

Priest: 'Me too, it's a miracle in its own right'

Now would that advertisement get past the religious thought police and onto our TV screens? I doubt it very much as it ridicules an important aspect of Christianity. Yet not a dissenting voice has been heard re the skit on spirit communication.

So how can we as Spiritualists get our message across in this age of television and the Information Super-Highway or Internet as it is most commonly called? I believe that we should all be prepared to speak out at every given opportunity using the media to our best advantage. All those that are invited into discussion on television or radio should ensure that they are properly prepared to answer the insults that are most certainly going to form at least a part of any interview. All those that can create web sites offering insights into the truth of eternal life should do so and seek to publicise the same. It is of great importance that we do not just sit back and permit the likes of Wiseman and Blackmore to expound their supposedly scientific interpretations of life after death. They would not do to Christianity, Islam or Judaism what they are attempting to do to Spiritualism. In fact they only get away with their activities because we are permitting them to do so. Now is the time to let the public know that eternal life is **NOT** conditional and subject to faith. Now is the time to act and promote our understanding of the truth of survival. If we fail to take action we most surely will face further decades in which the facts of our eternal existence are denied by pseudo-science, the established church and subsequently the media.

I for one do not believe that we should be prepared to have Spirit Communication lumped together with Zombies, Witch-Doctors, Werewolves and Monkey Men. Do the media think we are weird or something just because we talk to the 'dead'?

RESPONSE FROM Dr. Susan Blackmore to the above:

I would just like to mention how it seems from my point of view. After spending 30 years sincerely looking for paranormal phenomena and never finding any I honestly came to believe that they do not exist. This was not prior bias, nor fear of them, nor any other motivation of that sort. It was that I searched and did not find them. Then I found myself on numerous TV programmes where the agenda was clear – make the scientists look like completely closed-minded idiots who are biased from the start. In the end I had had enough and that is why I gave up. I was (and am) only interested in the truth rather than what people want to believe and it is terribly difficult sticking only to that. Most people want to believe in paranormal phenomena and will do so regardless of the evidence.

Chapter Seventy Nine

WORDS FROM BEYOND

In response to one of my recent Psychic World features on Electronic Voice Phenomena I received a letter from California USA which offered an account of a discarnate voice speaking through an electrical massage machine. The author of the letter, Moana Smith, wrote that in April 2009 she had purchased this machine to ease her back pain and that when she had switched it on a voice spoke to her. At first Moana believed that her mind was playing tricks and she was suffering from auditory hallucinations. Then, whilst using the machine in the presence of her sister Moana heard the voice again. This was also heard and confirmed by her sister who was amazed, as one may imagine. In response to Moana's letter I sent an email requesting further details of exactly what the discarnate voice was saying. Here are some examples of what the voice said:

The first thing spoken from the machine was an instruction: 'Write It Down...Write It Down'. Those were the first words and Moana switched it off. Then, some three days later when Monana again tried the machine she heard it speak her mother's name, the lady had passed to spirit in 1999. In shock Moana called her brother who said he thought she might just be a little crazy, like brothers do. Time after time Moana switched on the massage machine to hear it continue to speak names of her long departed family. As many of Moana's relatives came from distant lands the names were of foreign extraction and the machine uttered phrases in the language of their land i.e. in French and German. Before each name was spoken the words 'I am the vine' came also 'God is divine, praise the Lord'.

There were other names mentioned i.e. Aaban: Name of the Angel (Muslim) Abban: Irish 6th century Saint. Also a phrase in Spanish was spoken 'Arriba Arriba' which means up or up there. Moana's grandmother had a saying she often spoke in German and the machine gave this out too: 'Auch du Liebe' translated means 'Oh my dear'. The case of the talking massage machine is ongoing and I will report further on this subject in due course of time.

The well known actor and comedian Michael Bentine had many psychic experiences during his life and wrote about some of these in his brilliant book: Doors Of The Mind. One incident that Bentine recounted involved the phenomena known as Direct Voice. It was in the year 1979 whilst performing his touring comedy show at a country club in the county of Gloucestershire and staying in a room there he turned out the lights, climbed into bed and as he did so heard a deep booming voice that seemed to come from the centre of the room saying loudly 'Blood Sacrifice'. Somewhat shocked by this Bentine switched the lights back on, but the room was empty, there was no one else there. When he switched the lamp off again and tried to sleep once more the voice spoke, only this time it seemed closer to his bed 'Blood Sacrifice' it said and at that point Michael Bentine decided he would spend the rest of the night reading a book.

The next morning Benetine questioned the manager of the country club asking if the room he had occupied was known to be haunted, not so said the manager. That day Bentine drove back home and as he was passing BlenheimPalace he again heard the voice from nowhere saying exactly the same thing 'Blood Sacrifice'. By now Michael Bentine was becoming concerned. At home he told his wife about his experiences and went to relax in the lounge, quietly exhausted from his lack of sleep and the drive. As he sat dozing in the easy armchair with his wife sitting opposite Bentine was shocked awake by a loud and resounding explosion that came from within the wood of the occasional table beside him. Then again the words were spoken, only this time within his head: 'Blood Sacrifice'. In shock Bentime jumped out of his chair and as he did so the telephone in the hallway rang, his wife answered it. The news was really tragic, she told Michael that his close friend, the MP Airey Nieve had been murdered in a bomb outrage at The House of Commons. Bentine and Nieve had been serving officers together during WWII and Nieve was famous for being one of the few to ever escape from the notorious prison Colditz.

As Bentine sat reflecting on the terrible news he said, quietly, a prayer for the soul of his wonderfully brave and distinguished old friend Airey Nieve. As he did so suddenly, with a crack like a pistol shot, Bentine heard again an explosion from with the occasional table, then a voice spoke to him 'And all the trumpets sounded for him on the other side'. The words were loud and clear though his wife who was present did not hear them.

Some time later Michael Bentine attended the Memorial Service for Airey Nieve held at St Martin-in-the-Fields. He recalls he was sitting behind the organ contemplating the extraordinary career of Airey Nieve and reflecting on their friendship when suddenly he heard the words again 'And all the trumpets sounded for him on the other side'. This time he looked up and saw that they were being spoken by Margaret Thatcher the leader of The Conservative Party who was speaking in memory of Airey Nieve. Those words are taken from John Bunyan's book Pilgrim's Progress.

Chapter Eighty

DYLAN THOMAS

27th October 2014 is the centenary of the birth of Dylan Mariais Thomas. Dylan Thomas was born in Swansea, Wales and he is perhaps the best known of all Welsh poets. At the age of just 39 years Dylan Thomas was dead, he died on the 9th November 1953 of drink and middle age, so the poets say, but in fact his cause of death was diagnosed as being from pneumonia with various complications including a lung disorder. There was also the contributing factor of alcohol because Thomas had, according to a statement he made in the ChelseaHotel in New YorkUSA where he was staying, consumed 18 straight shots of whisky. You see Dylan Thomas was a notorious boozer, a riotous drunken wobble of a man who had to be locked into the wooden shed at his home The Boat House in Laugharne, Carmathenshire by his wife Caitlin to ensure he worked at his craft of poetry. Otherwise Thomas would have spent most of his time at Brown's Hotel in the village drinking beer till he was so intoxicated he could hardly stagger home.

I first encountered the work of Dylan Thomas during the Autumn of 1975 when I was a young man working in Wormwood Scrubs one of Britain's most notorious jails. Another member of staff there one Paul Collins suggested I listen to a recording of Under Milk Wood featuring the mellifluous voice of Richard Burton. I took the recording of the play to a quiet corner of the officers lounge and put the record on the player there: 'To begin at the beginning:It is spring, moonless night in the small town, starless and bible-black, the cobblestreets silent and the hunched, courters'-and-rabbits' wood limping invisible down to the sloeblack, slow, black, crowblack, fishingboatbobbing sea.' I was captivated by the imagery, suddenly I was no longer within the walls of a dark Victorian prison, I was running down the rain glistening cobbled lanes of a seaside Welsh village past Dai the bakers shop into Donkey Street where blind Captain Cat is sitting dreaming of long dead shipmates waiting for The Sailors Arms to open. It was absolutely magical and from that moment on I was hooked on the works of Dylan Thomas. The next day I found time to visit the local library and borrowed a copy of his collected works.

There is something sublimely spiritual about the way Thomas weaves his words into a mysterious poetry that, though at times obscure, has within it an eternal if rather ephemeral truth. One of Dylan Thomas' best known poems is titled: Do Not Go Gentle Into That Goodnight: Do not go gentle into that good night,/Old age should burn and rave at close of day/Rage, rage against the dying of the light. Though wise men at their end know dark is right/Because their words had forked no lightning they/Do not go gentle into that goodnight   Good men, the last wave by, crying how bright/Their deeds might have danced in a green bay/Rage, rage against the dying of the light Wild men who caught and sang the sun in flight/And learn too late, they grieved it on its way/Do not go gentle into that goodnight Grave men near death, who see with blinding sight/Blind eyes could blaze like meteors and be gay/Rage, rage against the dying of the light And you, my father, there on the sad height/Curse, bless me now with your fierce tears I pray/Do not go gentle into that goodnight/Rage, rage against the dying of the light.

What is that all about really? You may well ask so I will tell you what I feel about the poem. It is, for me a poem about the imminence of physical death, a final word to a dying man as he prepares to enter infinity. Look at the way Thomas uses images of nature, Lightning a force of nature, a green bay of the sea, the sun itself the source of light, meteors that blaze across the universe, in all those images Thomas is showing us that this life, which is ending now, has visited all the corners of this planet we call Earth and experienced much. There is regret in the poem as Thomas points out that too late we learn that actions and decisions taken in life usher in the dark. Throughout the poem there is the almost stentorian rhythmic chanting of Rage, rage against the dying of the light, like a militaristic command thumping out the message. In the end this poem works its mystical magic by allowing each of us to feel the almost forlorn falling into endless sleep of the loved one slowly slipping away. Do not go gentle into that goodnight.....

Over the many years since I first listened to Richard Burton reading Under Milk Wood I have seen and heard the play for words many times. In one reading of this play, at The Palace Theatre in Manchester, Dylan Thomas' daughter Aeronwy Bryn Thomas played the harp and it was most enchanting. I even went to a jaz music version of Under Milk Wood that was something else to behold, really mystical. There is something seriously special about the wonderful way Dylan Thomas works his craft with words and his collected poems are available to all. There are even many recordings of Dylan himself reading his poems and these are available on CD through Amazon etc. I would highly recommend listening to the poet reading his work he has an incredible voice, deep and booming, soaring and sensitive at the same time.

It is now one hundred years since the birth of Dylan Thomas and his poetry is as alive today and fresh as it was in the days directly after WWII when he wrote most of it. His short life was lived to the full though he was addicted to alcohol that did not prevent him from making an indelible impact on the literary heritage of Wales and Great Britain. There is a bronze statue to Thomas in his home town of Swansea and a blue plaque on the house where he was born. In CwmdonkinPark where he played as a boy there are a number of stone monuments each engraved with quotes from his work. My favourite is from his poem about lost youth 'Fern Hill' it reads 'Oh as I was young and easy, in he mercy of his means, time held me green and dying, though I sang in my chains like the sea'.

Dylan Thomas did not go gentle into that goodnight he drank 18 straight whisky's and slipped into a coma from which never was again able to rage against the dying of the light. He was buried at the church of St. Martin's in the village of Laugharne on the 24th November 1953. The wake for Thomas took place in his favourite pub, Brown's Hotel where he spent many happy hours drinking with his best boozing buddy his dear wife Caitlin.

Chapter Eighty One

'TEAM' John Myers Radio Days

John Myers is a name many will be familiar with he has been featured on television documentaries concerning the commercial radio industry and was for a time the head of Red Rose Radio in Preston, Lancashire. John has just written his Autobiography : 'TEAM' Its Only Radio published by Kenton Publishing. The book is an absolutely hilarious account of John's life and times in the radio business and it contains many outrageous insights into how the industry ran back in the eighties and nineties which is when I met John Myers. Today we have Psychic radio 'phone in shows all over the UK but few people know that it was John Myers that started this working with myself and the Bolton based psychic-medium James Byrne.

The year was 1991 and John Myers was the Programme Controller at Red Rose Radio, I recall listening to his morning show as I drove into work for Lancashire County Council. At the time I was working with James Byrne trying to get his career as a professional stage psychic-medium off the ground. In those days it was really quite difficult as there was no widespread acceptance of psychics, in fact many were openly hostile as James and I discovered. However it was John Myers that gave us a really positive opportunity when he called and suggested that James Byrne come into the studio at Red Rose Radio and broadcast a ninety minute show featuring him giving callers psychic messages. It was the first time that any commercial radio station had broadcast such a show and it caused quite a sensation. On the night the radio station was surrounded by Bible waving protestors demanding that the show be banned. The press had created a big storm of trouble for us by running a headline stating DEVIL WORSHIPPERS COME TO TOWN. That didn't help.

The first broadcast on Red Rose Radio of James Byrne passing messages from beyond the veil was a sensation and it made the national press. John Myers himself was so impressed that he offered James a regular show a late night psychic 'phone in and suddenly a door had opened and a new era for psychic presentations had begun. Within a matter of months commercial radio stations around the UK were running their own versions of our show. But it was John Myers that had the foresight and vision to make the decision and he contacted me to do it with him, using my then client the brilliant psychic-medium James Byrne.

The book by John Myers contains some really unusual admissions that opened my eyes to what really was going on back in the golden era of commercial radio. If you were around then in the late eighties I am sure you will recall the endless competitions that these local radio stations ran. The prizes were often really worth winning with brand new cars and amazing five star holidays on offer. But it was how these competitions were eventually won that will surprise you. I won't spoil the fun by telling you too much but let me just say that all was not quite what is appeared to be. Plus there were often serious mishaps as the radio stations made mistakes whilst trying to control the outcome of their competitions. On one occasion the station ran a crazy competition requiring callers to guess the number of onions packed into a French Renault car, a brand new on at that. So they actually did pack the raw onions into said car in the middle of an August heat wave and yes, they started to go off big style so that before anyone could win the car it had been virtually ruined by its content of by now rotten onions. How mad is that?

John Myers moved on from Red Rose Radio to run a commercial station in Carlisle his home town. So when I booked James Byrne in for a show at The Sands Centre it seemed to me a good idea to ask John Myers if he would run the Psychic 'Phone In show a few times in the weeks leading up to James appearing at The Sands Centre. As ever Mr. Myers was delighted to help and joined in the fun we had presenting James Byrne on his new radio station. It also proved to be immensely popular with the listeners as long before the date at The Sands Centre we had sold all the tickets. On the night of the show John Myers was kind enough to introduce James Byrne on stage and it was a great night.

There are within John's book many wise observations concerning the presentation of a radio show. John writes of painting pictures in the mind of the listener by descriptive language and a certain tone that is hard to define but is instantly recognised. Having worked with many of the biggest names in the radio business John Myers is uniquely positioned to direct and advise any aspiring radio presenter. The thing is John knows all the tricks, he invented most of them and in his book he openly discusses some of the incredible stunts he pulled over the years. There are stories about outside broadcasts that were virtually totally faked in the studio and because he knew how to do it no one ever discovered he truth, until now. So if you have any aspirations at all of being a radio psychic or presenter get John's book and pay attention to how not to do it. On one occasion the rather manic Mr. Myers used a heavy metal chain and padlock to secure the front entrance of BBC Radio Cumbria where he was working. On the front door he placed a sign announcing that is was for sale due to lack of public interest. The next morning the first crew of the day arrived at 5am but were unable to get in thanks to John's joke. He escaped the wrath of management by resorting to direct denial. You just need to read this book it is very funny.

Many years have passed since James Byrne and I first went to Red Rose Radio and since then the commercial presentation of psychic mediums has moved on to television. Indeed I myself was featured on TV3 in Ireland doing an infomercial two hour show called Psychic Readings Live. This was actually filmed live in a huge studio in the middle of Budapest, Hungary and broadcast on TV all across Ireland. I was on my own for the full two hours taking calls from the public in Ireland and giving them psychic messages and insights. I did eight straight two hour shows and the programme producers were impressed with the figures so within days of my return to the UK I was offered a long term contract and sent plane tickets to fly back. Unfortunately the Irish broadcasting authority did not like the show and it was taken off air. What we really needed was John Myers to sort them out in his very own personal way. To find out how John manages to manipulate situations read his book.

You can purchase the book 'TEAM: It's Only Radio' by John Myers published by Kenton Publishing ISBN 978-0-9546223-9-8 All proceeds go to charity 100% is divided between Cancer Research in memory of John's father, The Radio Academy and also Radio Tyneside a radio station in Newcastle for those in hospital. The book is available signed direct from John Myers himself just visit John's website www. myersmedia.co.uk cost is £10 including postage

Chapter Eighty Two

The Root of all Evil

Professor Richard Dawkins in his 2006 TV Documentary 'The Root of All Evil' came to the conclusion that 'The time has come for people of reason to say: enough is enough. Religious faith discourages independent thought, it's divisive, and it's dangerous.' Dawkins explained that in The Bible we have passages in The old Testament, (which he describes as the root of Judaism, Christianity and Islam) that preach violence and murder. As example he points to Deuteronomy 13 which instructs believers to kill any friend or family member who favours serving other gods, and Numbers 31 where Moses, angered at the mercy his victorious forces show in taking women and children captive, instructs them to kill all virgin girls, who are to be taken as slaves. This is a clear instruction to commit genocide and it is there for all to see in The Bible.

Dawkins also points out that there is a certain problem with the teachings of Paul in the New Testament which, at first, he describes as being a huge improvement from the moral viewpoint. But he is repelled by what he calls St Paul's nasty sadomasochistic doctrine that Jesus had to be hideously tortured and killed so that we might be redeemed – the doctrine of atonement for original sin– and asks "if God wanted to forgive our sins, why not just forgive them? Who is God trying to impress?' I must admit to being with Dawkins on that one, I mean I am not at all in favour of anyone being responsible for my sins and take exception to the idea that someone had to undergo public mutilation and death because I may have been a very naughty boy.

One point that Dawkins makes in the documentary is that religious beliefs can actually create evil by adherents to a strict doctrine being given what amounts to instructions to commit atrocities. He says: 'The god of the Old Testament has got to be the most unpleasant character in all fiction: jealous and proud of it, petty, vindictive, unjust, unforgiving, racist, an ethnic-cleanser urging his people on to acts of genocide.'

The question I want to address, as a Spiritualist, in this brief essay is this: Is religion really the root of all evil or is some other force more, or even partly responsible for the wickedness that clearly does exist in this world.

Exploitation of the masses by a powerful elite is, in my opinion, evil. By exploitation I mean the virtual slavery that is imposed upon the textile workers in China, who hand sew and stitch garments for major multi-national corporations that pay them an absolute pittance and hold them in near captivity. Many household name products with high priced designer labels are created in sweat shops run by gang-masters in the teeming back street factories of Beijing. There is of course nothing new in the exploitation of textile workers. In 1843 the poet Thomas Hood wrote 'The Song of The Shirt' here are the first two verses:

With fingers weary and worn / With eyelids heavy and red / A woman is sat in unwomanly rags / plying her needle and thread / Stitch! Stitch! Stitch! / In poverty hunger and dirt / And still with a voice of dolorous pitch / She sang the 'Song of the Shirt'.....Work! Work! Work! / While the cock is growing aloof! / And work work work / Till the stars shine through the roof / It's Oh! To be a slave / Along with the barbarous Turk / Where woman has never a soul to save / If this is Christain work!

Charles Dickens wrote books about the virtual slavery of the impoverished factory workers of the early Victorian Industrial Revolution. What he saw then, described in books like 'Hard Times' and 'Oliver Twist' we can still see today if we care to look in the broken back alleys of Beijing and Mumbai. But of course we do not look do we? We really do not, we just buy the designer label clothing and turn a blind eye to where it came from. It comes, very often, from the suffering of the poor exploited Chinese and Indian people who can not stand up and demand a fair days pay for a fair days work. Why is this so? Profit is the answer and that profit is expressed as money.

The days of Britain being the factory of the Western world are long gone. Have a look around your nearest city and try to find a factory that is manufacturing anything, I really mean anything and I believe that apart from a very few specialised products, such as nuclear precision engineering and a few, relatively few, cars you will find next to nothing. Why? Because the cost of employing one UK worker is around ten times more expensive than employing an equally able Chinese worker in China. So our people, the generations aged between 16 years and forty years, have virtually nowhere to work and, unless they are well educated will not find reasonable paid employment outside a burger bar. Virtually all our 'White Goods' that is washing machines, cookers, dishwashers, microwaves etc. come from what we currently term the Third World. All we do is buy them and use them. What you may well ask do we buy them with? We buy these goods with credit cards, loans etc. and the money that we pay in interest is profit to banks, the corporations and the elite that control these massive multi-national institutions. We have been doing this for many years, selling our virtual souls to the system and now the game is up, the time has come for the corporations to call in the cash and as most people can not pay, having no real jobs anymore, they are losing their property, their possessions and becoming seriously indebted. That is, in my opinion, evil.

The root of evil is, I feel, the pseudo capitalism that takes everything from the people and gives them back the modern day equivalent of bangles and beads to play with. I refer to things like the X-Box, the Sky-TV channels of rubbish like fake reality game shows and asinine imitation celebrities confusing the public with nonsensical bilge about who is dating who and divorcing etc. etc. Even the BBC TV News is flooded with banal garbage about so called football players and nasty mouthed uneducated foul-minded managers who seem to believe they are important! That is, in my opinion, evil.

The media have been feeding the public utter tosh, misdirecting the minds of people who really should know better. They are doing this, in my opinion, to sooth the pain, to sugar the bitter pill of unemployment and hopelessness that is the real news today. The media, TV, newspapers, magazines, radio etc. are all owned by the big corporations and their outlets report what they are told to report and it has nothing to do with the real news. The real news is that we are very quickly being transformed into mindless Yahoos programmed by the media to believe in a totally false reality. Rather like believing in a god that orders one to commit genocide and following those instructions to the letter, as some do and are still doing. That is, in my opinion, evil.

I say the time has come for Spiritualists and all sentient human beings to wake up and smell the coffee. The root of all evil is, I believe, ignorance. We are currently being programmed to accept ignorant explanations just like our ancestors were brainwashed from birth into believing in a jealous god that controlled the way, the truth and the light. We are being hoodwinked into accepting the reality of a make believe world where football managers are the high priests and 'A' list so called celebrities are the saints. As for the god of today, it's a fifty inch flat screen TV with surround sound and it tells lies. Just like the other gods.

Chapter Eighty Three

Reasons To Be Cheerful

As we enter a new year many of us will think something along the lines of 'Here we go again..another year...more problems'. The negative aspects of our lives can distract us from actually enjoying the day to day process of living. However, there are many reasons to be cheerful if we do but dare to dream. The author and philosopher Colin Wilson once considered his life useless and contemplated killing himself, these are his words: 'When I was 16, I decided to commit suicide. This was not a sudden emotional decision. When I made it, it seemed to me entirely logical.' Wilson had been working in a chemistry lab whilst studying to be a chemist and had lost all hope, he continues: 'I went into the other room, to the reagent shelves, and took down the bottle of hydrocyanic acid, with its waxed glass stopper. I removed this, and smelt that distinctive almond smell. I knew that hydrocyanic acid would kill me in less than half a minute. Mentally, I had already raised the bottle and taken a swig of the bitter liquid. Then an odd thing happened. I became two people. I was suddenly conscious of this teenage idiot called Colin Wilson, with his misery and frustration, and he seemed such a limited fool that I could not have cared less whether he killed himself or not. But if he killed himself, he would kill me too. For a moment I felt that I was standing beside him, and telling him that if he didn't get rid of this habit of self-pity he would never amount to anything. It was also as if this 'real me' had said to the teenager: 'Listen, you idiot, think how much you'd be losing', and in that moment I glimpsed the marvellous, immense richness of reality, extending to distant horizons. So I re-stoppered the bottle and went back to my analytical chemistry. I felt relaxed and light-hearted and totally in control of myself.'

Colin Wilson went on to earn wide critical acclaim for his international best-selling book 'The Outsider' published in the year 1956 when he was just 24 years of age. Since then Wilson has continued his successful career with over a hundred books published world wide. Colin Wilson has produced many philosophical works based on his belief in positivity i.e. that no matter how dismal it all may seem there are, if we really try, always reasons to be cheerful. I have been a Colin Wilson reader for over forty years and I find his philosophy inspiring and even inspirational. Wilson argues, as does his one time colleague the eminent psychologist Abraham Maslow (they taught at the same American University) that as a general rule we live our lives on automatic pilot and only when faced with an emergency or some moment of extreme interest do we overtake the robot and assume command. Such moments Maslow termed as being 'Peak Experiences'. When Wilson reached for the bottle of acid and lifted the stopper he experienced just such a moment, replaced the stopper and became alive.

There are numerous other gifted individuals that did not resist the urge to end the tedium or pain of life. I Think of Van Gogh who, before shooting himself in the stomach wrote a brief suicide note: The misery will never end'. Yet in his work there appears to be a delight in living, look at 'A Starry Night' or 'Road with Cypress and Star' both paintings contain uplifting images but Van Gogh, no doubt in a moment of despair, took the negative pathway and failed to recognise the truth of eternal hopefulness and life that his own work depicted.

The philosophy of John Paul Sarte may offer an insight into the despair that obviously grips many individuals at certain times in their lives. Sarte suggested that 'hell is other people' and his constant theme is one of alienation. That is summed up by Sarte in these words: 'Man can will nothing unless he has first understood that he must count on no one but himself; that he is alone, abandoned on earth in the midst of his infinite responsibilities, without help, with no other aim than the one he sets himself, with no other destiny than the one he forges for himself on this earth.' Sarte's philosophy is a mistake, he argues that we are all alone, that life is meaningless and he is

wrong. Colin Wilson's argument is that we are living in a world of infinite possibilities which we can see if we will just open our minds to them.

As Spiritualists we accept that beyond this sometimes troubled material world there is another dimension, another life that we will live once this short journey is at an end. What we find when we do eventually walk through the doorway called death will have been prepared by us, for as we have sown in this life so we will reap in the next. That is why I agree with Wilson and strongly disagree with the negative nihilism of Sarte. Hell is not other people, hell is not trying, hell is accepting the little defeats that life deals us and hell is giving in. We each owe ourselves a duty to try and make our lives a success within the limitations of the possibilities presented. But, believe me, there are many exciting possibilities and the limits are surprisingly distant. All that is holding one back is the lack of self belief. If you can summon the strength to dream, if you can visualise yourself succeeding and achieving a certain target or goal, then you are halfway there already.

Colin Wilson had to sleep rough on Hamstead heath in London whilst he researched his first book 'The Outsider'. He was virtually penniless, had no Oxbridge education and yet he had a dream of being a writer, and a philosopher. Against all the odds he succeeded. For us all there exists hope and we should find in each day reasons to be cheerful. 2011 looks like being a difficult year, so let's start by deciding that no matter what it brings we will face it with determination. We are such stuff as dreams are made of, so dream on.

Printed in Great Britain
by Amazon

33057832R00194